Teachers, Ideology and Control

WITHDRAWN

Teachers, Ideology and Control

A Study in Urban Education

Gerald Grace

Faculty of Education
King's College, University of London

Routledge & Kegan Paul

London, Henley and Boston

First published in 1978
by Routledge & Kegan Paul Ltd
39 Store Street,
London WC1E 7DD,
Broadway House,
Newtown Road,
Henley-on-Thames,
Oxon RG9 1EN and
9 Park Street,
Boston, Mass. 02108, USA
Set in Compugraphic Baskerville
and printed photolitho in Great Britain by
Ebenezer Baylis and Son Ltd,
The Trinity Press, Worcester, and London

British Library Cataloguing in Publication Data

Grace, Gerald

    Teachers, ideology and control.
    1. Education, Urban – Great Britain – Political
    aspects
    I. Title
    371.1'02'0941   LC5136.G7   78–40714

    ISBN 0 7100 0014 6
    ISBN 0 7100 0015 4   Pbk

For

June, Claire, Helena and Dominic Grace
who made the writing possible

and for

all teachers in urban schools,
for whom the writing was done.

Contents

Preface

I wish to acknowledge the considerable help I have received from Basil Bernstein and from Michael Young, both for critical readings of early draft chapters and for valuable discussions concerning the focus of the analysis. Their formative if sometimes conflicting advice has shaped this work in important ways and my intellectual debt to their published works is obvious.

Although the responsibility for the writing is my own, Karen Mallett, my assistant between 1975 and 1977, contributed to the work; in transcribing the research interviews, in helping with the historical inquiries, and in discussing with me possible interpretations and implications. The finished work – and the fact that it is finished – owes much to her efforts, enthusiasm and energy. The research activity upon which this work is based has been funded by the Social Science Research Council.

I am conscious that the work has been influenced from many sources. Stuart Hall's essay, 'Education and the Crisis of the Urban School' and Rachel Sharp and Tony Green's book, *Education and Social Control* had an early and I believe fruitful effect on the project. I have also gained much from discussions with various people during the course of the writing, particularly with the members of the MA (Sociology of Teaching) seminars at Gordon Square; with the members of the MA (Urban Education) seminars at King's College; and with Margaret and David Brook.

My thanks and acknowledgment are due to the Inner London Education Authority; to Marten Shipman and Hilda Cole of the

Research and Statistics Department, ILEA, and to a number of writers who are also practising urban teachers. Those who produce such journals as *School Does Matter*; *Radical Education*; *Libertarian Education*; *Great Brain Robbery*; *Teaching London Kids* and *Teachers' Action* make available interpretations of the social reality of urban schools which challenge conventional wisdom in provocative and necessary ways.

To those teachers and headteachers who have generously cooperated in this study in the hope that 'it might do some good' I am very grateful and I sincerely hope that the result will not be a disappointment to them.

Acknowledgments

The author and publishers would like to thank the following for permission to reproduce copyright material: Hodder & Stoughton Education for *Things I Cannot Forget*, by P. B. Ballard (1938); Link House Publications Ltd for *Lux Mihi Laus* by T. Gautrey (1937); Professor A. H. Halsey and HMSO for *Educational Priority: EPA Problems and Policies*, vol. 1 (1972).

Introduction

*Social Science deals with problems of biography, of history, and of
their intersections within social structures.*

C. WRIGHT MILLS

This work attempts to take seriously the view advanced by C. Wright
Mills (1970, p. 159) that biography, history and society are 'the co-
ordinate points of the proper study of man'. An attempt has been
made to examine certain features of state education in urban areas in
this country using biographical, historical and sociological material.
Its specific focus is upon a strategic but neglected social group – the
teachers of the urban working class.

  Bernstein's writings (1975, 1977) in the field of cultural transmission and reproduction and the writings of the new school of
'critical' sociologists of education[1] have led to a heightened awareness of the social and political embeddedness of the educational
system. The current preoccupations of the sociology of education
are, among other things, to investigate and make explicit the relationships between various forms of educational experience and
various forms of social control; to examine the social organization of
curricula and pedagogy and to suggest ways in which issues of power,
ideology and control are implicated in educational arrangements. It
is apparent that central to these preoccupations must be some
attempt to provide a socio-historical location of teachers in state
schools. Such teachers constitute, within any type of social formation, a crucial sector of the agents of cultural and social reproduction

1

and a *crucial sector of the agents of symbolic control.*[2] At present, however, comparatively few sociological or historical studies have examined this occupational group in any detail, either at the level of social structure or at the level of consciousness. This general neglect of socio-historical studies of teachers, especially those in the ideologically sensitive arenas of urban working-class schools, appears at first sight surprising. What explanation is there for it? Historically, the most obvious reason is the comparative obscurity of the professional and working lives of those whom Derwent Coleridge (1862), called the 'teachers of the people'. While we have detailed accounts of the lives and philosophies of 'great teachers' – a term generally synonymous with the headship of public schools – collected material which throws light upon the 'experience of being a teacher' in the public elementary school tradition, is still sparse. The teachers of the working class have few written histories which document their philosophies and aspirations, struggles and achievements.[3]

There are, however, more general reasons for this neglect which apply to both historians and sociologists. These have to do with pervasive images of the teacher within state education which have emphasized features of constraint and control in the teacher's social world and have thus tended toward the production of a 'social puppet' view of the teacher. At one level, this has involved taking for granted the compliance and conformity of the teachers to the public policies, dominant ideologies and given structures within which they have worked. Such a view has, of course, a strong historical basis. The teachers of the urban working class in particular can be seen historically *to have been* the objects of class control and supervision but this emphasis has overshadowed study of the ways in which some of them resisted the system of which they were a part and sought to turn it to other ends.

Sociology has contributed little to a modification of this situation. Until recently the majority of sociological studies concerned with teachers and teaching have been derived from a functionalist form of role theory. Although the concept of social role has many possibilities for empirical analysis, the particular version of role theory which has dominated the field has been, as Turner (1962, p. 37) puts it 'a refinement of conformity theory'. In practice, role theory has led to an emphasis which characteristically sees the teacher on the receiving end of other people's expectations and which underplays the teacher's own view of his activities and the meanings he attaches to them. Thus very few sociological studies of teachers exist which capture the existential reality of what it is to be a teacher or which depict the social world of school and classroom through the medium of the teacher's discourse. Much of what has passed for the sociology of teaching has tended to perpetuate the 'social puppet' view of the teacher.

Recently, however, the work of Keddie (1971) and of Sharp and Green (1975) has been important in going beyond such studies to make explicit aspects of teacher consciousness and, especially in the latter study, in relating these to the constraints of the work situation. There is now a growing recognition within the sociology of education of the need for more studies which attempt to locate teachers in state schools in relation to some notion of an 'objective' social reality concerned with class relations and changing modalities of social control and some notion of a 'subjective' social reality concerned with the constitution of teacher consciousness within the constraints of the work situation. This study is intended to be some contribution to that end. At the same time, it is intended to be a contribution to urban education studies. The writer shares with Pahl (1975) the conviction that metropolitan cities provide the arenas *for the making visible of fundamental social contradictions* within the wider society and of the ideological and political conflicts associated with such contradictions. State schools within such cities, particularly those situated within inner rings of deprivation and powerlessness constitute a context within which issues of power, ideology and control become unusually salient and thus available for examination.[4] The schools of the urban working class within such localities have always been schools of confrontation and struggle – in a classroom sense, in a cultural sense, in an ideological sense and in a socio-political sense.[5] The developing field of urban educational studies in this country and in America is concerned to locate and to document such struggles.[6]

A basic assumption of the present work is that attempts to locate the teachers of the urban working class as a strategic occupational group must involve some examination of their historical origins and formation and some examination of their position at the nexus of continuing ideological conflict within state education. While this has been done it is necessary to specify the limitations of the attempt. The first two chapters provide an historical context against which contemporary sociological material can be read and interpreted. These chapters cannot claim to be 'history', since they violate many of the conventions of historical scholarship and use history explicitly as a resource for other purposes. Their intention is not to provide a detailed chronological examination of the origins and formation of the 'teachers of the people' (although this urgently needs to be done) but to provide an *historical sense* of some of those elements which were crucial in the genesis of this occupational group. It will be for historians to say whether or not this historical sense is seriously misleading.

Part I is also concerned with the attempt to locate the teachers of the urban working class both historically and contemporarily, in relation to a notion of ideological conflict within education. The particular use of ideology in this context must be explained.

Ideology in one of its classic Marxist senses[7] is understood to be a system of ideas and beliefs whose function is to legitimate and render 'natural' (through the diffusion of a false consciousness) the domination of the bourgeoisie. It is understood to be variously a system of ideas, 'world views' or 'knowledge' which is grounded in the material interests of a particular social class. For Marxists, therefore, the notion of ideological struggle within education refers essentially to the attempts by a dominant social order to impose hegemonic control and to the attempts by those who are dominated to resist such control.[8] While not denying that this manifestation of ideological conflict within urban education is 'in the last instance', the most profound, the focus of this particular study is upon ideological conflict *within* a social class rather than between social classes. The concept of ideology used here refers essentially to systems of ideas about and prescriptions for the education of an urban working class – ideologies which are located in different and conflicting interest groups within the middle class. Plamenatz (1970) and Gouldner (1976) suggest that the investigation of intra-class differences is a necessary part of the analysis of the complex nature of ideological conflict within mature industrialized societies, and a number of writers have begun to trace the nature of such conflict with especial reference to education (Williams (1971), Hoare (1967), Bernstein (1977), Finn, Grant and Johnson (1977)). What is attempted here is to show the ways in which the teachers of the urban working class and the 'problem' of urban working-class schools have been constituted in different ideological formulations within the middle class both in the recent past and at a present time of 'urban education crisis'.[9]

Part II provides some empirical grounding of these issues with particular reference to a group of teachers working in ten inner-London comprehensive schools.[10] An examination is made of the complex of social expectations and ideological and other pressures which focus upon the teachers within these schools. The exploration of constraint and control in urban education is undertaken with reference to contemporary social constructs of the 'good' teacher; the demands of the work situation and to notions of autonomy and of professionalism. The ways in which various groups of teachers characterize their pupils, the educational process and the experience of inner-city teaching are also made explicit and related to features of their working world.

In 1971, Young (p. 5) called for 'very detailed case studies . . . which treat as problematic the curricula, pedagogic and assessment categories held by school personnel'. There are still comparatively few sociological accounts of an empirical nature which provide such detail. Chapters 7 to 10 of this work are concerned with adding to our knowledge and understanding of such categories and the circumstances in which they are generated.

Kay-Shuttleworth, writing in 1862 (p. 582), saw the teachers of the urban working class as 'the pioneers of civilization'. Althusser (1972, p. 260-1) sees them as 'professional ideologists' engaged in the transmission of 'a variety of know-how wrapped up in a massive inculcation of the ideology of the ruling class'. The following chapters represent an attempt to examine these and other typifications of the teachers' role and to relate these typifications to an exploratory study of teacher consciousness and their work situation.

Teachers in deprived urban working-class localities, (along with policemen and social workers in such situations), have provided easy targets for critical attack, without sufficient effort having been made to locate them, historically, within their work situations or within the wider contradictions of society or to appreciate their attempts to deal with these contradictions. This study attempts such a location and such an appreciation.

Part One

Socio-historical Context

Chapter 1

Teachers of the Urban Working Class: socio-historical location

The 'urban problem' and education

Marx saw the city as the epitome of industrial capitalism and as the context for its overthrow. The concentration together in metropolitan and urban areas of vast masses of the industrial proletariat and their families in conditions which were economically exploitive and socially oppressive provided an opportunity for political action which the state of 'rural idiocy' had never made possible. But Marx was not alone in that realization. The Victorian middle class, or at least some of its more socially conscious and perceptive members, was fully alive to the dangers as well as the advantages of industrial 'progress' and urbanization. The disruption of existing social patterns and cultural mores, while it might liberate the necessary impetus for 'progress', might at the same time liberate the forces of anarchy. James Kay-Shuttleworth (1862, p. 428) was one who gave expression to this fear:

> the state of the manufacturing poor is that which awakens the
> greatest apprehension. The labour which they undergo is
> excessive and they sacrifice their wives and their infants to the
> claims of their poverty and to the demands of the intense
> competition of trade. Almost everything around them seems to
> materialize and inflame them. They are assembled in masses –
> they are exposed to the physical evils arising from the neglect of
> sanitary precautions and to the moral contamination of towns –
> they are accustomed to combine in trades unions and political
> associations – they are more accessible by agitators and more

readily excited by them. The time for inquiry into their conditions is passed – the period for the interference of a sagacious national forethought is at hand.

Thus stated, the dilemma for one section of the Victorian middle class was how to facilitate industrial progress while at the same time containing anarchy. The answer was to be found in a whole array of social and ideological agencies among which educational institutions in the form of ragged, industrial and elementary schools and mechanics institutes were to play an important part. A new 'trained' occupational group was created to act as one of the bulwarks against anarchy – the 'teachers of the people'.

The Victorian middle class was, however, a very heterogeneous group[1] and while it might be united in an agreement that there was an urban problem, the significant characteristics of the problem and the solutions thought necessary were seen to vary considerably. The basic imperative to control co-existed with a genuine humanitarian and Christian impulse to help, a radical interest in equipping the people for political membership, a capitalist interest in rendering them competent and efficient as workers, a religious interest in making them 'good' and a liberal/cultural interest in 'elevating' and 'refining' them to an appreciation of a higher order of culture. That many of these interests were nothing more than *variations* on the basic theme of control is clearly an arguable position. While recognizing the difficulty of interpreting most contemporary statements of *intent*, Johnson (1970, p. 119) concludes that

> the early Victorian obsession with the education of the poor is best understood as a concern about authority, about power, about the assertion (or the reassertion) of control. This concern was expressed in an enormously ambitious attempt to determine, through the capture of educational means, the patterns of thought, sentiments and behaviour of the working class. Supervised by its trusty teacher, surrounded by its playground wall, the school was to raise a new race of working-class people – respectful, cheerful, hard-working, loyal, pacific and religious.[2]

Teachers as agents of social control: the missionary ideology

There is no doubt that, whatever other intentions he had for education, social control was an enduring concern for James

Kay-Shuttleworth, the architect of popular education in England in the 1840s and 1850s, and significant definer of the role and function of the teachers of the people. His appreciation of the 'urban problem' was well grounded in his early experiences in the slum areas of Manchester and in his later appointment as an assistant Poor Law Commissioner. For Kay-Shuttleworth (1862, p. 61) 'alarming disturbances of social order generally commence with a people only partially instructed. The preservation of internal peace, not less than the improvement of our national institutions depends on the education of the working class'. The teachers were to be central to this enterprise in the role of social and cultural missionaries – a kind of secular priesthood dedicated to the work of 'civilization'. This was the established model of the teacher at Battersea Training College and subsequently it was to become a powerful constituent in the occupational socialization of elementary school teachers for the rest of the century and beyond.

The ideology was expressed in a religious rhetoric (Kay-Shuttleworth, 1862, p. 309):

we hoped to inspire them with a large sympathy for their own
class. To implant in their minds the thought that their chief
honour would be to aid in rescuing that class from its misery of
ignorance and its attending vices. To wean them from the
influence of that personal competition in a commercial society
which leads to sordid aims. To place before them the
unsatisfied wants of the uneasy and distressed multitude and to
breathe into them the charity which seeks to heal its mental
and moral diseases.

The successful establishment of a missionary ideology for teachers was not, however, without its problems. Would such a preparation be sufficient to combat tendencies to self-assertion and criticism of the existing social order from among the teachers; and would it of itself sustain them in their difficult role as agents of social cohesion? Kay-Shuttleworth (1862, p. 401) was concerned with both of these questions:

in the formation of the character of the schoolmaster, the
discipline of the training school should be so devised as to
prepare him for the modest respectability of his lot. He is to be
a Christian teacher following Him who said, 'He that will be
my disciple, let him take up his cross'. Without the spirit of

11

self-denial he is nothing. His reward must be in his work. There should be great simplicity in the life of such a man.

If such a regime was not effective, the 'teacher of the people' 'might become *not* the gentle and pious guide of the children of the poor but a hireling into whose mind have sunk the doubts of the sceptic and in whose heart was the worm of social discontent' (1862, p. 401). Even if the initial socialization of the teachers was success-fully accomplished, would such preparation render them 'capable of contending with the greater difficulties of town schools?' (1862, p. 391). Kay-Shuttleworth was acutely aware of the problems which teachers in urban schools faced and in the following passage he gives a vivid account of what he saw to be the 'reality shock' for young teachers in such situations (1862, pp. 391–3):

> Such a position is in the most painful contrast with his previous training. He exchanges the comparative seclusion of his residence in the normal school for the difficult position of a public instructor on whom many jealous eyes are fixed. For the first time he is alone in his profession – unaided by the example of his masters – not stimulated by emulation with his fellows, removed from the vigilant eye of the principal of the school – separated from the powerful influences of that corporate spirit which impelled his previous career – yet placed amidst difficulties perplexing even to the most mature experience and required to tax his invention to meet new circumstances before he has acquired confidence in the unsustained exercise of his recently developed powers. He has left the training school for the rude contact of a coarse, selfish and immoral populace whose gross appetites and manners render the narrow streets in his neighbourhood scenes of impurity. He is at once brought face to face with an ignorant and corrupt multitude to whose children he is to prove a leader and guide. His difficulties are formidable.

It would be necessary to sustain (and control) the teacher in such situations by ensuring that his social superiors in the locality took a close interest in the management of schools. Johnson (1970) has pointed out how the writings of Kay-Shuttleworth and of the School Inspectorate in early Victorian England legitimized a missionary ideology for teachers by presenting a picture of demoralized and dis-organized working-class life, attributable in the main to the personal failings of the class, rather than as a consequence of the social and economic structure. This legitimation was to have a long history. Established in the bold, explicit prose of the Victorians, it was to be transmuted over time into the language of social science – into the vocabulary of 'deprivation' and 'maladjustment', of 'immediate gratification' and 'low achievement motivation', of 'special needs' and 'compensatory education'.[3] The attention of the teachers of the people continued to be firmly fixed upon *ameliorating* activity, upon a social pathology view of the working class, and away from any serious analysis of the structural conditions which required such amelioration. Such an emphasis was to be characteristic of the régime of teacher training colleges and colleges of education until well into the twentieth century.[4]

A missionary ideology for teaching in the popular system could then serve a number of social functions. It could help to sustain teachers in the face of considerable pedagogical and other difficulties which they faced in the large classes of urban elementary schools; it would preoccupy them with a Christian and humanitarian concern for amelioration and rescue; and it would serve as a powerful means of occupational control through its associations with notions of vocation and humility and relative unconcern for political, economic and social status questions.

Controlling the teachers: the ideology of respectability and professionalism

While endorsing the need for 'dedication' among teachers, other contemporaries recognized that this large and strategic occupational group, recruiting as it did from among the more intelligent and ambitious youth of the working class, would not be successfully managed by a missionary ideology alone. There were expectations for social mobility and social status, for a recognition of the worth of the teachers' activity and for their acceptance into the 'respectable' ranks of Victorian society. If these expectations were wholly frustrated then the 'teachers of the people' might well turn to political activities, to undue identification with their own class, so that they might become not the agents of social stability, but 'active emissaries for misrule' (quoted in R. Johnson, 1970, p. 115). Since it was unthinkable that teachers should be regarded as the equivalent of clerics or lawyers, some intermediate social position had to be found to which would be attached aspirations and expectations both indivi-

13

dually and collectively for increased respectability. These expectations might, of course, be very delayed in their realizations, but while
they existed they would provide a powerful means of attachment to
the existing order. Derwent Coleridge, Principal of St Mark's Training College, made these understandings explicit. An appeal should
be made, he wrote (1862, p. 30),

> to that keen sense and appreciation of social respectability,
> together with that energetic desire of social advancement which
> unite to form at once the moving spring, the self-acting safety-
> valve and self-adjusting regulator of that great machine which
> we call the British community; that sentiment which, with all
> its follies and excesses has reconciled in this country the largest
> amount of social progress with the most intense conservatism
> ever found in combination in the history of nations; a
> sentiment, which may in the last resort be absorbed in the
> prevalence of religious motive but which meanwhile it is our
> business to moderate, to control, to direct. . . .

In his book, *The Teachers of the People*, published in 1862,
Coleridge argued a thesis which sociologists would now call a functional theory of social mobility. The position of the teacher 'must not
be foreclosed against all possible advancement' (1862, p. 34). The
teacher, 'must if possible have something in prospect – it need not be
much – it need not be sure – something before him. He may not
strive, he may not even wish for advancement, but it will not be
closed against him. He will therefore be content' (1862, p. 34). To
those who feared that such aspiration and such mobility would
threaten the existing order of society, Coleridge (1862, p. 41)
returned a classic answer which foreshadowed almost exactly the
conclusion which sociologists of education were to come to a century
later:

> Ill indeed do the upper classes understand their own interest if
> they see in this movement any danger to their prerogative. *Its
> real tendency is to preserve the existing map of society while it
> softens its demarcations* [my emphasis]. . . . A few individuals
> will, indeed, shoot upwards from below, their path being
> marked by a stroke of light. Such men act as a bond between
> the classes.

Tropp (1957) has shown how the 'social condition' of the elementary school teacher was the subject of frequent comment in teacher

journals and conferences throughout the nineteenth century.[5] These early aspirations for respectability and advancement were to find their expression subsequently in the language of professionalism. No attempt to locate the teachers of the people historically and sociologically can escape their long preoccupation with notions of professionalism and with the concept of a profession. Here was an ideology at times complementary to and, at times opposed to, the missionary imperative. For the teachers it could serve as a legitimation for individual and group social mobility, for greater occupational control and for claims for greater autonomy in their day-to-day teaching activities. To be a professional was to attain to greater social honour, increased economic reward and freedom from 'obnoxious interference' (Tropp, 1957, p. 134). For their employers on the other hand it could serve as a device to separate the teachers from the rest of the working class and from any tendencies to militant unionism by encouraging loyalty in anticipation of greater social honour and by associating professionalism for teachers with the notion of vocation and disinterested dedication. Professionalism in the latter sense became the 'modern' version of the missionary ideology.[6] The need to control the teachers of the people by keeping before them anticipations of respectability and social honour epitomized in the concept of a profession, was a strategy which was to have a long history.

But control through professionalism cannot be seen as an unproblematic part of a 'conspiracy theory' of the working of society. While some middle-class writers saw in professionalism the means to keep the teachers loyal to the existing order and strategically separated from the rest of their class, others were concerned that it generated discontent, over-confidence in relation to superiors and dangerous aspirations towards autonomy. There co-existed, therefore, with an impulse towards the 'embourgeoisement' of the teachers, an impulse to keep them in their place and these contradictions were perceived by the teachers who were ready to advance their own constructions of what professionalism should involve.[7]

Unlike a missionary ideology, professionalism was a double-edged weapon. It might be used as an effective means of occupational control by the educational establishment – on the other hand it might provide a legitimation for teachers to claim greater economic rewards and a real measure of control of their own activities. It was the intention of a significant group among the Victorian middle class that the former should dominate the latter.

15

Socializing the teachers in the training colleges

The training colleges were the institutional contexts within which missionary and professional ideologies were realized in varying degrees of intensity. In the initial selection of students heavy emphasis was placed upon the moral and religious qualities of the candidates, estimations of their 'character' and knowledge that they originated from the 'respectable' section of the working class. Goodness and steadiness were much to be preferred to cleverness for those who occupied the strategic position of educators of the people. Intellect without a moral and religious commitment was a potentially dangerous force. The régime of the colleges followed a model which Goffman (1970) has called 'the total institution'. An attempt was made to encapsulate the students, to facilitate the process of socialization for their role, and to 'elevate' them (though not too far) from their class of origin. A report to the Popular Education Commission (Newcastle Commission, 1861, vol. 4, p. 403) notes that 'there is very little opportunity for the students of training colleges to indulge in irregularities or to consort with improper companions . . . no set of young men of the same age . . . are kept under such close restraint'.

A necessary part of the socialization process was that students should not become involved with controversial issues, especially political questions. Reports to Commissions are full of assurances that 'there is very little active feeling with regard to political or ecclesiastical questions among the students' (Newcastle Commission, 1861, vol. 4, p. 404).

The régime of the colleges was designed to produce an occupational group characterized by hard work, informed by religion and respectability, committed to ideas of rescue and improvement, who would act as the cohesive agents for an industrialized and urban society. It was desirable that these agents themselves should be apolitical and ideologically bland.

There were always doubts, however, as to whether the socialization process alone was a sufficient means of controlling such a crucial cultural position. Middle-class concern can be seen in direct attempts to expropriate the role of the elementary school teacher (Tropp, 1957, pp. 23 and 148) and in warnings to the nation that the occupational group must be closely monitored. The rise of socialism gave these warnings an added urgency. One such account, written in 1908, noted that 'it is a serious matter what sort of men the schoolmasters are to be, especially those of the elementary schools. They will be able to do more in a day for any creed or principle they hold than the House of Commons could do in a whole parliament', and warned that

> the socialist leaders already perceive what a splendid field the elementary schools afford for their peculiar propaganda. What better career can they offer to their sons and daughters than to enter the teaching profession and in a discreet way play the socialist missionary.

If the middle class seriously desired to check socialism and unionism 'they would supply teachers of their own class – men and women free from the bias and envy of a narrow upbringing' (Lawson, 1908, p. 214; Tropp, 1957, p. 148). That such attempts at expropriation were largely unsuccessful gave added significance and importance to the socializing activities of the training colleges.

Taylor (1969) has argued that the value orientations of the colleges continued in the twentieth century to represent an apolitical and consensus-seeking tradition. Nineteenth-century concern with improvement and with the socially disruptive consequences of urban life found expression in a new vocabulary – the language of social criticism focusing upon the undesirable effects of materialism, affluence and permissiveness (but essentially a criticism 'of "culture" rather than social structure') – and a language concerned with a sense of community and 'replete with terms such as synthesis, integration, consensus and wholeness' (Taylor, 1969, pp. 286–8). Teachers destined for elementary schools, and later for secondary modern schools, were exposed in their training institutions to an emphasis which sought to induce in them a moral and social concern which was abstracted from serious analysis of structure and context and expressed in essentially individualistic terms. This situation of political and sociological naïveté was long established and was not to be seriously threatened by the formal introduction of sociology into college curricula after 1963. As Young (1971) has argued, the particular forms of sociology of education mediated to teachers were to provide a 'scientific' legitimation to many of the existing preoccupations of the colleges – the concern with order and stability, functionalist theories of social mobility and a social pathology view of working-class life and culture. What they did *not* do was to expose to serious examination the social organization of curricula and the problems associated with control, knowledge and questions of cul-

17

tural relativism. Such sociology did not challenge existing hierarchical notions of knowledge and culture or bring seriously into question the assumption that the teachers of the urban working class were agents of cultural enrichment or raise the possibility that they could be agents of cultural domination.

Teachers as agents of cultural transmission

The different sectors of the Victorian middle class had different prescriptions for the contents of the education of an urban working class. Faced with what they generally perceived to be a class in a state of ignorance and barbarism some looked for 'civilization' as a result of religious education, others looked from a 'rational' approach to knowledge and others from the opposed positions of instrumental efficiency in basic skills or the refining effects of high culture. Each of these ideologies embodied a distinctive view of the role of the teachers of the people and the story of elementary education is one of struggle for dominance among them. The religious prescription was the most tenacious.[9] The culture of religion, it was believed, would 'enable the poor to govern and repress the workings of their passion; it would render them patient, humble and moral and would relieve their present lot by the prospect of a bright eternity' (quoted in Hughes, 1936, p. 8). The teachers of the people were to be important agents in the transmission of this bright vision into the social world of the urban working class.[10] As a consequence they themselves were subject to a whole array of ideological screening devices and ideological pressures designed to ensure their commitment to this religious enterprise. Such pressures were to continue until well into the century, although the teachers individually and collectively kept up a steady resistance to the more extreme manifestations of religious control. Others put their faith in the diffusion of 'rationality'.

Young (1971) has pointed out how 'what it is to be rational' is a social construct which can have a temporal and cultural relativity. One particular use of 'rationality' can be seen in the prescriptions which a section of the Victorian middle class held for the education of the people. A curriculum was sought which would facilitate the process of making the working class 'rational' by demonstrating to them that the existing organization of the means of production was logically justified by the 'laws' of political economy and operated to the advantage of all members of society.[11] Elementary school teachers could diffuse these truths among the population and by so doing contribute to that state of harmony and order associated with a rational appreciation of the best interests of all. Kay-Shuttleworth (1862, p. 63) wrote:

> the ascertained truths of political science should be early taught to the labouring classes and correct political information should be constantly and industriously disseminated among them . . . the poor might thus also be made to understand . . . that they are infinitely more interested in the preservation of public tranquillity than any other class of society; that mechanical inventions and discoveries are always supremely advantageous to them; and that their real interest can only be effectively promoted by displaying greater prudence and forethought.

It was also suggested that

> the relation between the capitalist and those in his employ might prove a fruitful source for the most beneficial comment. The misery which the working classes have brought upon themselves by their mistaken notions on this subject is incalculable, not to mention the injury which has accrued to capitalists and to the trade of this country.

To make the working classes 'rational' through the dissemination of the truths of political science and political economy can be seen as an impulse in both elementary education and adult education. It was not, however, to become a dominant influence. To make the teachers explicit agents of the culture of capitalism, to focus their attention directly on the organization of the means of production was a hazardous undertaking. While they might become the instruments of economic rationality they might also become 'irrational' and attracted by 'artificial systems, socialist and communal'.[12] The failure of political science and political economy to find a significant place in the elementary school curriculum can be explained by the conviction of a section of the Victorian middle class that the risks were too great and that the interests of capitalism would be better served by ignoring direct study of these questions and by relying instead upon pervasive notions of the 'common sense' and 'normal' character of the existing political and economic structure.[13]

If making the working class 'rational' was too problematic, making them 'efficient' seemed less so and became an increasing imperative as foreign industrial competition made itself felt. With the recognition that 'upon the steady provision of elementary education depends our industrial prosperity',[14] the teachers of the urban working class were expected to produce a disciplined and functionally literate and numerate workforce. These expectations were manifested in an emphasis upon basic skills, precision and accuracy, a growth in scientific and technical elements in the curriculum and physical training régime which provided the necessary socialization for the industrial context. An economistic ideology with its model of the teacher as agent of industrial progress was, however, itself opposed by a powerful alternative – an ideology of 'harmony through culture' and a view of the teachers of the people as agents of 'sweetness and light'. The writings of Matthew Arnold in his strategic position as an inspector of schools, provided a powerful legitimation for this view. Arnold, like Durkheim, was concerned with what he saw to be the tendencies to disintegration of an industrialized and urbanized society – its tendency towards anarchy. Faced with the fact that the urban working class was 'beginning to assert and put in practice an Englishman's right to do what he likes' some new principle of social solidarity, of order and control had to be found. For Arnold (1935, p. 70), the answer was a notion of culture which 'is the study of perfection' and which 'seeks to do away with classes, to make the best that has been thought and known in the world current elsewhere. The control elements of this ideology can be clearly discerned' (1935, p. 50): 'culture indefatigably tries not to make what each raw person may like, the rule by which he fashions himself, but to draw ever nearer to a sense of what indeed is beautiful, graceful and becoming and to get the raw person to like that.' In arguing that culture would 'make all men live in an atmosphere of sweetness and light' (p. 70), Arnold (1935, p. 82) was confident that

> light shows us that there is nothing so very blessed in merely doing as one likes . . . that the really blessed thing is *to like what right reason ordains and to follow her authority* [my emphasis], then we have got a much wanted principle, a principle of authority to counteract the tendency to anarchy which seems to be threatening us.

While Arnold was critical of the aristocracy (Barbarians) and the middle class (Philistines), he saw the threat to social order arising from the working class (Populace). The elementary school system provided a means of transmitting notions of culture among that class which would ameliorate the divisive effects of the class system – 'a community having humane manners is a community of equals' – and a means to establish the authority of 'right reason' (Connell, 1950, p. 84). Who was to determine the nature of 'perfection', 'the best' and 'right reason' in cultural terms is nowhere made explicit, but the implication is that it would not be the Populace. In effect a legitimation was given for the transmission of selected aspects of middle-class culture especially in literature and poetry in terms of the refining and civilizing qualities which they possessed. Arnold and others were concerned that the teachers of the working class should themselves be suitably 'cultured' in order to undertake this function and looked to the training colleges to provide this. The socialization of the teachers of the urban poor involved, therefore, an exposure to the process of 'being cultured' – a process which implicitly or explicitly denigrated the culture from which they themselves had originated.

Mathieson (1975, p. 45) has pointed out how the Arnoldian emphasis on harmony through culture was to be repeated in an influential report on the *Teaching of English in England* (Newbolt Report, 1921):

> like Arnold the contributors to this Report insisted upon the desirability of uniting society's divided classes by means of a literature in a common language. They expressed their faith in its 'unifying tendency' in the national literature's power to serve as a 'bond'. Like Arnold they referred to teachers as the 'missionaries of culture'.

The ideology of 'the special mission of the English teacher' had elements of romanticism, anti-urbanism and social control, compounded together with genuine concern for notions of 'quality' in aesthetic experience. As a dominant emphasis it was to be challenged later by radical interests who saw in it nothing more than a gloss on cultural invasion of the working class and the mystifications of cultural élitism.[15]

Teachers in the popular system of education were, therefore, at the meeting point of diverse expectations and ideologies arising from different sections of the middle class. They were expected to save and gentle, elevate and refine, make rational and efficient an urban working class whose existence constituted a potential threat to the social order. In such a matrix of expectations, what it was to be a 'good teacher' was a social construct partly dependent upon the ideology dominant at a particular time and partly upon the scale of priorities of the particular authority figure doing the defining.

The social construction of the 'good teacher' and the 'good school'

The various constructions of 'good teacher' and 'good school' which can be found in nineteenth-century educational writings reflected the difference in ideology and emphasis already referred to. The 'good teacher' might be variously a person religious and dedicated; cultured; efficient in the management of seventy children; successful in the transmission of basic skills; an exponent of 'intelligent' teaching. Ideally he might approximate to all of these things – certainly he would have been the cause of no trouble to the head-teacher or the managers. The 'teacher as paragon' epitomized the early conceptions of the teachers of the people as a kind of secular priesthood. An ideal type of pedagogical goodness was constructed which, as a goal of emulation, appeared equivalent to sainthood. Thus Kay-Shuttleworth (1862, p. 368) quoted with approval M. Guizot on 'what the school teacher ought to be':

> A good schoolmaster ought to be a man who knows much more
> than he is called upon to teach, that he may teach with
> intelligence and taste; who is to live in a humble sphere and yet
> to have a noble and elevated mind that he may preserve that
> dignity of sentiment and deportment without which he will
> never obtain respect and confidence of families; who possesses a
> rare mixture of gentleness and firmness; for inferior though he
> be in station to many individuals in the parish, he ought to be
> the obsequious servant of none; a man not ignorant of his
> rights but thinking much more of his duties; showing to all a
> good example and serving to all as a counsellor; not given to
> change his position but satisfied with his situation because it
> gives him the power of doing good; and who has made up his
> mind to live and to die in the service of primary instruction
> which to him is the service of God and his fellow creatures.

While this model existed as an abstract ideal for teachers, the inspectorate were the agents closely involved in the day-to-day reality of elementary education and it was they who had the power, subject to the constraints of official codes, to impose definitions, to label teachers and schools and to evaluate pedagogy. While they could not ignore the requirements and expectations of official policy, especially

22

during the period when a utilitarian and 'payment by results' ideology was dominant, they were never merely its creatures and some of them, notably Matthew Arnold and Edmond Holmes, produced powerful critiques of the systems in which they acted.

Her Majesty's Inspectors (HMIs) as definers of pedagogic excellence

How, then, did the inspectors define 'good teachers' and 'good schools', especially in relation to urban working-class education? There was general agreement that the position of teacher of the people required energy and organization. Reports mention the need for 'vigour' to contend with the exigencies of urban teaching and define the 'cardinal virtue of a schoolmaster' as 'untiring, unceasing, remorseless energy which tolerates no waste of time or remissness of attention'. The result of such energy allied to organization would be the creation of a good school of machine-like efficiency. An example is reported to the Popular Education Commission (Newcastle Commission, 1861, Vol. 2, pp. 222–3) as 'one of the noblest specimens of the class':

> There could hardly be a more striking sight to the
> understanding eye than the interior of this school, in which I
> have seen 600 children present at one time, all under the most
> perfect command, moving with the rapidity and precision of a
> machine and learning as though they were learning for their
> lives. It is difficult indeed to overrate the greatness of the work
> which Mr James Wrigley, to whose intelligence and unflinching
> energy the success of the school is entirely due, is effecting in
> the town.

Indications of the success of a school were looked for in rising enrolments and in parental opinion. The report noted that 'it is a subject of wonder how people so destitute of education as labouring parents commonly are, can be such just judges as they also commonly are, of the effective qualifications of a teacher'. The success of schools in working-class areas was seen to be related to 'the rule of maintaining exact order and ready and active attention as the first necessity and after that as much kindness to the children as is compatible with a habit of entire obedience' (Newcastle Commission, vol. 2, 1861, pp. 258–9). Working-class parents and their children, it was claimed, were attracted to schools where 'thorough order' was maintained.

Models of the 'good teacher' and the 'good school' which emphasized 'energy', 'organization' and 'exact order' were generated in a social and pedagogic situation where the function of education was to control and civilize, where physical space was restricted, where classes were large and where the time-scale for the whole process was short. If the teachers of the people were to be successful in such conditions these were the qualities required – it could hardly have been otherwise.

But successful teachers and successful schools had also to produce results according to criteria defined in official codes and manifested in written and oral examinations. For some inspectors, a teacher would be 'good' whose pupils exhibited a technical mastery of the competencies required; for others the goodness of the teacher had to be shown in the intelligence of his teaching and the understanding as opposed to the retention of his pupils. For Matthew Arnold the teacher was essentially 'good' if he introduced his pupils to the humanizing and harmonizing influences of great literature.

While results were an important part of the social construction of the 'good teacher' and the 'good school' there was a recognition by some that these had to be judged relative to context. Those with a close knowledge of the ecology of schools in urban areas were aware of this: in 1861 HMI Mitchell wrote that

> the establishments in the east of London, are of an entirely
> different order . . . the conduct of these schools is much more
> laborious and complicated. The difficulties of the managers
> arise from deficiencies of funds and the more independent
> character and condition of the parents and scholars, the
> absence of the higher classes among the residents and the
> continual change of abode of the operatives.

He noted that 'the difficulties of the teachers arise from the careless insubordination of the children who not infrequently are submitted to no control at home'.[16] In a later report he also observed that 'in one of the large schools at the east of London the clergyman examining the boys found it impossible to get out of them any idea of what was meant by "betters" in the catechism . . . some persons seem to imagine it an insult to suppose that they have any betters'.[17]

The Inspector for the Marylebone Division gave a detailed account in his report for 1873 of differences in educational achievement which he related to the social context of the schools:

> In certain parts of my district a much higher standard of
> efficiency is attained than in others. It is higher, speaking
> generally in the richer, longer settled and more permanently
> inhabited parts of it. Paddington takes the lead. A Paddington
> boy reads and spells more than twice as correctly than a St.
> Pancras boy; his arithmetic is nearly 17 per cent more accurate
> than that of a Hampstead boy . . . It is not surprising that in
> St. Pancras the results of schooling are less satisfactory. Not only
> are the schools in it fewer in proportion but they have much
> less wealthy support to lean on. In some large districts in it as
> Somer's Town and Kentish Town, progress has been retarded
> by the displacement of population, the rapid increase of
> population and those frequent removals which affect
> attendance so seriously.

He found it, however, 'not so easy to understand why Hampstead as a
whole falls behind'.[18]

The Inspector for Southwark, writing in 1881, noted the effect of
social area and school size:

> all the work of a school is indisputably influenced by the social
> position of the scholars. Assuming the ability and industry of
> the teachers to be equal in two schools, the one attended by
> children from clean and tidy homes, with parents of regular
> habits and careful of their offspring, where books and
> conversation and correspondence are not unknown . . . ; the
> other filled with poor neglected things from the squalor and
> misery of a single room, bare of furniture and too often of
> food, there can be no question which school will excel in an
> examination.

Observing that 'several Board schools of very poor girls have fallen
into a sad disorder and disorganization . . . even where the mistresses
have been wisely selected', he felt that large schools were inappropriate in such situations: 'I deprecate most earnestly the collection of
such large numbers of undisciplined girls, as fruitful in evil of many
kinds.'[19]

The difficulty of achieving good results in the face of irregular
attendance by the pupils was recognized by many inspectors. The
Inspector for Marylebone noted that London teachers had to contend with 'drafts of neglected and mutinous children who come when
they are compelled and stay away until they are compelled again'

and with 'the continuously shifting attendance . . . mostly the result of that influx and efflux of labour which is always going on in this huge capital'.[20]

The level of truancy might also be taken as a measure of the relative success of teachers and schools. While some inspectors saw truancy as a natural outcome of the disorganization and economic stresses of working-class life, others saw it as a measure of 'the interest taken by the teachers'. HMI Graves reported to the Committee of Council on Education in 1895 (p. 132) that

> in one of the lowest neighbourhoods of London, a change of
> teachers . . . raised the average attendance from less than 70
> per cent to upwards of 90 per cent. . . . In this case the routine
> of school work and the exceptional discipline has scarcely
> varied: the greater sympathy and evident desire to benefit the
> scholars has produced the change. Make the school attractive
> and only a few confirmed truants will be absent.

While, therefore, a basic model of the 'good teacher' existed in which 'energy', 'organization', 'good order' and the ability to produce results were important constituents, the more perceptive and socially aware inspectors related these evaluations to the social context. The impact of teachers on the local area, parental reactions and levels of interest in education as shown by enrolments and truancy rates were also important in the labelling of 'good teachers' and 'good schools'.[21]

As definers of pedagogic excellence, the inspectors were, like the middle class of which they were part, *never a homogeneous dominant group* and never mere reflections of an official policy.[22] In some cases they were the source of powerful alternative models which challenged the system and dominant ideology in which they worked. The most dramatic example was that of Edmond Holmes, a former Chief Inspector of the Board of Education, who, in 1911, published a fierce critique of elementary education and a programme for progressive reform. In a long criticism of the 'path of mechanical obedience', Holmes (1911, p. 141–2) argued that the only motive force in the system was 'the hope of external reward' or 'the fear of external punishment'.

> From highest to lowest, from the headteacher of the school to
> the youngest child in the bottom class, all the teachers and all
> the children are subjected to the pressure of this quasi-physical
> force. The teachers hope for advancement and increase of

salary, and fear degradation and loss of salary, or at any rate
loss of the hoped-for increment. The children hope for medals,
books, high places in their respective classes, and other rewards
and distinctions, and fear corporal and other kinds of
punishment. The thoroughly efficient school is one in which
this motive force is duly transmitted to every part of the school
by means of a well-planned and carefully-elaborated
machinery. . . . Only those who are intimately acquainted with
the inside of the elementary school can realise to what an
extent the machinery of education has in recent years
encroached upon the vital interests of the school and the time
and thought of the teacher. In schools which are administered
by business-like and up-to-date Local Authorities, this
encroachment is becoming as serious as that of drifting sands
on a fertile soil. Time-tables, schemes of work, syllabuses,
record books, progress books, examination result books, and the
rest, – hours and hours are spent by the teachers on the clerical
work which these mechanical contrivances demand. And the
hours so spent are too often wholly wasted. The worst of this
machinery is that, so long as it works smoothly, all who are
interested in the school are satisfied. But it may all work with
perfect smoothness, and yet achieve nothing that really counts. I
know of hundreds of schools which are to all appearance
thoroughly efficient, – schools in which the machinery of
education is as well contrived as it is well oiled and cleaned, –
and yet in which there is no vital movement, no growth, no
life. From highest to lowest, all the inmates of those schools are
cheating themselves with forms, figures, marks, and other such
empty symbols.

Far from blaming the elementary school teachers, Holmes saw them
as 'the victims of a vicious conception of education' of 'thirty years or
more of Code nepotism and "payment by results"'. He (1911, p. vi)
acknowledged that his programme of reform had been strongly influenced by 'a noble band of pioneers' among such teachers and by
'the brilliance of their isolated achievements'.

As Selleck (1972) has argued, the impact of Holmes' book gave a
powerful legitimation to the ideology of 'progressive' education in
England. Later in the century different models of the 'good teacher'
and the 'good school' from those of the nineteenth-century elementary tradition were to become influential.

Chapter 2

The Working World of the 'Teachers of the People'

One of the imperatives of historical and of sociological research is the clarification of the world of everyday life as experienced by members of particular social worlds at particular times. That this imperative has been largely ignored in the study of Victorian popular education has been suggested by Silver (1977) and a similar position obtains in sociology of education. As Dale (1973, p. 179) puts it: 'many existing sociological studies of education describe what happens in terms of a reified social system rather than in terms of the actor's own view of his situation.' In this chapter an attempt is made to avoid reification and to recover something of the existential social and pedagogic world of the teachers of the urban working class, through their own accounts of it. This chapter is concerned not only with a description of the everyday life of the classroom but also with an examination of *the process of constitution*, i.e. 'the process whereby actors generate and maintain their view of the social world . . . the process by which members' typifications are formed' (Dale, 1973, pp. 177–8).

An attempt to recover some aspects of the social reality of urban working-class schools of the last century will be necessarily limited and fragmentary at the level of description (owing to a relative lack of accessible historical material) and problematic at the level of interpreting processes of constitution and typification. Nevertheless the commitments of this study make such an attempt necessary. It is important, however, to note Sharp and Green's (1975, p. 25) observation that 'the sociologist should go beyond the phenomenological preoccupation with human meanings . . . to try to develop some sociology of situations, their underlying structure and interconnections and the constraints and contingencies they impose'.

In the following pages, accounts of the life-world of the teachers of the urban working class will be related to the sociology of the situations in which such teachers were located. However, given that those teachers who constructed detailed accounts of their working lives are likely to have been atypical of the occupational group as a whole (i.e. having been 'successful' and generally having attained the position of a headteacher or an inspector), such an analysis cannot claim to be a comprehensive view of that social world, but a view from some of its more articulate and successful members. [1]

The sociology of the urban elementary school

The sociology of the schools of the urban working class is inextricably associated with conflict – of class and culture, of ideologies and social processes. The very architecture and physical structure of elementary and Board schools proclaimed their function as citadels of a dominant order and culture set in the midst of hostile and barbarous territory. The social imagery employed by their creators drew upon military and colonizing metaphors. Such typification can be seen in Derwent Coleridge's (1862, p. 24) argument that 'every good school is a citadel of national defence', and in his hope that there would soon be 'a garrison in every town and in every village'; in Kay-Shuttleworth's (1862, p. 583) review of the first stages in the battle for popular education, 'this core of teachers has been like the raw recruits of an army suddenly raised – brought into the field in successive battalions on the verge of immature manhood and placed as soon as drilled in the front of difficulties and dangers. . . . They have been the *pioneers of civilisation*'; and in the reports of the inspectorate, 'every new Board School erected in the midst of the crowded and joyless streets of Walworth or Peckham . . . becomes a new centre of civilisation and intelligence'. [2]

Into these 'citadel schools' there came, in addition to the clean and amenable children of some of the artisans and lower middle class, the children of the less 'respectable' sections of the industrial proletariat, 'swept' and 'netted in' by the enforcers of compulsory attendance. While HMI Fitch felt able to report in 1882 that every new Board school in his division of London was 'eagerly welcomed by the parents' there were many parents whose definition of the situation was at variance with that of the establishment and who continued in sturdy resistance and guerilla warfare against such schools, their teachers and their intentions. The elementary school classroom was the immediate context in which such conflicting definitions of the situation were to meet. Within this arena the life-world of the teachers of the people had its 'paramount reality'.[3] Two of the salient characteristics of the social world of the elementary school classroom were the *emphasis upon order* and *the reality of constraint*. The emphasis upon order, conceived of in terms of a culture of silence and immobility for the pupils (associated with ritual or stereotyped verbal and physical expression at designated times), was a response both to official intentions for the socialization of the people and to the actual limitations of the physical setting. Constraint was manifested temporarily – in the short period available for the instruction of the children; spatially – in the crowded classrooms with their fixed furniture; and pedagogically – in a controlled and inspected curriculum designed to produce results as formulated by official codes and inspectors. Such situations severely restricted the possibilities for any notion of 'role making' on the part of the teachers and the pressures upon them to perform a prescribed role were considerable. The situations similarly generated an understandable concern with qualities of assertion, vigour and crowd control. The inspectorate recognized that urban working-class schools thus constituted would 'demand all the energy and knowledge of well-trained masters in perfect health and vigour', and frequent references were made to the need for these qualities and the limits within which they could be expected to work: '60 scholars . . . is the largest number . . . that a skilful and robust teacher can teach and manage with advantage. A teacher without skill and sound health is quite out of place in a London Board school'.[4]

Faced with sixty children in cramped conditions, with irregular attendance and parental hostility as real factors in the situation, the position of the urban school teacher was vulnerable and stressful. This vulnerability was frequently exacerbated by insecurities arising from the teachers' own social and cultural background[5] and, at particular periods, by the system of pedagogic accountability under which they operated. Those who wrote accounts of their social world, give some insight into the responses which were made to these exigencies and to the processes of generation and maintenance of teacher consciousness in such situations.

The working world of the urban school teacher

Lee Rainwater (1967, p. 2) has described the situation of social workers and youth workers in urban ghettoes in America, as the 'dirty workers' of society who are 'increasingly caught between the silent middle class which wants them to do the dirty work and keep quiet about it and the objects of that dirty work who refuse to continue to take it lying down'. He points out that 'often they must carry out their daily duties with fear for their physical safety'.

The position of the urban school teacher in the nineteenth century was in a number of senses comparable to this. The teacher was at the focal point of class antagonisms which he was expected to ameliorate and contain. He faced the concrete manifestations of poverty, misery and exploitation and its associated bitterness and 'lawlessness'. He was not infrequently attacked and abused in his attempts to 'civilize' the people and his ability to survive in such a situation depended upon personal resilience and tenacity, the evolution of a system of 'management' and the sustaining effects of a Christian or missionary ideology. An account of 1850 vividly describes the social world of the poorest urban schools in 'Extracts from the private diary of a master of a Ragged School'. The writer observed of his pupils that:

> In decency of behaviour or in respect for the teacher or in discipline of any kind, they are totally unparalleled. No school can possibly be worse than this . . . the very appearance of one's coat is to them a badge of class and respectability; for although they may not know the meaning of the word, they know very well, or at least feel, that we are the representatives of beings with whom they have ever considered themselves at war.[6]

Teaching had to be attempted in the face of many difficulties:

> I had occasion to punish a boy slightly this morning: he swore and blasphemed most horribly and rushed from the school. I took little notice of this display and sat down calmly to hear the class with which I was engaged. . . . I was suddenly startled by a large stone passing my ear. . . . I got out of reach of stones thrown through the window and continued the lesson. Several followed: half a dozen at least. He was ready in the court with a brick in his hand to have his revenge when I came out. With some difficulty I got out of the lane without being obliged to

31

run. . . . I considered it best to call at the police station to ask for a convoy. This was readily granted.[7]

In its early days the school was in a state of siege and was frequently invaded:

> seven women rushed into the school; the stairs were full besides and outside at least fifty women had collected. These were the mothers and friends of the girls who had fought. Having abused me in no measured terms . . . they proceeded to fight. . . . The women swore and shrieked . . . those outside responded. Never surely was such a noise heard before. I did not believe that human beings resident in this Christian metropolis could so behave.[8]

To sustain any activity the teacher had to evolve a strategy for survival which 'worked' in such a context – 'they will not be managed by sheer force nor by kindness – a mixture of all kinds of legitimate expedience must be used',[9] and he was to write later that 'we have found that a cold silent reserve towards the unruly has more effect than scolding or foregiveness'.[10] The account describes how the teacher was able to bring the school into a state of 'order' over a period of time by the use of such strategies and by coming 'to understand something of the natural history of them and their families'.[11] Value differences distressing to the teacher remained as did differences in conceptions of the uses of literacy: 'I did what I could to convince my pupils that people learn to write for other and far different purposes than merely to be enabled to pen their own begging letters.'[12]

This teacher's account may be taken as typical of the schools of the most submerged section of the Victorian working class – the ragged schools and the free schools – which dealt not only with the poorest sections of the indigenous population but also with the children of Irish immigrants in the industrial centres.

What does such an account reveal of the consciousness of a particular teacher in such a situation? What is clearly revealed is the teacher's sense of shock at a social and cultural reality never previously encountered, and a sense of revulsion from the values, language and behaviour of the members of that world.[13] This is shown in typifications of pupils as 'utterly destitute of feeling or propriety' and as 'lazy and degraded'. Accompanying these initial reactions and labellings is an urgent search for a *strategy* whereby these unsocialized beings might be managed in order to be civilized. The beginnings of what might be called a more critical consciousness are, however, apparent in the later sections of the teacher's account. From a tendency to find explanations in terms of personal deficiencies of working-class children and parents, *the writer begins to appreciate the effect of their objective social and economic situations*:

> I am forced to acknowledge that such conduct . . . is just what might be expected from youths who have been bred in courts and lanes and not in homes. . . . ideas of personal decency and self-respect no sooner bud than they are blasted in these crowded rooms. . . . these people do not require the schoolmaster so much as they need some municipal act for the regulations of lodging-houses and dwelling houses generally. [14]

The realities of the work situation were to generate for a number of urban school teachers this type of critical consciousness which looked beyond the immediate world of the school. The radical nature of many metropolitan teachers (especially London teachers) when compared with their provincial colleagues was partly a correlate of their direct experience of the social and personal miseries resulting from a *laissez-faire* industrial society and expressed in concentrated form in large cities.

Accounts from a later period show the essential continuities of the stressful characteristics of urban classrooms. Three former Board school teachers who subsequently became inspectors wrote accounts of their working conditions and experiences. In the writings of Phillip Ballard (1937), G. A. Christian (1922) and F. H. Spencer (1938) something of this pedagogical world can be recovered. Ballard's description shows how even liberal and sensitive teachers were virtually compelled to establish an initial dominance through physical coercion. Their objective social situation and the expectations of their pupils regarding 'discipline' and the proofs of a 'proper' teacher [15] gave little possibility of other courses of action. While the 'tyranny of the situation' forced them towards one course of action, the policies of liberal School Boards – especially the London School Board – prohibited such action. The teachers were thus caught up in a conflicting matrix of liberal expectations, personal and formal and the seemingly inexorable demands of an impossible working situation [16] Their responses to this dilemma were various. Some were defeated by it and left teaching altogether. Others

resorted to illegal physical coercion accepting this as a painful but
necessary 'initiation by ordeal' into the world of the elementary
school classroom which, once accomplished, would permit them in
practice to employ subsequently humane social relationships and
progressive pedagogic approaches. Yet others came to confuse the
idea of teaching with coercion, order and dominance, and in order
to maintain an essentially precarious position, used social distance
and a 'frozen' presentation of self as strategies. Phillip Ballard (1937,
p. 62) accepted initiation by ordeal:

A little fighting spirit was of great value to the London teacher
in those early days. (1885) If he had it not he was pretty sure to
go under. So large were the classes, and so unruly the boys,
that . . . one could not educate, one could only subjugate . . .
As I stood before my class of boys at Settles Street school on
that first memorable morning in 1886, I saw at once what I was
up against. We eyed one another, the class and I, like two
opponents in the ring, each taking each other's measure. For,
make no mistake about it, we were not co-operators, we were
antagonists. With a few consoling exceptions, the boys resisted
as far as they dared all attempts to tame them or to teach
them. It was a trial of strength between us: I pulling one way
and they pulling another.

As the youngest teacher on the staff I was given the lowest
class. A miscellaneous class it was, a class of oddments. It
contained boys who, either from lack of brains or from lack of
opportunity, had not passed Standard I at the annual
government examinations. Hence it had in it, mixed among the
boys of normal age and normal intelligence, a fair sprinkling of
older boys with freakish histories. Some were illiterate emigrants
from Poland or Russia, others were vagrants who had not long
before been captured and clapped in school.

The softening influence of popular education had been at
work on the London poor for a decade and a half, and the
bulk of the parents were still unschooled and unlettered. In the
case of conflict between teacher and child they nearly always
sided with the child. And it sometimes seemed as though the
School Board did too. For the corporal punishment regulations
were stringent in the extreme. The headmaster alone was
allowed to inflict corporal punishment, and even so under
restricted conditions. No assistant, however well-qualified or

however experienced, was allowed to touch a child. The
consequence was that discipline was terribly difficult to
maintain. For the boys were often openly defiant and held a
poor opinion of a teacher who fell back on the aid of the
headmaster.

. . . I had in my class a hulking lad almost as tall as myself.
Weight for weight he was probably my superior. And he was a
brute and a bully. He had been hauled up before the
magistrates three times for cruelty to animals. One day I found
him sticking pins into the leg of a smaller boy who sat beside
him. When I called him out he refused to budge and stared at
me defiantly. I quietly walked up to him as though I were
coming to argue with him, then suddenly seized him by the
collar and shot him out. He turned around, put up his fists and
made for me. I had to fight him then and there; and I had to
win or throw up my job. . . . How I hated the whole coercive
business. How I should have loved to find gentler methods
equally effective. It was clear that these lads had to be civilised;
and in my heart of hearts I did not believe in force as a
civilising agent. I had to find a substitute. My first task seemed
to be to get around the boys – to turn hostility into friendship,
and to make moral suasion take the place of physical coercion.
And as time went on, and especially as I took my boys up the
school, they began to see that our interests were at root the
same. At any rate they got to like me, which was the main
point. And the more liking there was on their part the less the
need for caning on mine.

. . . The odds were heavily against the disciplinarian who
wished to employ humane methods . . . he had to contend not
only with large classes, ignorant parents, and graceless homes,
but also with a scheme of studies that was arid and desolate.
The grind for the annual examination drove all human culture
out of the school. There was no belief in the goal and no joy in
the pursuit. And in so bleak an atmosphere it was not easy to
kindle enthusiasm or to cultivate friendship between teacher
and taught.

Similar accounts of *the initial struggle for dominance* are given by
Christian (1922) and by Spencer (1938). Christian (1922, p. 19) notes
that 'teachers were frequently waylaid on their journeys to and from
school', and Spencer (1938) records that 'in those rough days the fate

of a teacher who, in a boys' school with a roughish clientele, failed to establish personal authority independent of the head of the school was, after a struggle of indescribable misery, to have to go as a failure'.

D. H. Lawrence who was himself an elementary school teacher, also recreates the tensions of this world through the eyes of Ursula Brangwen:

> It seemed she scarcely saw her class the next day. She could only feel her will, and what she would have of this class which she must grasp into subjection. It was no good any more, to appeal, to play upon the better feelings of the class . . . she, as teacher, must bring them all, as scholars, into subjection. She had become hard and impersonal, almost avengeful on herself as well as on them, since the stone throwing. She did not want to be a person, to be herself any more, after such humiliation. She would assert herself for mastery, *be only teacher*. She was set now. She was going to fight and subdue.[17]

The classrooms of urban elementary schools were thus arenas in which were enacted basic struggles for dominance. The physical context and the expectations of colleagues, parents and pupils that the first business of a teacher was to govern, made this a paramount reality of the teacher's world. Young teachers entering such situations had, in the view of one writer (Macnamara, 1896, pp. 13–14), 'all their fine theories knocked out of them within the first month' or 'they fight tenaciously for the newer, the more human, and the more educational way and after a brief and unavailing struggle against the Stolidity of the Established rule, go under and pass out into the bitterness reserved for those who fail'.

The working world of the elementary school teacher was not only constrained by physical space and social expectation but was also powerfully determined by the systems of evaluation and accountability within which they operated. The reputation of a school and the salaries and professional standing of the teachers were closely bound to the production of results as defined by official codes and as assessed by visiting inspectors. The particular injustice of this system was the application of an absolute standard across all schools regardless of social location and composition. Teachers in the poorest schools who felt the greatest need to vary curriculum and approach had in practice to exercise a fierce narrow concentration on the 'paying subjects'. Teachers' accounts of the time and contributions in professional journals recreate that experience. G. A. Christian (1922, p. 17) recollected this aspect of his working life at Alexis Street Board School, Bermondsey:

> Had one been able to ameliorate the requirements, the task would have been easier, but added to the annual strict Government exam was a similar individual test given by the school-board Inspector halfway through the school year to ascertain whether the school was satisfactorily progressing towards the annual goal. . . . schoolwork in the 'seventies' and 'eighties' was undeniably hard. . . . the reputation of both scholars and teachers turned very largely – in some influential quarters almost exclusively – upon the percentage of passes. . . . If the teacher sought to achieve anything outside the prescribed limits, he incurred a great risk of reducing his percentage of passes and damaging his reputation.

There are frequent references in teacher journals to the *oppression* of the code and to the impossible task which it imposed upon some teachers. The *Board Teacher*, 2 July 1883, noted that a recent survey in one part of London had revealed that 871 families each occupied only one room. It asked,

> how can the best teacher cope with overwhelming difficulties such as this – which are typical of a large number of schools of the London School Board? The teachers of Tower Street work with all the energy they can and ability they can command . . . all they seem to do is direct a handful of children to school in time to learn (but not to understand) a few tests and a few facts from the Bible and about 70 per cent (on average) to learn imperfectly the subjects prescribed for them by the Code. To the half-starved children of Lisson Grove, the feeding of the five thousand with five loaves and two fishes seems too commonplace to them to be an astonishing miracle.

The article continues with the assertion that 'the results of teaching of these children compared to more highly favoured suburban school children are necessarily very meagre until steps are taken to improve the homes of these children'.

On 1 September 1884 the journal observed that 'the work of the elementary teacher is far harder than any other kind of toil known to civilised communities . . . the teachers have more to do than flesh and blood can bear . . . the only way of escaping official reprimand is to put the screw on the child'.

The *Teachers' Aid*, 22 January 1887, in an article entitled 'the Difficulties of Teachers, and How to Overcome Them' argued that

> the life of a teacher in an elementary school is one of continual care and anxiety: the conditions under which he (or she) labours are such that it is impossible for it to be otherwise . . . the bright, the fairly intelligent, the slow, the dullards and the idle all go into his daily bill of fare. He has to bring all these widely differing natures to the standard of an inexorable code, and by that code his work is measured and he is stamped by it as a successful or unsuccessful teacher.

The social world of the elementary school frequently witnessed the death of idealism, of spontaneity and of humane social relationships. Constrained as it was spatially, temporally and pedagogically and created essentially to 'domesticate' the urban working class, it became a *real context for alienation*. Teachers and pupils were caught up in a system of mental and cultural production which mirrored the oppressiveness of the wider social and economic order. The possibility of meaning, of creation, of co-operation and of change was heavily circumscribed. Notions of autonomy and initiative were unfamiliar. For both teachers and pupils the 'real' world was external and constraining and characterized by hierarchy and order. Power was located outside of themselves in headteachers, inspectors, managers, Board members and distant Whitehall masters. In the consciousness of a few teachers the wider aspects of this oppressive reality were understood and strategies of resistance were formulated. In the consciousness of the majority, issues of day-to-day survival and 'work production' were paramount. Such pre-occupations concentrated their attention upon the nature of the pupils and the homes they had to deal with, rather than the nature of the society in which they operated.

Typifications of urban working-class pupils and their homes

Anthony Platt (1969) has shown how the 'child-saving' movement in America, responsible for the 'invention' of delinquency as a social category, used as part of its ideological justifications, *images of urban corruption*. The child-savers and the social pathologists, strongly influenced as they were by rural values,[18] came to see the city as a context within which the development of children became stunted, distorted and morally contaminated. The pattern of life of the urban working class, especially in its lower reaches was perceived to be disorganized and impulsive and its children to be in need of rescue and the reforming effects of a structured and orderly environment.

Many of the teachers of the people in nineteenth-century Britain saw their pupils in a similar light, and the vocabulary of their accounts reveals the typifications employed. Since such teachers were necessarily preoccupied with notions of 'order', 'morality', 'civilization', and 'getting results', their perceptions of their pupils focused upon characteristics related to these goals and particularly, upon features which impeded their realization. Where their own social background was rural, the reality of child-life in inner-city areas was, for them, in many senses shocking. Even those who originated from the urban working class itself had rarely experienced the total social and cultural spectrum of this large and heterogeneous social group. Selected from the 'respectable' families, they often found themselves in daily interaction with the children of the improvident and lawless. Throughout their accounts, typifications of such children as 'indisciplined' and 'precocious' co-exist with strategies to change these characteristics. A master of a ragged school saw his pupils as 'without one exception . . . precocious. They require more training than teaching. The great city has been their book and they have read man as such boys alone can do' (*English Journal of Education*, vol. IV, 1850, p. 6). G. A. Christian (1922, p. 17) records 'what impressed me most here [Alexis Street Board School, Bermondsey] was the raw and undisciplined character – the result it seemed to me, of generations of moral and intellectual indiscipline – of a large proportion of the boys'. Thomas Gautrey (1937, p. 90) describes how in one of the earliest London Board schools 'the boys came from the streets undisciplined, coarse in speech and manners'. Articles on discipline studied in relation to the nature of the child were frequent in teacher journals. The *Teachers' Aid* for 1887 advised that regularity and punctuality were the 'foundation stones' of good discipline. Discipline was understood to be the control of 'a strong, latent force in children', and this force could be controlled by a plan of management. The *Teachers' Aid* advised on such a plan for dealing with 'quick, restless, fidgety children', 'the fairly intelligent', 'the idle', and 'the dullards'. A problem of discipline was that what might be labelled in one context as 'indiscipline' and as such, morally condemned, might in another context be regarded as 'independence' and as such, morally approved. Some of the earliest teachers in popular education were caught up in this dilemma. Faced with members of an 'independent' working class who refused to recognize a hierarchy of 'betters', the domesticating enterprise upon which they were engaged brought them into conflict with qualities, which in other persons and in other contexts they might have esteemed. At the same time the teachers were also concerned to produce hard-working pupils who would submit themselves to the mechanical demands of the formal curriculum and thus become 'schooled' and more 'rational' beings. The children of some sections of the urban working class, especially those in the inner areas, were seen to provide a challenge to this enterprise because of their *volatile natures*: 'they do things by a kind of impulse . . . they have not fixedness of purpose, or ideas of individual application or exertion'. In the view of one writer, they had 'no originality of thought apart from their wit'.[19] The master of the ragged school attempted to introduce a sober, solemn tone into the lessons as an antidote to 'the flippant, irreverent, thoughtless, gabbling manner to which they are very prone'. James Runciman (1887, p. 6) observed that 'the power of paying attention was almost wanting in them', and typified such pupils as having 'the fluid mind of the true barbarian'.

The structure of the urban elementary classroom generated 'paying attention' as a prime requirement and virtue for the pupil and 'getting attention' as a primary necessity for the teacher. With a predominantly oral mode of instruction, a class of sixty pupils, a prescribed curriculum and visible and measurable results to be achieved in a short space of time, *the question of 'attention' was paramount*. The volatility and restlessness[20] of many of the pupils meant that they failed to conform to the ideal pupil role engendered by such a system and were, thus, frequently perceived by their teachers as failing to be 'good scholars'. Not only did their behaviour depart from the required norms, but the manifestations of their intelligence and ability were frequently unacceptable. Teachers' accounts of the time show that such pupils were often typified as 'sharp' and 'acute', but an intelligence which had been forged by the exigencies of working-class urban life, an intelligence of resistance and survival, a quickness to see through pomposity and pretension, and a sharp critical wit was *not* the construct of intelligence which the formal pedagogy required, or to which the hard-pressed teachers could usually afford to respond. This 'unsocialized intelligence' was

often irritating to the teacher, since it did not contribute produc-
tively to the business in hand. It is apparent that for these reasons
teachers perceived some of their pupils as not having the qualities
required for 'scholarship' and of being troublesome, cheeky or
insolent.

In addition to such typifications, the teachers in some schools had
daily experience of departure from other norms, particularly those of
cleanliness, diet and personal appearance. Runciman (1887, p. 6)
wrote, 'some of the boys were cowed and sly but vicious and some
were dulled into semi-imbecility by hunger, disease, ill-usage'.
Thomas Gautrey (1937, p. 11), beginning his teaching career at
Settles Street Board School, Whitechapel, in 1885, recognized that
though he had been used to poverty, 'it had been clean poverty, not
sordid, grimy, heart-rending poverty like this'. In a chapter on
poverty and illiteracy in London Board schools, he (1937, p. 91) gives
an account of this aspect of the working world of the urban elementary school teacher:

> In the early days, in the poorest districts, the children used to
> attend in a verminous condition. . . . I knew of schools where
> the women teachers had, as a matter of course, to change their
> clothing on arriving home in the evening . . . many of the
> children's heads were infested with lice and the mistresses,
> especially in the earliest days, had immense difficulty in
> remedying this. Some mothers were indignant at receiving
> requests for their girls to be sent to school with clean heads.
> Their outraged dignity led them to visit the schools and even to
> assault the mistresses.

Gautrey saw the London School Board as engaged in a battle
against 'three great enemies . . . illiteracy, bad manners and dirt'.
While appreciating the objective reality of the poverty in which many
children lived, Gautrey (1937, p. 91) and other teachers saw the
failure of many working-class mothers to overcome this as evidence of
personal deficiencies in the home.

> One potent incidental effect of the Education Act was the
> beneficent influence on the homes in the slum areas. The
> enforcement of habits of regularity and cleanliness reacted on
> the parents. The mothers especially were gradually forced to
> overcome their own slothful tendencies and their own tolerance
> of dirt. In innumerable homes the school became the pioneer of
> improved social conditions.

41

While, for some teachers, the existence of dirty, under-fed children was evidence of the social disorganization of poor working-class families, others saw them as victims of an oppressive economic system and sought to relieve their immediate needs by ameliorative social welfare. Gautrey (1937, p. 138) reports the crusading activities of Mrs E. M. Burgwin, headteacher of Orange Street School, Blackfriars, who faced with the reality of a school filled with poverty-stricken girls, 'became an iconoclast and realist'.

The inner-urban school was often the context for the radicalizing of teachers. If the typifications of urban working-class pupils and their homes were unsympathetic on the part of some teachers, this was often a reflection of *the pressures under which they were working* and the added burdens which volatile, dirty and hungry children placed upon them. Doubtless, those who had seen their own mothers triumph over adverse circumstances found it difficult to avoid explanations of an individualistic, personal deficiency kind. Some saw answers to the 'problem' in reform of the homes, others in the development of social-welfare policies. A few, crystallized in their work situation a political consciousness which suggested that the whole social and economic framework was in need of radical change.

Reaction to official control of pedagogy and curriculum

The teachers of the urban working class, like that class itself, were constrained and controlled in many ways, but like sections of that class, some of them resisted the apparently inexorable demands of their situation. The beginnings of a collective consciousness appeared moderately in the National Union of Elementary School Teachers after 1870, and among London teachers more militantly in the Metropolitan Board Teachers' Association. As Tropp (1957) shows, organized teachers in the popular system took action to improve their working conditions and prospects; sought to gain effective government of their own occupational group in terms of control of membership; sought to establish teacher autonomy and, as a concrete expression of the latter, increasingly resisted curriculum prescription and inspectorial evaluation. As a weapon in this struggle, the teachers used the ideology and rhetoric of professionalism. They claimed, with increasing confidence, expert knowledge on the nature of 'true' education and with a sense of professional authority, condemned much of the curriculum, pedagogy and evaluation of the elementary school. Against what were seen as the oppressions of the Revised Code 'the teachers individually and collectively protested against it as a cramping and unworthy instrument'. Gautrey (1937, p. 13) records that 'the best-equipped and most conscientious teachers were the strongest and the most persistent in their protests'. A denunciation at the Nottingham Conference of 1879 is typical (quoted in Gautrey, 1937, p. 119):

> What is the first question asked by the manager visiting a school or engaging a teacher? 'What percentage did you pass last year?' Upon what is the salary, nay, reputation, of a teacher made to depend? Upon his ability to turn out so many yards of reading, writing and arithmetic from his human machines at 3s. per yard? What is the foundation of those lists of schools in order of merit with which some of Her Majesty's Inspectors embellish their reports? The percentage of passes in reading, writing and arithmetic. How utterly unworthy this educational ideal is of the worship bestowed upon it, and how easily it can be appreciated by unworthy means teachers know full well, and it is only just to some of Her Majesty's Inspectors to say that they have pointed out the illusory character of percentages as the test of the state of a school.

James Runciman, described by Gautrey (1911, p. 131) as 'the most gifted and capable elementary school teacher I have known', published his critique in the form of an ironic parody of the system, in *Schools and Scholars* (1887, p. 230): 'The smart inspectors play tricks with the human animals that they drive and they never think of the cost at which their brilliant results are produced. "We must raise our standards next year. I shall expect. . . ."' Runciman (1887, pp. 236–7) reports the case study of a young teacher who 'would have liked to teach geography, for instance, in an intelligent way. He had constructed a model of England which showed the elevations of mountains, the course of rivers and so forth. The lads saw a fairly accurate representation of their native country and they were not puzzled by the mystery of maps. But what use was a model in an examination which ran, "What is the next river to the Tweed?"'

Teachers such as Runciman, generally metropolitan teachers and those who had attained headships early, maintained a strong resistance to the pedagogical system in which they were located. They recognized that the knowledge made available for their pupils was arid and narrow, that the pedagogy expected was mechanical and repetitive and that the evaluation of outcomes was arbitrary and

43

unjust. They were not afraid to say so publicly. Gautrey observes that the first headteachers of the London Board schools 'were men of courage, strong personality and independence'. They saw themselves caught up in a system for the production of objects, rather than intelligent beings, and they resisted. 'What is the primary object of education?' asked a writer in the *Board Teacher*, 5 December 1901, 'is it to do mechanical things with great accuracy? No – or is it rather to develop all the latent powers of the child?'

To writers such as Runciman the control of knowledge was a concrete reality both at the level of the pupils and of young teachers in training. He (1887, p. 141) saw that 'they were taught to abhor Cromwell, de Montfort . . . Wilkes and all the other persons who ever defied Authority' and of the training colleges he was certain 'that a young teacher could only escape intellectual ruin by successfully resisting the culture which his official superiors prepared for him'.

Strategies of adaptation and resistance

The majority of urban elementary school teachers, as the accounts show, found themselves in a pedagogic and social situation which determined to a high degree their possibilities for independent action. As a consequence of their socialization for teaching and the real constraints they faced in schools, many of them were caught up in a system of social and cultural reproduction, the imperatives of which were difficult to escape. At the same time some teachers individually and collectively adopted strategies of adaptation and strategies of resistance.

Strategies of adaptation consisted in meeting the system on its own terms, achieving 'good results' in a formally defined sense and on the strength of the reputation thus acquired, subsequently introducing some variations of curriculum and pedagogy. Such a strategy of system management was often seen as demonstrating 'controlled resourcefulness', and could lead to promotion to a headship or the Inspectorate.

Strategies of resistance to the prescribed curriculum were pursued collectively by teacher unions, especially the Metropolitan Board Teachers' Association and the National Union of Elementary Teachers. Such strategies included 'a stream of suggestions' sent annually to the Education Department, 'by deputation, memorial, petition and letter' (Tropp, 1957), political lobbying and continued public statements designed to project 'professional' and 'expert' condemnation of the curriculum to the widest possible audience. Such resistance made an important contribution to the eventual abolition of 'payment by results' in 1895.

Despite this formal victory, the world of the elementary school was not to be immediately transformed. A culture of classification and repetition, of dominance and subordination, and of measurement, had sedimented itself over time and was not to be easily dispersed or recreated. While formal pressures had reduced, *informal pressures* and parental-pupil expectations continued as real factors to inhibit change. Given the structural isolation of teachers in their work situation and an ethic of individual survival in many schools, group or team approaches to questions of curriculum and pedagogic change were unlikely. Alternative pedagogies tended to be the work of individual 'hero-innovators'[21] such as Edward O'Neill.

O'Neill was an elementary school teacher and subsequently headteacher in the Blackburn area of Lancashire who, in the early twentieth century, attracted considerable attention as a pioneer of 'progressive' pedagogy in working-class schools. In his own account of his work, delivered as a paper, 'Developments in Self-Activity in an Elementary School', to the Conference on New Ideals in Education at Oxford in 1918, he claimed to have generated this alternative pedagogy as a pragmatic response to the difficulties of the situation in which he was located (O'Neill 1918, pp. 110–24):[22]

> I did not set out to work to any fixed theory. I found myself in a difficult school. In overcoming the difficulties, I introduced new methods in every subjects and in the end found that I had developed a self-active school in which class teaching had no place. My attitude towards school work was largely influenced by what I found inside the school, by what I saw outside. . . . In school, apathy and listlessness, an absolute imperviousness to all oral lessons. . . . Outside school, I was appalled by the great gulf which lay between their mode of life and that of educated people.

O'Neill proceeded on progressive assumptions of 'faith in the child' and of the value of heurism, as the rhetoric of his account shows:

> let the child's reach exceed its grasp. The teacher should not say 'No' to the child who wishes to step out beyond the thing planned for children of his age . . . this idea that the child could attempt

anything accounted for the success of the handwork and all other work. We said continually 'we can make anything' – in the handwork I wished to make the boys inventors and discoverers. The men who moved the world forward were not taught, they discovered.

These methods were applied to all subjects including science:

> I think the history of science shows quite clearly that science is only advanced by the men who work on free lines. I provided a science table. . . . I drew up a book of suggested experiments designed to make boys discover the scientific laws for themselves. . . . I put on the table glass tubing, lumps of lead, electrical apparatus as well as all my books on the subject. . . . I was sure that on these lines boys could make mighty strides in their knowledge of science, the teacher just being there to discuss the results. . . .

Some elementary school teachers in this way established alternative pedagogies in the face of considerable institutional constraints and formal sanctions. They were a minority – part of Edmond Holmes's 'noble band of pioneers'.

What was the *social genesis* of such pedagogies in working-class schools? It seems clear that they were partly a reaction against the dehumanizing and mechanical pedagogy dominant in such schools in the latter part of the nineteenth century, and partly a more general reaction against the culture of industrial life and urban existence. They were a response to 'the hideous depths of the Lancashire valleys and their mills and mill-life', a response to 'white-faced dwarfed mill women' (O'Neill, 1918, pp. 118–24). The missionaries of progressive pedagogy in urban working-class schools were concerned to bring dignity, self-confidence, creativity, beauty and enrichment into the lives of working-class children as an antidote to the perceived lack of these things in their general environment. They were concerned to improve the quality of life and to associate the notion of education with happiness and self-fulfilment. They believed that education thus conceived could be a real factor in the transformation of the lives of the working class, rather than being a mere formal acquisition quickly discarded. But this concern for cultural transformation did not extend to any wider concerns for socio-economic transformation. The writings of both Holmes and O'Neill were essentially idealist and utopian.

For all its criticisms of industrial life and society, O'Neill's account reveals no explicit socio-political consciousness – no suggestion that the real enemy of human dignity, creativity and fulfilment might be in the organization of production. There were those among the teachers of the people to whom this was apparent and who felt that the arena of politics rather than of pedagogy was the crucial context for action.

Political involvements

It seems likely that the intentions of a section of the Victorian middle class to keep the teachers of the people apolitical and ideologically bland, were largely successful. The initial selection of candidates, the socialization process, the dominance of women in the occupational group, the influence of missionary-professional ideologies and the sanctions against 'controversial' views, all worked in that direction. At the same time the concrete manifestations of poverty, misery and exploitation encountered by teachers in inner-city schools were phenomena which could, and did, activate a radical and political consciousness among some urban teachers. Inner-urban schools in particular were likely to contain more 'political' teachers for at least three reasons. Young socialist teachers positively sought employment in them as an act of political and ideological commitment;[23] the schools themselves engendered 'radical conversions' and the exigencies of teacher supply weakened the operation of ideological screening by appointing committees.[24] For these reasons such radical political consciousness as there was, was located essentially among urban teachers, especially inner-urban teachers, but while it received vigorous expression, it was not representative of the occupational group as a whole.

Some of the expressions of this consciousness are to be found in 'an increasing rapprochement between the National Union of Teachers (NUT) and working-class associations' (Tropp, 1957, p. 150) and, although a formal vote to affiliate the NUT to the Trades Union Congress was lost in 1895 by 9,721 votes to 4,911, certain district associations attempted to work with trades councils – the Metropolitan Board Teachers with the London Trades Council and the Bradford Teachers' Association with the Bradford Trades Council (Tropp, 1957, p. 150).

That teachers who became actively and visibly associated with politics, especially socialism, were in a vulnerable position, is clear from the events of the Burston School Strike. Thomas Higdon, originally a London teacher, who took up appoinments in Norfolk, became involved in a long dispute (1914–39) with the authorities which, while contested ostensibly on educational and management issues, was at base political (see van der Eyken and Turner, 1969, pp. 69–96). The prolonged attempts to remove Higdon from his position were clearly related to his known socialism and his activities as local organizer for the Agricultural Labourers' Union. In his own account, *The Burston Rebellion*, Higdon (1924, pp. 4–11) argued that school managers would not tolerate 'active, propagandist Socialist teachers' and that the essence of the issue was that 'these Socialist Agitating Teachers were to be got rid of'. He was particularly disillusioned with what he regarded as the weak support given by the NUT during the struggle: 'then what is the use of a teacher – at least of a Socialist teacher – being a member of the NUT?' Ultimately, with trade union support, an independent Strike school was established, described as 'the first Trades Union School in England' (quoted in van der Eyken and Turner, 1969, p. 94).

Socialist teachers and trade union leaders attempted to influence Labour Party policy on education in the 1920s. A motion before the TUC in 1918 asserted (quoted in Barker, 1972, p. 146):

We want our point of view . . . emphasized inside the elementary schools. When compulsory education was introduced into this country it was said by a certain statesman, 'You will be educating your masters'. That gentleman was unduly apprehensive. He did not know that the people in schools could so teach the children that they would believe that the domination of the community by one particular class was a just and natural thing, and that kind of teaching has continued and, unfortunately our class has believed it.

An attempt to form an alliance between the NUT and the Labour Party was lost in 1921 by 29,743 votes to 15,434 votes, but Labour members of the Union formed a Teachers' Labour League in 1922. The Teachers' Labour League attacked Labour Party educational policy for being preoccupied with structure, rather than the content of education (quoted in Barker, 1972, p. 148):

It was not sufficient for the Labour Party to aim at the extension of Education of the existing type . . . that was all right but it did not go far enough. What they wanted was a revolution in the present type of Education . . . the aim of which was largely to provide efficient wage-slaves for the capitalist system.

Attacks were made on what was seen to be the political bias of existing school curricula, particularly 'the widespread reactionary and imperialistic teaching in the schools' and 'the use of history and other text books with an anti-working-class bias'.

In 1926 a resolution was carried at the Labour Party Conference calling for the establishment of a 'Workers' Committee of Inquiry', one of whose duties would be (quoted in Barker, 1972, pp. 148–9):

> To determine the part Education must play in abolishing the present and creating a new Order of Society. . . . To prepare a report as to how far the present books . . . and the predominant methods of teaching and disciplining children, foster a bourgeois psychology, militarism and imperialism and as to how far, under a workers' administration, this might be counteracted and a proletarian attitude . . . might be cultivated.

Despite this formal victory, Barker (1972, pp. 150–2) notes that attempts to establish 'the ideological character of school curricula' as a significant issue in the Labour Party education debate achieved little subsequent success, and in the year that the Teachers' Labour League was expelled from the Party (1927) Conservative Teachers' Associations were being formed to 'combat the teaching of Socialism and Communism in schools'.

The working world: an overview

This chapter has attempted to reconstitute some features of the working and socio-political world of the 'teachers of the people' between 1850 and the 1920s, with particular reference to teachers' accounts of this world and of their actions within it. As a socio-historical analysis it is gross and crude because it has not been possible, within the limitations of the present work, to locate these accounts in relation to a detailed analysis of socio-political developments and developments in educational policy and administration in this period. This would require a study in itself. Nevertheless the analysis here is defended as providing some 'historical sense' against which the analysis of accounts by the contemporary 'teachers of the people'

can be interpreted and defended, also as providing some complement to what Silver (1972) has described as the 'top heavy' nature of
writings on popular education concerned predominantly 'with the
provision and administration of education' to the neglect of content
and process.

While accepting that the teachers' accounts are largely de-contex-
tualized they nevertheless provide a beginning of the process of seeing
the social world of popular education from viewpoints other than
those 'at the top'. They bring the teachers out of the role of marginal
men and women in history.

From these accounts it is clear that many teachers were caught up
in a system of social and cultural reproduction which because of its
many exigencies and constraints, preoccupied them with questions of
order and management, of personal and professional survival and of
producing results, within a narrow framework of definition. Their
work situation determined to an important extent the ways in which
they related to their pupils and the ways in which they understood
what 'being a teacher' involved. Faced with the grim realities of
urban working-class life some sought to transform or at least
ameliorate its worst manifestations by school-based social-welfare
measures or by the diffusion of a more progressive pedagogy which
might effect a cultural transformation, within these grim realities.
Socialist teachers, and those who became 'iconoclasts and realists' as
a result of working in deprived urban schools were convinced that
more profound forms of structural transformation were necessary.

These various responses were to continue to characterize the urban
teachers who inherited the elementary school tradition.

Chapter 3

Change and Continuity in Urban Education

The schools of the urban working class in inner-city areas today are both arenas of change and repositories of continuity, and as such they reflect the social configurations of the localities in which they stand. Within their immediate environment, the architecture of the tower block co-exists with that of the Victorian terrace; the cultural manifestations of the 'new commonwealth' with that of an indigenous population; the ideologies and activism of radical consciousness – feminist, black, Marxist – with that of working-class conservatism and 'apathy';[1] the paraphernalia of affluence with the marks of poverty. Within the schools themselves change is more visible and dramatic than continuity. The elementary school tradition as a class-based and narrowly conceived educational experience for an urban working class *appears* to be extinguished in schools whose architecture, pedagogy and rhetoric proclaim openness and equality of opportunity. The progressive pedagogy of many infant and junior schools in the inner-city stands in marked contrast to the controlled uniformities of their predecessors. The comprehensive school celebrates an ideal of social harmony through class and ethnic mixing and an ideal of curriculum richness in modern languages, physical and social sciences, creative arts and integrated studies. The ideology of community works to undermine the concept of the 'citadel school', to integrate the learning resources of school and community and to begin a process of transfer of real control of the schools to the members of the community. Within the schools, the rhetoric of participation is apparent in the election of parent governors and the creation of school councils and staff associations. Notions of hierarchy and boundary weaken in the face of mixed-ability grouping, integrated studies, the community school and the community curriculum. [2]

Teachers in contemporary inner-city schools are socially and ideologically more differentiated than their predecessors – more middle class, more cosmopolitan and less firmly associated with the training college tradition. Unlike their predecessors they do not face the constraints arising from the curriculum prescriptions of an official code, close inspectorial evaluations, uncertain tenure and classes of sixty children.

The sociology of the situations in which many contemporary urban teachers are located appears therefore, in many important respects, to be radically transformed when viewed in historical perspective. In the place of curriculum and pedagogic prescriptions, teacher autonomy *appears* as a salient characteristic of the schools. The long struggles of teachers as an occupational group to liberate themselves from 'obnoxious interference' seems to be realized in their relative independence of parents, employers and inspectors, and their possibilities for control of curriculum and evaluation. Indeed, the extent of this apparent liberation has caused concern to some writers. Musgrove and Taylor (1969) for instance have argued that such autonomy has gone too far – the teacher 'claims the right to disregard his client which no other professional worker enjoys. Unlike the lawyer or the architect he is the arbiter of ends as well as the expert in means. The basis of this position in moral and social philosophy is far from clear' (Musgrove and Taylor, 1969, p. 79).

The world of the urban working-class school appears transformed when set against the visible constraints of an earlier time, but preoccupation with the surface structure of change ignores the *deep structure of continuities*. Continuity is as much a feature of the urban school as is change and particularly from the perspectives of radical teachers, the latter is seen as largely cosmetic, while the former, it is claimed, constitutes the 'real basis' of an essentially unchanged enterprise. Continuity is most obviously proclaimed in the essentially working-class character of contemporary inner-city schools. In this they remain the direct heirs of the elementary school tradition and this tradition is especially visible in those inner-city comprehensive schools created from the amalgamation of under-resourced and unpopular secondary modern schools. These are still the schools for the urban working class into which some of the children of the 'new' middle class have entered, for ideological and other reasons. The working class for which they exist has become more cosmopolitan in character and, in some areas, more affluent, but the population of these schools reflects the most impoverished, disadvantaged and powerless sections of the city. They are characteristically the schools of the black urban proletariat. As in earlier times, they contain the greatest number of 'poor' schools and of 'sink' schools, and the children of the inner-city continue to fail in tests of educational achievement in greater numbers than do children in other areas. Such manifestations would be familiar to a Victorian inspector of urban schools.

These continuities pattern others. The teachers themselves, although as an occupational group more internally differentiated and located in a situation of apparent autonomy, *remain in the same essential position in the matrix of class relations as did their Victorian predecessors.* They find themselves at the meeting point of classes; at the point where 'official' culture with its understandings, values and world view meets alternative realities; where middle-class prescription meets working-class resistance; where elaborated language meets directness and where the contradictions of liberal educational reform become apparent. While there are among the teachers pedagogic commitments to 'integration', 'heurism', 'critical intelligence', 'creativity' and 'cultural pluralism' these have to find their expression within a framework increasingly concerned with the formal definitions of educational certification. The contemporary radical critique of such schools argues that the essentials of the teachers' position are unchanged. Teacher autonomy is seen to be only real in the 'soft' areas of school life, such as choice of teaching style and mythical in the 'hard' areas, such as the social determination of knowledge and its evaluation. Where autonomy has consequences for power relationships as in knowledge definition and assessment, its existence, it is argued, is more rhetoric than reality. Teachers in urban working-class schools in the perspective of this critique are, despite surface features of change, essentially engaged in a domesticating and job-selecting activity for a capitalist economy. 'Autonomy' is merely a liberal gloss on this reality. While the thesis of this critique is clearly open to argument, its *existence* serves to underline the notion of continuity in urban schools – in this case, the continuity of ideological conflict and of different conceptions of the function of schools.

Ideological conflict

Teachers in contemporary inner-city schools are exposed to many prescriptions for action in the name of 'discipline', 'standards', 'literacy', 'self-expression', 'critical consciousness' and so on. At a simplistic level the ideological contest appears to be mainly pedagogic and to be polarized in a struggle between progressive forms and traditional forms or between Red Papers and Black Papers. *In fact, the ideological struggle is, as it always was, a matrix of class, educational and political issues.* [3]

Bernstein (1977, p. 85) has argued that the way in which a society 'selects, classifies, distributes, transmits and evaluates the educational knowledge it considers to be public, reflects both the distribution of power and the principles of social control'. Curricula and pedagogy do not exist in abstraction from social and political contexts. An educational code which celebrates received knowledge, boundary strength, teacher direction, hierarchy and approved stages for initiation and 'progress' enshrines a particular model of man and a particular model of society – its implications for social control are clear. An educational code which emphasizes the learner's own capacity to make sense of the world in notions of 'curriculum as practice'[4] and 'conscientization'[5] and which opposes hierarchy, authority and boundary, postulates a different conception of man and a different social and political order. The contemporary urban school, especially the inner-city school, is at the focus of an ideological struggle among various interest groups which, while carried on largely in the rhetoric of educational debate and, apparently, in terms of conflicting educational codes and pedagogies, is inextricably involved with wider social, political and economic issues. Just as the various sections of the Victorian middle class advanced their conflicting prescriptions for the education of an urban working class, so, too, do contemporary groups largely active in middle-class contexts. [6] *Conservative* theorists argue that inner-city schools reveal the anarchism inherent in modern tendencies which undermine the imperatives of organized social life: externality of order, specificity of roles and hierarchy of power and evaluation. The situation in their view can only be retrieved by renewed emphasis on order and discipline; strong leadership and 'good teaching' and a reassertion of the absolutes of 'standards' and of received cultural forms.

The ideologies of liberalism have alternative messages, but are themselves internally differentiated. A form of *liberal pragmatism* diagnoses the problem of inner-city schools essentially in terms of their functional inefficiency, particularly in poor administration of management systems and in the existence of low expectations by teachers for the achievements and behaviour of their pupils. Such a view leads to an ideology of salvation through management and through increased pedagogical optimism, but its structuralist approach is of a technical rather than a political nature and it remains in terms of the latter, essentially naïve. So, too, in many ways, do forms of *liberal romanticism* which look for the regeneration of urban schools in a more progressive and relevant curriculum and pedagogy which in meeting 'the needs of the child' and in creating conditions for self-expression, it is believed, will overcome alienation, pupil resistance and problems of under-achievement. [7]

At a more consciously political level, *liberal social democracy* [8] represents one of the most powerful ideologies in contemporary British urban education. Legitimated at both government and local authority level, its prescription for positive discrimination in favour of deprived areas and for the creation of urban community schools and community curricula, seen to be the means for generating active and responsible local democracy, have had a wide appeal. The ideology of liberal social democracy works to try to ensure that inner-city schools are one of the agencies whereby inequalities in the social and political structure can be counteracted and ameliorated.

Against system-approved liberalisms stand the ideologies of the varieties of *radicalism* [9] and *Marxism*. The crisis of the urban school in the perspective of the former is seen to result from the processes of cultural and personal domination in which the schools are engaged and from the forms of resistance which pupils raise against them. Until urban schools cease to be essentially custodial and authoritarian; until they realize an educational practice based upon a relativist and non-hierarchic view of knowledge, language and logic and of categories such as 'teacher' and 'pupil' then the urban school crisis will continue. Urban education from this view must become 'the practice of freedom' and not a continuing enterprise of cultural invasion and domination.

Marxist formulations explicitly view the schools as reproducing the social relations of a capitalist mode of production and of constituting a crucial part of the 'ideological state apparatus' (see, for instance, Bowles and Gintis, 1976; Althusser, 1972). Inner-city schools are seen to be contexts in which these processes can be resisted and a critical political consciousness generated. An important part of the problem of the urban school, in one Marxist perspective, is that the teachers in the main are seen to be the victims of a false consciousness derived from the ideology of professionalism. A crucial purpose of such schools, it is argued, is the creation of a sense of solidarity among both teachers and pupils with working-class movements in general and this involves a rejection of notions such as 'being professional'; the formation of a syllabus which helps to generate a critical political consciousness and an engagement in militant union activity.

A more detailed examination of the 'messages' which each of these ideological positions carries for teachers in urban schools will be undertaken in the following chapters. For the present, it is necessary to comment upon their historical locations and upon their contemporary social structural location.

Historical locations of differing ideologies

A sense of historical continuity is most apparent, as one would expect, in conservative educational ideologies and can be discerned in the Arnoldian cultural emphasis of writers such as Bantock (1975) and in the traditionalist emphasis upon order and structure in the writings of Boyson (1975). In a similar way, Victorian preoccupations with 'school management' are clearly alive, although in new executive and organizational forms, in a contemporary liberal pragmatism which seeks a solution to the urban education crisis through technical changes in structures, communication procedures, improving teacher morale, and so on.

The ideology of contemporary educational progressivism and the emphasis upon a child-centred pedagogy *within state schools* is a continuation of that impulse generated in the writings of Edmund Holmes (1911) and diffused by the sponsorship of a fraction of the middle class in the Conferences on New Ideals in Education in the early part of this century (see Selleck, 1972).

Finn, Grant and Johnson (1977, p. 153) have characterized a social democratic ideology of education as being a particular formation of British 'Labourism' and have distinguished it historically from radical and Marxist positions:

> We can see . . . that the British Labour Party's educational object was not, and never has been, its own class or classes. It is interesting to find Labour intellectuals later in this tradition, actually disavowing what they regard as a 1920s 'continental'

and Marxist model . . . (Crosland, 1962). As a national party
. . . it was never an educational agitational movement. It did
not have a starting point in some conception of Socialist
education. Nor did it set out from the cultural and educational
resources of existing working-class communities. Its educational
policies, like its general politics, were posited instead on a pre-
existing machinery – in this case a structure of State schools
and a particular distribution of formal 'educational'
opportunities. It was these that the party set out to reform.
Thus the party began as, and remained, an educational
provider for the popular classes, not an educational *agency of*
and *within* them.

This analysis is persuasive and convincing and goes a long way
towards explaining the contemporary disjuncture between social
democratic analysis of, and prescription for, the urban education
crisis and those emanating from other 'Left' positions.

Contemporary radical and Marxist formulations have diverse historical origins – from working-class movements in the nineteenth
century, from socialist and Marxist writers and from forms of
anarchism and libertarianism. The tensions between radical/libera-
tory ideologies of education and explicitly Marxist formulations can
be traced historically to a corpus of writings embodying different
conceptions of the essential nature of human oppression and different conceptions of the means for achieving liberation. Joel Spring
(*Libertarian Teacher*, no. 9) provides some historical location for a
radical/liberatory tradition and Richard Johnson (1976) has begun
to examine the revival of socialist educational and cultural politics
from the 1890s.

In general, it is apparent that while contemporary ideological
conflict, which focuses upon the crisis of urban schools, is carried on
in a vocabulary different to that of the nineteenth century, its historical linkages with earlier conflicts are clear and many of its essential concerns are unchanged.

However, there are two important changes in the nature of this
conflict which must be noted. The first is that the conflict has now
become mediated by different groups of teachers working *within* the
schools rather than being essentially fought out *around* the schools.
The second is that some significant fraction of the teachers and
generally some significant fraction of the agents of symbolic control
now take up positions which explicitly relate real transformations of

educational practice to real transformations of the social and economic base of society. While Bernstein (1977, p. 128) takes the view that 'the opposition between fractions of the middle class is not an opposition about radical change in class structure but an opposition based upon conflicting forms of social control', this does not appear empirically to be the case. There has emerged an influential and articulate group located in schools and in institutions of higher education who *are* in opposition on questions of radical change in class structure rather than merely on questions of social control or of symbolic form. The emergence of such a group gives contemporary ideological conflict in education an added sharpness and an added dimension.

Social structural location of differing ideologies

In following Gouldner's (1976) observation that 'ideologies always further some interest', an attempt must be made to locate ideologies in urban education in terms of their relationship to various middle-class interest groups.[10]

The conservative/traditionalist segment of the middle class clearly provides both intellectual and political support for the defence of 'quality', 'standards', discipline and hierarchy in education which are seen to be threatened by a lack of nerve among liberal school reformers and through positive subversion by egalitarians. This segment contains those who take on the role of the guardians of high culture and 'excellencies transcending class' (epitomized in Bantock, 1975) and also those who adopt an aggressive doctrine of tough-mindedness and the work ethic (epitomized in Boyson, 1975). Such a position probably receives widespread support from among that section of the middle class which is directly involved in commerce and industry and from among those recently upwardly mobile from the working class with a conscious sense of 'scholarship' success.[11] *Its wider interests are essentially in the preservation of existing socio-economic, political and cultural categories coupled with appropriate amounts and realizations of sponsored mobility for those with 'talent'.*

'Liberal pragmatism' can be located in a section of the middle class which sees a need for 'modern', functional and technical responses to changing social and economic requirements. Attempting a stance of political neutrality, the liberal managerialists, frequently responsible for the administration of 'personal service' organizations and institutions, interpret crisis and contradiction in terms of system dysfunctions which require more efficiency, more managerial skills, better communication, higher expectations, etc. Their interest in managerial solutions is in one sense liberal in that it leads towards system change, but it is in another sense conservative: as Gouldner (1976, p. 213) puts it, 'to have a purely "technical" interest is tacitly to have *an interest in maintaining the larger social system in which such technical specialism is encouraged and supported'*.

The interests of liberal social democrats are constituted in that segment of the middle class which embraces *the possibility of evolutionary socialism* through political and social action 'within the system'. By this group, the education system is seen as one of the mechanisms for redistributive justice in an unequal society, and as having the potential to be the instrument and facilitator of a more democratic and egalitarian social order. This position, which is epitomized in the writings of Halsey (1972, 1975) and Midwinter (1973, 1975) represents the reformist tradition of educational thinking within middle-class Labour party circles and probably receives much of its support from among 'moderate' Labour party academics, teachers, local government administrators and politicians.

The ideology of child centredness is most associated with the colleges of education as institutional contexts. In its emphasis upon the regenerating possibilities, especially for urban schools, of a child-centred, open and active pedagogy; in its individualistic stance and in its relative lack of concern for social structural and political issues, it continues in a new form the apolitical and ameliorative preoccupations of the earlier colleges and of the socialization ethos of the 'teachers of the people'. While liberal at the individual level, it is ultimately conservative at the social structural and political level and romantic in its belief that pedagogical arrangements can and should be looked at in isolation from wider structural issues. *The interests of the colleges in combating their low status academic position by legitimating a new pedagogical expertise and the parallel interests of primary school teachers as an occupational group are clearly involved in the constitution of a progressive-romantic ideology of education.* It receives much of its support from among teachers in primary education and from that section of the middle class which sees itself in terms of a liberated aesthetic and inter-personal consciousness.

Radical ideologies variously derived from the writings of Illich (1973) or Freire (1972a, b, 1974) or from the 'critical' studies of the new sociologists of education have their strongest appeal and their strongest location among young teachers, sociologists and community workers. More younger members of educational, social or community enterprises, especially in metropolitan areas, characteristically have a critical awareness of the pervasiveness of oppression at State, institutional, bureaucratic and cultural levels; are concerned to oppose such oppression, and in general see problems of human liberation in their widest sense as central preoccupations. Such a stance often involves *scepticism* about the liberatory potential of established institutions and scepticism also about established political formations as a means to that end. This leads its proponents often to locate themselves in the category of 'the unattached Left'.[1 2]

Gouldner (1976, p. 214) observes that 'ideologies are grounded in interests of which they may not speak with ease and freedom' and this must apply to radical as to other ideologies. It can be argued, without detriment to the notion of serious commitment, that *other interests are implicated when younger members of middle-class professions subvert the authority and the conventional wisdom of an older establishment.*

Marxist ideologies in education are more widely located in terms of generation and status position among the 'Left middle class'. As far as teachers are concerned, it seems likely that the majority of Marxist teachers are to be found in urban working-class schools, especially those situated in the inner rings of metropolitan cities. However, it is apparent that there are sharp divisions within the 'Left middle class' working in education. Members of the 'Old Left', particularly members of the Communist Party, occupy important positions within teacher unions and also as headteachers and deputies in inner-urban schools. Such activity is seen by the 'New Left' of young Marxist teachers as evidence of incorporation by the system. This has produced the paradox of ideological conflict *within* the 'Left middle class' rather than essentially between the Left and liberal-reformist or conservative formulations.[1 3] Despite these internal contradictions, *the interests of the 'New Left' have been to continue to demonstrate that the crisis of urban schools is one of the more visible aspects of the wider crisis of contemporary capitalism and that its solution can only be looked for as a consequence of wider social and political action.*

It is apparent that the analysis of ideological conflict undertaken here has utilized the analytical device of the ideal type and it follows from this that these ideologies may not be found empirically in pure form, nor may it be possible to locate any given writer or group of teachers conveniently within one category. The empirical complexity of the world is otherwise. However, these positions appear to describe at least the parameters within which the contemporary urban education debate and struggle takes place.

Classroom struggle

The continuity of struggle and conflict in urban schools exists not only at the level of ideology but in the day-to-day realities and praxis of classroom life. The context of this particular struggle has changed in important respects since the nineteenth century. Unlike the nineteenth-century teacher, the contemporary teacher of urban working-class pupils has a work situation characterized by apparently more possibilities for education as opposed to schooling. The contemporary teacher faces a population less obviously marked by physical neglect and poverty and more characterized by signs of physical and social maturity and of the egalitarian confidence and 'cool' of metropolitan adolescents.

For all these changes, two central accomplishments of the world of the classroom remain in a sense timeless – the accomplishment of a 'definition of the situation' and working relationship and the accomplishment of 'progress' in the form of valid realizations of knowledge and skills. Teachers, as always, have to find classroom situations which 'work' for them and, as always, have to meet the expectations of colleagues, parents and pupils for what are understood to be 'results'.

Waller, in 1932 (1965, p. 296), saw conflict among various definitions of the situation as central to the sociology of the school:

> the schools may be viewed as an agency for imposing preformed definitions of the situation. Education, as has been truly said, is the art of imposing upon the young the definitions of situations current and accepted in the group which maintains the schools. The school is thus a gigantic agency of social control. It is part of its function to transmit to the young the attitudes of the elders, which it does by presenting to them social situations as the elders have defined them. . . . From the fact that situations may be defined in different ways and by different groups arises

> a conflict of definitions of situations and we may see the whole
> process of personal and group conflict which centers about the
> school as a conflict of contradictory definitions of situations.
> The fundamental problem of school discipline may be stated as
> the struggle of students and teachers to establish their own
> definitions of situations in the life of the school.

This 'fundamental problem' remains in contemporary urban
schools.[14] Young teachers still have to establish or 'negotiate' a definition of the situation and, in some inner-city classrooms, to undergo
an 'initiation by ordeal' not essentially dissimilar to that which faced
the nineteenth-century elementary school teachers. This 'ordeal' may
be constituted in various ways. The young teacher from a middle-
class background, carefully separated from the majority of his peers
during adolescence and socialized in selective secondary schools and
institutions of higher education, is likely to experience shock at the
realities of the inner-city classroom. Having established notions of
the 'normality' of the educational process in ordered, hierarchic,
bookish and domesticated contexts which have been largely exclusive
in social class and ethnic terms, his career as teacher now locates him
in a social world which appears to him pathological: pathological in
its apparent lack of 'order', in its lack of respect for hierarchy and
authority and in its apparent resistance to learning; disturbing and
threatening in the directness of its relationships, language and
behaviour and the unpredictability of its unsocialized intelligence
and wit. Above all, it is threatening in the very low regard which its
members give to his status as teacher (thereby compounding his own
insecurities on this issue), and to the academic specialism to which he
has devoted a large part of his formative years. While his nineteenth-
century predecessor was equipped with a missionary and colonizing
ideology and with strategies for 'management', the young contemporary urban teacher will have been exposed to a greater or lesser
extent to the ideology of progressive education but to very few prescriptions for action. He will have generally absorbed the notion that
definitions of the situation in modern schools should not be and
probably cannot be imposed, but must be negotiated. The problems
of negotiation are, however, considerable. The class seems disinclined
to take him seriously, especially when he represents the fifth teacher
of French or physics who has started negotiations with them during
the course of a school year. The humane and non-authoritarian relationships which were the ideal of his preparatory course seem diffi-

cult to accomplish in practice within the context of compulsory schooling and interactions with thirty children set in the slots of a time-grid. The failure of the class to act in a 'responsible manner' and the suggestions of some older colleagues that college ideology can never work in the 'real' world, add to the sense of ordeal.

Radical young teachers in particular face the sharpest crisis and the greatest contradictions. As messengers essentially of human liberation and of the potentially transforming effects of critical consciousness, they find themselves caught up in structures and processes which in their view deny these possibilities. The working-class pupils and parents of the inner-city – the particular population to whom their message is addressed – reveal a scepticism and conservatism which some of them had not allowed for.

The working-class conservative, both at pupil and parent level, remains a dilemma and a paradox for young radical teachers. As a population most obviously, in a radical perspective, the object of a bureaucratic and controlling school system, in which most of their children 'fail' and are processed for low-status jobs in a capitalist economy, these are pre-eminently members of a social world who might be expected to welcome liberation. In practice, important sections of this population want 'discipline' for their children, support unliberated concepts, such as school uniform and single-sex schools, expect to see visible and early signs of achievement in basic competencies, and want their children to 'get on' within the existing social and economic order. In addition, many pupils and parents have a construct of a 'proper' teacher which associates that position with an ability to produce order and work by imposition and alternative strategies are interpreted in terms of 'softness', rather than positive liberation. While it is possible to explain these phenomena in terms of the 'false consciousness' of such pupils and parents, this recognition does not seriously affect the existential challenge of the situation for the young radical teacher. Classroom struggle remains a reality.

Continuity and change, therefore, co-exist within contemporary urban schools. The 'classless' institution – the comprehensive school – remains in inner-city areas the school of the urban working class; the more extensive curriculum remains a curriculum in which most children fail; teacher autonomy is real for some and unreal for others. Ideological struggles continue to focus upon the schools, although some of the ideologies have altered. The changed contexts of inner-city classrooms are still arenas which witness conflict and the

death of idealism, and yet, at the same time, witness also the generation of radical consciousness[15] – in this sense they are both the cradle
and the grave of ideas of social change.

Chapter 4

The 'Problem' of the Urban School: conservative and liberal formulations

Brian Fay (1975) has argued that implicit in all social theories and explicit in some are questions of control, policy and political action. In other words, social theorizing is an activity inextricably bound up with consequences for changing the world even though the theorist may disclaim such intention and point to his 'analytic' or 'objective' stance. The ideologies which focus upon the urban school are in a sense conflicting social theories giving different accounts of that world and advancing different prescriptions for action. What is common to all of them, however, is the notion that there is a problem in relation to urban schools. Conflict arises out of the different social constructions of the problem and the action seen to be necessary.

The conservative critique

The conservative perspective as represented in the Black Papers and especially in the writings of Rhodes Boyson, points to the existence of a 'crisis' in state education, particularly in inner-city areas. *Black Paper, 1975* (Cox and Boyson, 1975, p. 3) gives this account of the crisis:

> surveys of reading standards of 11 and 15 year olds indicate that literacy is declining. Half the adult illiterates are below the age of 25. Industry complains of increasing innumeracy. Some 650,000 children play truant every day from our schools and teachers flee from city schools because of lesson resistance and insolence by the pupils.

The 'Problem' of the Urban School

An anonymous young teacher writes in 'Experiences in a London Comprehensive' of 'the nihilistic behaviour of many pupils' as being responsible for widespread feelings of failure and futility among young teachers in city schools.

These manifestations of crisis are seen to arise from a number of sources among which, lack of discipline and good teaching; the effects of large schools; progressive education and the politicizing of education are salient. The account of 'young teacher' (Cox and Boyson, 1975, p. 33) asserts that

> the home environment remains the most powerful influence in the development of the child and the responsibility for the growing wilfulness and ineducability of modern youth can, in most cases, be laid at the feet of the parents. In most homes in the area of London where I taught the children ruled their parents. . . .

Central to the problem of the urban school in a conservative perspective are notions of loss of identity, status and function at the level of teachers. The instrumental task of the teacher – to be the agent of learning – is seen to have become diffused in socializing, administrative and pastoral functions, and this position is compounded by a reward and promotion structure related to the latter rather than the former. Urban schools it is held, could be regenerated by the recovery of 'teaching' as a central and highly valued activity – 'teachers should be teachers again and not social workers . . . the teacher by becoming a second-grade social worker has become a third-grade teacher'. The lowering of the pupil-teacher ratio in city schools is seen (Cox and Boyson, 1975, pp. 3–4) to have 'allowed the best teachers to leave the classroom for counselling and administration and the calibre of the classroom teacher has fallen. Indeed the status of the classroom teacher is reduced by the fact that only apparent failures remain there. If every deputy head, counsellor, year master and housemaster in the large London comprehensive schools returned to teaching . . . there would be far fewer disciplinary problems because the most capable teachers were teaching again'.

Throughout the conservative critique of schools, especially city schools, the question of size is important. Large schools are seen to generate bureaucracy to the detriment of 'teaching'; to threaten the possibility of identity creation through lack of consensual values and ritual; to create problems of control in terms of both deviant pupils and deviant teachers; and to weaken the paternalistic authority of the headteacher. *Large urban working-class schools are in this sense regarded as contexts for anarchy.*

Progressive education

Anarchy is seen to be realized in these schools in the form of progressive education. Progressive education within this critique is understood to mean a weakening of structure and boundary both within and between academic subjects, within authority relations and roles and between institutions. 'Teaching' is increasingly replaced by 'discovery', 'sequence' by 'flexibility' and 'application' by 'interest'. High culture and the accepted forms of knowledge lose their absolute and classless status and are frequently represented as forms of middle-class domination to be opposed by other realizations of culture and knowledge – especially that of the working class.

The conservative critique uses a notion of progressive education socially constructed in these ways as an important part of its theory explaining the malaise of urban schools. [1] Schools especially in inner-city areas are regarded as being particularly vulnerable to the ideology of progressivism because of above-average proportions of young and radical teachers, lack of established traditions and continuity in many reorganized schools and lack of close parental involvement in and monitoring of the schools' activities. Various conservative writers point out that progressive education thus constituted is not only inappropriate for many children from working-class and immigrant backgrounds but will *place them at a disadvantage in a competitive society.* Bernice Martin (1971, p. 311–13) argues the disruptive effect of discontinuities in socialization:

> working-class children . . . typically experience a more
> structured pattern of family relationships, more rooted in group
> belonging and more based on ascriptive roles . . . the irony is
> then that all progressive reforms expressly designed to tease out
> his true potential, are in fact radically inimical to the pattern
> of relationships and responses to which his family experience
> predisposes him

and,

> it should be noted that most of the immigrants, except perhaps
> the West Indians, have a tight family structure and rigidly

67

ascriptive role pattern which is extremely ill fitted to take the progressive mode.

In referring, in a later paper, 'to some of the more problematic consequences of the Expressive Revolution in our schools' she (1975, p. 59) claims that 'the tendency to devalue useful skills because they are vocational and instrumental will also be more detrimental to working-class than to middle-class children because they above all *need* specific competencies and not just sensitive souls with which to confront the labour market'.

Bantock (1975) in reasserting the Arnoldian view of culture as excellencies transcending class, criticizes 'the current deprecation of middle-class culture as a form of social tyranny intended to keep "the poor in their place" and the search for "validity" elsewhere'. Arguing for the notion of 'autonomy of the culture as something to be come to terms with, submitted to and grappled with in its own terms', he (1975, p. 19) dismisses the credibility of the notion of working-class culture:

> It is only possible to pretend that the working-classes today have a culture if one juggles with the meaning of the word culture. Clearly, if it is interpreted in its anthropological sense as a way of life, the working-classes can be said to have a distinctive life-style; but in its evaluative sense, the old folk-culture has been destroyed by industrialization.

The work of city schools in particular is seen to be undermined by the ideologies of radical sociologists of knowledge and Bantock (1975, p. 19) quotes a comprehensive school headmaster 'on teachers who cause difficulties' as containing among them 'those involved with newer notions about repressive middle-class culture – those who come out of college with "Knowledge and Control" in the bloodstream'.

Particularly influential in the conservative critique of urban schools are the writings, public speaking and political activity of Rhodes Boyson. As a polemicist within the urban education struggle and debate, he has drawn upon his experience as headteacher of two inner-London schools over a period of thirteen years. In Boyson the conservative critique has its authoritative expert – a status produced by grassroots experience, a flair for publicity,[2] vigorous advocacy and clear-cut prescription. Such status has been the more easily created because of Boyson's radical departure from what might be called *the norm of headteacher reticence*. This norm has meant in practice that most headteachers in inner-city schools and elsewhere have generally confined their public statements about education to factors relevant to their own schools and have abstained from general pronouncements which might seem to imply a criticism of their colleagues or of the pedagogic practices of other schools. The existence of this norm has been socially determined by a variety of influences among which, notions of professionalism, distaste for publicity and questions of protocol, *vis-à-vis* the local authority, have been important. In his decisive breaking of this norm, Boyson became the highly visible and articulate expert of the urban education crisis. In his book, *The Crisis in Education*, Boyson (1975, p. 45) condemned 'the collapse of order, structure and external discipline' and argued that 'secondary schools without rules are alien to the working-class, however popular they may be with the middle-class and the school advisers'. Community schools were attacked (1975, p. 60) as appealing to 'a strange suffocating nostalgia' and current trends in curriculum change in urban schools were seen (1975, pp. 101–2) to be subversive: 'it is the rejection by the egalitarians of any belief in a classless "high culture" which is most dangerous'. The essential markers of the urban education 'crisis' serve as chapter headings – 'illiteracy', 'collapse of confidence', 'retreat from Authority', 'use of the discovery method', 'the fashion for change', 'the comprehensive school', 'de-streaming – the new frontier', 'the egalitarian millenarians', 'the myth of reverse discrimination', 'the attack on examinations', 'fall in the calibre of teachers and teacher training'. Colleges of education are seen to have lost their strictly instrumental functions of selecting and training teachers in becoming diffuse liberal arts institutions serving as 'vehicles for the propaganda of "progressive" educational methods which are ineffective in the schools'. Above all, the notion of teaching as a profession with its associations of 'quality', 'responsibility' and non-militant and apolitical activity is seen to be seriously undermined, especially in London (Boyson, 1975, pp. 115, 118, 138):

> while half the membership of the NUT is below the age of 35, two-thirds of the teachers in London are below 35 and one-third are below 25. This has both increased the teacher militancy and the Rank and File movement and the disciplinary problems of the schools. Many such teachers, while pretending to protect the child, have taken every opportunity to strike and attack 'the system'.

Particularly singled out as contexts for extremists are English Departments in inner-city schools:

> it was reported in 1974 that at Tulse Hill School . . . the efforts of the caring staff were 'being ruined because some members of the staff are telling the boys that their chances of success in society as it exists today are nil'. It is significant that most of the 'group of extremist teachers, a dozen or twenty', at that school, came from the English Department.

The reassertion of control

In the same way in which conservative social theory tends to find explanations of the problems of industrial societies in the breakdown of various forms of control, so too does the conservative theory of urban education crisis. Control of pupils, of teachers, of curriculum and of standards has from this perspective been lost by the excessive development of principles of autonomy. *The answer to the problem of the urban school is to be found in the reassertion of control.* Thus Boyson (1975, pp. 141–2) writes:

> these problems can be solved only by making schools again accountable to some authority outside them. The necessary sanction is either a nationally enforced curriculum or parental choice or a combination of both

and argues that despite its unpopularity with teachers,

> the Revised Code did improve reading standards because teachers had to concentrate on skills and not on indoctrination.

Such a prescription is repeated in *Black Paper, 1975* (Cox and Boyson, 1975, p. 4) when the editors argue that 'teacher and school liberty has become licence to the deprivation of pupils who suffer from the whims and prejudices of teachers'.[3]

The continuities of conservative theory with the preoccupations of the Victorian establishment, are apparent in Black Paper concern with control, in Boyson's preoccupation with 'standards' and in Bantock's (1975) continued assertion of the Arnoldian tradition of culture. It continues to represent an important element in the ideological struggle.

The ideologies of liberalism

The various liberal ideologies which focus upon the urban school have a common commitment to the reform of a problem situation, but characterize the problem in different ways and advance different prescriptions. While internally differentiated as a category, they nevertheless may be distinguished in significant ways from 'conservative', 'radical' or 'Marxist' positions. Characteristically the *political implications of education*, especially in terms of a class-conflict model, are absent or of low salience and emphasis is placed variously upon notions of social justice, positive discrimination, community regeneration, or improved technical organization.

Regeneration through higher expectations and changed organization

For some liberal ideologists *the* problem of the urban school is essentially one of educational under-achievement with its associated social injustice, especially for the children of the inner city. While the notion of crisis is accepted, conservative prescriptions for discipline, traditional culture and testing are rejected in favour of a policy of higher expectations and improved organization.

An example of this perspective is provided by the publications of the Right To Learn group. In a manifesto published in July 1973 this group of practising comprehensive school teachers in inner London claimed that the crisis in education within the Authority 'results more from what goes on in the schools than from any alleged social or cultural deprivation'. Distinguishing themselves from 'community' educationists such as Eric Midwinter (1973, 1975), and from Black Paper (Cox and Boyson, 1975) prescriptions, the group advanced proposals for reform 'based on successful practice by teachers at present in ILEA schools' (see Right to Learn, 1973).

In a subsequent publication, *School does matter; organisation for achievement in the inner-city* (1974), the group developed their critique and policy proposals. Starting from the fundamental orientation that 'we think the just and rational aims of comprehensive education are endangered because of bad policies and insensitive organisation', various dysfunctional elements were isolated. Important among these were low expectations:

we believe that the poor attainment and low level of literacy shown to exist among London school children is a result of

71

many schools' low level of expectation and is not due to an
innate lack of ability on the part of the children;

a social pathology view of working-class children and their homes:

we maintain that the number of really difficult and disturbed
children and of grossly inadequate families is very small. The
sweeping assertion recently made that one in five of London
children are 'disturbed' is based on completion of the Rutter
behaviour scale . . . originally devised as a screening test for
children with psychiatric disorder;

inappropriate curriculum:

it is too easy to blame chaos and under-achievement on the
problems which the children bring into the schools with them.
Schools make problems too. When schools offer children
diluted courses with a minimum content of real learning –
simply because they happen to live in a certain postal district –
then schools themselves are the agents of deprivation;

and maladministration:

administrators operate from their offices, remote from the
children and out of touch with the pressures which day-to-day
teaching imposes on the classroom teacher. . . . the
administration structure as it exists at present allows for several
members of staff either to do no teaching at all or at most to
teach only half a timetable.

It is argued that these dysfunctions could be overcome by higher
expectations, a 'normal' as opposed to a 'pathological' view of urban
working-class children, good subject teaching and a changed
administrative context. The latter represents the most radical suggestion of the group. Against existing models of the urban
comprehensive school with differentiated administrative, pastoral
and teaching functions, associated with power, status and reward
differentials, a unified and non-hierarchic model is proposed in
which all teachers share in administrative, pastoral and teaching
activities. Separate administration and pastoral systems would be
abolished and 'the school will be run by the teachers. That is,
educational and administrative decisions will be taken by the people
who actually teach the children and not by a special team of highly-
paid administrators' (*Right to Learn,* 1974, p. 1).

Within the Right To Learn perspective the increasing division of labour which has characterized the large urban comprehensive school has *not* resulted in a harmonious situation of 'organic solidarity' but a situation in which many teachers feel alienated and powerless. Their answer is a return to a simpler model of 'mechanical solidarity' with composite roles and consensual commitment to social, emotional and intellectual development. The end of the division of labour in this sense, will end the system of hierarchy and differential reward.

The Right To Learn critique and policy prescriptions make few explicit references to questions of social control or to political implications. What is declared is a commitment to a construct of the 'best interests' of urban working-class children based upon the authors' own experience of 'bad social conditions' and significant experience of inner-city teaching. This leads them to take the middle ground on issues of class and education – distinguishing themselves from Black Paper critiques: 'we do not associate ourselves with the denigration of working-class culture', and from some radical pre-scriptions: 'but we would not restrict learning to it', and in con-demning some Marxist perspectives: 'we find it hard to stomach the arrogance of those who declare that nothing can possibly be achieved in schools until these social abuses are put right. . . . We are not so foolish as to imagine that social injustice can be cured by offering a good education to every child. But we do believe that "until the revolution" it is our duty as teachers to maximize the potential of every child' (*Right to Learn*, 1974, p. 13).

Regeneration through 'efficiency' and pastoral care

Other liberal ideologists see the problem of the urban school as one of *lack of management expertise* at local authority, school, departmental, classroom and human relations levels. The prescrip-tions of educational administration and management are not, of course, confined to specifically urban areas, but the situations of urban education, and especially the large urban comprehensive school, are seen as particularly appropriate contexts for admini-strative and managerial skills and lack of such skills is seen to be associated with crisis and malaise. That such a view has received official recognition is apparent in the sponsoring of 'administration and management' courses by the ILEA and other urban authorities and by an increase in publications concerned with these issues. In one of these, *Management Development for the Education Profession*, Glatter (1972) argues that:

> the concept of the teacher's role as that of a *manager* of a set of learning resources, including other more or less skilled staff, pupils' time, ability and motivation, furniture and software and hardware of all kinds, is increasingly being put forward as a more appropriate model for the present and future than that of the class-based instructor and discipline enforcer. We fully agree with this point of view, although, because of its far-reaching organisational implications, the model will, unfortunately, not become a working reality for teachers for some time yet.

The view that all teachers, but particularly urban teachers, need to be efficient managers has been powerfully diffused by the writings of Michael Marland (1974, 1975), a leading exponent of what might be called liberal managerialism. The basic thesis advanced is that all schools, but particularly urban schools, have been confronted with a number of 'challenges' arising out of increased size and complexity, a changed clientele and enlarged conceptions of their social and educational function. The response of many schools to these challenges has been unsatisfactory because of *failure to establish adequate management systems* in terms of role definition and specification, communication and participation, systems of care and classroom strategies. The basic premise of the critique (Marland, 1974, pp. 92–104) is that 'confusion has been institutionalised at the core of the school' and that 'schools cannot continue to organise themselves as sloppily as some of them have in the past. The role of each person, spheres of responsibility and the links between them need careful planning *as a total system* if the individual pupil is to have the care he or she needs and if the school is to be a well-ordered community'.

Such a view, with its stress upon system and the need to find equilibrium maintaining responses to new challenges, represents a classic functionalist position. The prescriptions of this particular perspective are contained in publications such as *Head of Department: leading a department in a comprehensive school; Pastoral Care: organizing the care and guidance of the individual pupil in a comprehensive school* and *The Craft of the Classroom: a survival guide to classroom management.*

In the latter, the problem of the urban school is presented in terms of heightened challenge (Marland, 1975, pp. 2-5):

> inner-city social conditions have deteriorated rapidly. A general
> 'decline in deference' has made it harder to look after young
> people. It is not that they have become 'tougher' or more
> 'violent' but they have certainly become more choosy, less easy
> to organise, less easy to impress and less easy to lead (and yet
> still wanting leadership!).

Against this construct of challenge, a rationale of classroom management is advanced in these terms:

> the central art of the teacher is to manage the classroom; the
> paradox is that good classroom management makes *personal*
> teaching possible, for it frees the individual from constant
> conflict and only then can the teacher be truly personal;
> contrary to superficial impressions, most, very nearly all, pupils
> like good order and are happier if the classroom is 'in control'.
> The very word 'control' is unfashionable and has perjorative
> associations. Yet a teacher must face up to the fact that
> 'controlling' is part of his task and if he fails in that he will fail
> in much else.

A construct of the 'good teacher' is produced based upon pupils'
responses to this issue. The crucial characteristics are seen to be:

> a sense of caring, of never giving up. . . . (Love alone cannot
> guarantee success but it is necessary – a rather hard, remote,
> balanced, ungushing kind of love), making complicated things
> simple; being in control – a good teacher is a good classroom
> manager.

An important element in this particular liberal ideology is that
urban schools need to be efficient and caring and that these two
concepts are not in opposition as many radicals suppose but functionally interrelated. Thus it is argued that 'humanity is not possible
in schools without efficiency' (Marland, 1974, p. 204).

Pastoral care represents an epitome of liberal concern for
efficiency with humanity. Its ideology in many urban areas is
officially legitimated and it is powerfully institutionalized in inner-
city schools. It represents for many the acceptable face of a liberal
educational system, while for others its existence is profoundly disturbing.[4] In this sense it constitutes one of the concrete manifestations of ideological conflict in urban education. The liberal rationale

75

for pastoral care is based upon an assumed increase in 'pastoral need' among pupils, particularly in urban areas, which requires schools in such areas to take on a responsibility for the total welfare of the pupil. In addition it is argued that care systems are needed to respond to various sets of problems which may occur (Marland, 1974, p. 16): 'if, for example, there is a sudden influx of immigrants into the neighbourhood, a policy of slum clearance . . . , the middle-class element in the locality increases, there is an exodus of staff. . . .'

Pastoral care and counselling are an important part of the liberal answer to the problem of the urban school. Nevertheless there is continued conflict as to whether teachers in the pastoral care role represent the necessary liberal responses to the distresses and complexities of urban society or whether they are, in fact, the agents of social control in liberal disguise.[5]

Regeneration through progressive pedagogy

In chapter 2 it was suggested that some elementary school teachers in urban working-class schools reacting against the de-humanizing and mechanical pedagogy of the time and against the cultural manifestations of industrial life and urban existence, found a gospel of regeneration in educational progressivism. This progressivism, sponsored by important middle-class interest, hoped to find an answer to the problem of the urban school and the problem of urban society by bringing, through a different school experience, dignity, self-confidence, creativity, meaning, wholeness, beauty and enrichment into the lives of working-class children as an antidote to the lack of these things in their day-to-day lives. This form of progressivism was 'romantic' in the sense that it looked substantially to education for social regeneration and was naïve about, or tended to disregard, external power realities.[6] The ideology of progressive education in this liberal romantic tradition is an important feature of the contemporary urban education scene. Offering as it does a pedagogic mode which celebrates openness, co-operation and integration, it stands in attractive antithesis to constraining, competitive and divisive aspects of urban living. In inner-city areas, its associations with variety of experiences and resources, with 'inquiry, making, and dialogue' seem to offer the valuables of a middle-class educational experience to the poorest children. For these reasons, liberal urban authorities have facilitated the development of such pedagogy, particularly in primary education, although these have always been critics and sceptics of such policies.

At secondary school level, alienation from the curriculum is counteracted by 'curriculum development', inter-disciplinary inquiry and notions of integration. Widespread truancy from city schools, is seen to be, among other things, a reaction against out-moded, meaningless and fragmented knowledge and the liberal answer is to find the necessary functional reforms. These may be realized in a number of ways: in heurism, the aural-visual and 'concepts rather than facts' (as in 'new' science, modern languages and mathematics); in a wider cultural perspective, as in black studies and comparative religions; in the creativity of English and the expressiveness of movement, design and artistic studies; in the finding of 'relevance' in sociology, social studies, community education, urban studies, human relationships and child care; in the utility of technical studies, computer studies and office practice. Above all, *the search for meaning in the curriculum finds its expression in the impulse towards integration*. From this viewpoint the problem of the urban school is the problem of alienation, boredom and truancy and this is seen to result from the stratified and compartmentalized nature of secondary school experience, both at the level of curriculum and of working groups. Regeneration, interest and harmony are looked for in an ideal of *integrated school experience*, concretely expressed in integrated knowledge codes and integrated or mixed-ability grouping. Integration is enshrined at the heart of contemporary progressive pedagogy and for many young teachers in inner-city schools it represents both the doctrine in which they have been socialized and an attractive and 'common-sense' solution to the discontinuities of urban living. In so far as young urban teachers may still be viewed as missionaries to the inner city, many of them take with them a gospel of 'pastoral care' and 'integration' in place of their predecessors' gospel of 'civilization' and religion.

Bernstein (1975, 1977) has examined the social genesis and ideological contexts of moves from 'closed' to 'open' schools, from collection to integrated codes, and from 'visible' to 'invisible' pedagogy. In essence such changes are seen to be related to 'a shift of emphasis in the principles of social integration – from "mechanical" to "organic" solidarity'; important changes in patterns of socialization, particularly among the middle class, and to an intensified ideological conflict within the middle class. From the basic premise that 'the ideologies of education are still the ideologies of class', Bernstein (1977, p. 124–6) argues that the origins of progressive pedagogy and integrated codes can be located in a section of middle class – the 'new middle class' – 'the new agents of symbolic control' who have 'interrupted' traditional patterns of socialization, asserted alternative values – 'variety against inflexibility, expression against repression, the inter-personal against the inter-positional' and sponsored progressive pedagogy in state schools (1977, p. 124–6).[7] The diffusion of progressive pedagogy and of integrated knowledge codes as an answer to the problem of the urban school is seen to be romantic in its naïveté (Bernstein, 1977, pp. 145–6):

> the movement to invisible pedagogies realised through integrated codes may be seen as a superficial solution to a more obdurate problem. Integrated codes are integrated at the level of ideas, they do *not* involve integration at the level of institutions, i.e. between school and work. Yet the crucial integration is precisely between the principles of education and the principles of work. . . . *the liberal tradition . . . masks the brutal fact that work and education cannot be integrated at the level of social principles in class societies* [my emphasis].

The liberal romanticism of progressive pedagogy which has frequently found its expression in urban schools, especially those in inner-city areas, is thus regarded as problematic in terms of the real benefits it can bestow upon urban working-class children. Such a view is argued from a wide range of ideological positions, including both Black Paper and Marxist orientations and pressure groups of the liberal middle ground. The group, Right To Learn (1974, p. 17), for instance, takes the view that 'we should be suspicious of schemes which integrate subjects in working-class areas, while it is still widely felt that separate subject teaching is appropriate for middle- and upper-class children'.

Insistence is made, however, in the writings of Bernstein (1975, 1977), that progressive pedagogy 'has the potential of making visible fundamental social contradictions'. Radical and Marxist ideologies, which will be examined in the next chapter, are particularly concerned with facilitating this process.

Liberal social democracy: educational priority areas and community education

In both Britain and America influential and government-backed liberal intervention programmes have attempted to grapple with problems of educational under-achievement among working-class pupils, especially those in inner-city areas. Each of these intervention programmes has its supporting legitimations and ideology which serve both as credos (though supported by scientific 'works') and as levers upon policy makers and funding agencies. Three of the most influential have centred around notions of 'compensatory education'; 'positive discrimination/action research' and 'urban community education' and the issues raised by these notions have generated a considerable debate within sociology of education and urban education contexts.

Compensatory education programmes originating essentially from America have been premised on the liberal assumption that the under-achievement of many lower working-class and negro children was not based upon genetic limitations but upon cultural and environmental limitations relating to their early socialization and home background. Given that the relative lack of educational success by many children in inner-city areas could be 'explained' by cultural rather than innate deficiencies, the logic of liberal concepts such as social justice and equality of opportunity led to policies of early cultural intervention designed to 'remedy' this situation. Thus (Morton and Watson, 1973, p. 46):

the programmes generally aim at 'compensating' children pre-
empting the growth of deficits by exposing the children to an
'enriched', stimulating, pre-school environment. The main
objective is to equip such children to compete with more
'privileged' groups of children in the school system from the
earliest possible age.

The rhetoric of such programmes has become an integral part of discussions concerned with urban education problems in this country and the language of 'disadvantage', 'cultural deprivation' and 'compensation' is part of the professional vocabulary of many urban school teachers.

The critical attacks on such programmes and the assumptions and ideologies underpinning them are by now well known (see, for instance, Keddie, 1973). From radical and Marxist perspectives such programmes constitute nothing more than a liberal gloss on a cultural invasion of the urban working class and diversionary ameliorating activity designed to draw attention away from the real basis of inequality in the social and economic structure. Such critiques are able to draw upon Bernstein's (1973, p. 82) criticisms of the concept of compensatory education, that 'it distracts attention

79

from the deficiencies in the school itself and focuses upon deficiencies within the community, family and child' and upon the ideological critique of Morton and Watson (1973).

In examining the relationship between compensatory education and contemporary liberalism in the USA, Morton and Watson (1973, p. 49) assert:

> It is our contention that the ideology of compensatory education is a specific expression of the liberal ideology. From this standpoint the formulation of social problems in psychological terms such as 'maladjustment', 'linguistic or sensory deprivation' and 'poor motivation' can be seen as the scientific counterpart of the individualistic approach to social problems which characterises the liberal perspective.

Liberal ideology is seen to involve 'social change in piecemeal fashion, within the existing framework of social institutions' and the isolation of problems by the 'special areas approach':

> by implying that 'the problem' whether that of poverty or educational disadvantage is limited to certain areas and to a small minority of the total population, such an approach tends to deflect attention from the full extent of the problem and its root in the overall social system. This approach is exemplified by such concepts as 'the inner-city' and 'educational priority areas' which together focus attention away from rural and small-town problems and the educational disadvantages encountered by working-class children everywhere. [8]

In the view of Morton and Watson (1973, p. 49), the liberal perspective on compensatory education is nothing more than 'a variant of conservative ideology'.

Positive discrimination and action research: the EPA Programmes in Britain

In Britain the impetus for liberal intervention has stemmed largely from the recommendations of the Plowden Report (1967), particularly those relating to notions of positive discrimination, educational priority areas, action-research and the community school. The Report, in recognizing that 'in our cities there are whole districts which have been scarcely touched by the advances made in more fortunate places', called for special action in response to 'special need' (Plowden Report, 1967, Vol. 1, paras. 138, 151–3):

> We ask for 'positive discrimination' in favour of such schools and the children in them, going well beyond an attempt to equalise resources. Schools in deprived areas should be given priority in many respects. The first step must be to raise the schools with low standards to the national average; the second, quite deliberately to make them better. The justification is that the homes and neighbourhoods from which many of their children come provide little support and stimulus for learning. The schools must supply a compensatory environment. . . . Objective criteria for the selection of educational priority schools and areas will be needed to identify those schools which need special help. . . .

In addition to such special action in favour of deprived areas and schools, especially in urban centres, the Report (1967, Vol. 1, para. 177) called for 'research to discover which of the developments in the educational priority areas have the most constructive effects'.

The prescriptions of the Plowden Report have been powerfully mediated both as ideology and as practice by the EPA programmes directed by A. H. Halsey (1972). The publications generated by these programmes have considerable significance in the ideological struggle which focuses upon inner-city schools. They represent variously, 'official' policy on urban education; the epitome of the liberal middle ground; the most extensive collection of action-research findings on education in inner-city areas; and a strongly developed ideology of the community school. Their distinctive sociological orientation contrasts with the psychological origins of many American compensatory programmes.

Specifically in the writings of Halsey (1972, 1975), the liberal perspective on problems in urban education receives its most sophisticated expression. There is in the rationale for EPA action a clear recognition that education alone cannot compensate for society; that 'special areas' approaches are problematic (Halsey, 1972, p. 181);[9] that compensatory education may legitimate a deficit view of working-class culture and even within its own terms be ineffectual.[10] At the same time there is a recognition that *in the absence of radical political action which changes the whole basis of society*, educational and social strategies are required to overcome palpable disadvantage and to engender a critical consciousness which in the long term may

81

lead to radical political action. Thus, in stating the general objectives of the programmes as being '(1) to raise the educational performance of children (2) to improve the morale of teachers (3) to increase the involvement of the parents in their children's education and (4) to increase the "sense of responsibility" for their communities of the people living in them' (Halsey, 1972, p. 172), it is accepted that 'too much has been claimed for the power of educational systems as instruments for the wholesale reform of societies which are characteristically hierarchical' and that 'the school is only one influence among others, and in relation to the phenomenon of social stratification, probably a fairly minor one' (Halsey, 1972, pp. 7–8). While the limited nature of educational intervention alone is fully acknowledged, there is an optimistic orientation towards its potential for regeneration (Halsey, 1972, p. 30):

> it is possible too, that educational programmes may make considerable impact on the political consciousness of the poor, a process that has certainly accompanied the development of compensatory education in the United States. Such political awakening may be the most effective means of ensuring that the gross inequalities between social and ethnic groups are eradicated.

The urban community school

In recognizing the many contradictions and dilemmas of liberal educational reform, some resolution of these is sought in the concept of the community school. *The ideological appeal of this concept is considerable because it appears to offer a mode of working 'within the system' while at the same time encouraging critical opposition to it.* The urban community school in particular makes a comprehensive ideological appeal. In celebrating the values of 'community' knowledge as against 'academic' knowledge and in suggesting complementary rather than compensatory education (see Halsey, 1972, p. 118), it is responsive to radical critiques of cultural invasion in working-class areas. In representing permeability of boundary between school and neighbourhood, it manifests the powerful impulse to integration – to the end of the 'citadel school', the weakening of specific 'teacher' identities and in the long term to the very category of 'school' itself. In its associations with notions of 'community', 'urban regeneration', 'active involvement', 'home-school co-operation', it can appeal simultaneously to conservatives, liberals and radicals; to romantics and pragmatists; to political activists and to urban planners; to those who wish to see ideological struggle and conflict in urban areas intensified and those who wish to see it defused and contained.

Plant (1974) has shown how the concept of community with its wide range of social meanings and value connotations has been variously used by social analysts and reformers. From the conservatism of Tönnies 'Gemeinschaft' to the egalitarian fraternity of Marxist notions of community, the concept 'has been used by both conservative and radical critics of industrialism or industrial capitalism to formulate the predicament of man in modern society' (Plant, 1974, p. 19). It is clear that notions of the community school and of community education derived as they are from this elusive and ideologically catholic concept will generate considerable conflict. Indeed, it could be argued that conflict among the various ideologies or theologies of community and community education will be the contemporary equivalent of the religious struggle which focused upon urban schools in the nineteenth century.

In this struggle the liberal social democratic perspective is at present the most powerful and the most widely diffused, particularly in the writings of Halsey (1972, 1975) and Midwinter (1973, 1975). In *Educational Priority: EPA Problems and Policies* (Halsey, 1972), the liberal construction for community education in urban areas is presented as 'the *essential* principle along with that of positive discrimination in a policy for educational priority areas'. It is a rationale based upon concerns for integration, 'relevance', urban regeneration and active social democracy. Thus the argument is made that 'to put the matter in its broadest perspective the problem at all stages is to integrate school and life. That is the concept of the community school'; 'the community school seeks almost to obliterate the boundary between school and community, to turn the community into a school and the school into a community' (Halsey, 1972, p. 189). Among the many advantages to be gained by such integration it is claimed, would be the end of the Victorian 'citadel school' in urban working-class areas, with its colonizing and military associations – 'at worst the teachers drive through enemy-occupied territory at 9 a.m. to withstand siege until the 4 p.m. withdrawal'. A new concept of shared enterprise could be established: 'the community school holds out the promise of peace and co-operation between teacher and parent' (Halsey, 1972, p. 18).

83

The reconstructed urban community school would no longer serve to perpetuate the historic functions of its predecessors in gentling the masses and in sponsoring an 'able minority' for higher things, but would perform essentially populist action in *raising the general level of competencies and consciousness* towards the transformation of the immediate community context and the power realities beyond this. This argument is contained in two important sections of the report – an initial questioning about the functions of education (Halsey, 1972, p. 11):

> The debate could be taken beyond equality of educational opportunity to a third phase which involves reappraisal of the functions of education in contemporary society. Education for what? . . . What assumptions could or should be made about the world into which our EPA children would enter after school? Were we concerned simply to introduce a greater measure of justice into an educational system which traditionally selected the minority for higher education and upward social mobility out of the EPA district, leaving the majority to be taught, mainly by a huge hidden curriculum, a sense of their own relative incompetence and impotence – a modern, humane and even relatively enjoyed form of gentling the masses? Or could we assume a wide programme of social reform which would democratise local power structures, and diversify local occupational opportunities so that society would look to its schools for a supply of young people educated for political and social responsibility and linked to their communities not by failure in the competition but by rich opportunities for work and life.

and a later, more explicit, prescription (p. 117):

> This argument may be couched in political as well as pedagogical terms. If we are concerned with the majority of children who will spend their lives in EPAs, rather than only with the minority who will leave them for universities and colleges and middle-class occupations elsewhere, then the schools must set out to equip their children to meet the grim reality of the social environment in which they live and to reform it in all its aspects.

and (p. 144):

EPA community education presumes that the EPA should be radically reformed and that the children should be 'forewarned and forearmed for the struggle'. This does not mean that the teacher should form a revolutionary cell in the classroom but that both teachers and children should develop a critical but tolerant attitude to a range of social institutions, ideas and aspirations.

Anticipating criticism of narrowed educational horizons and social determinism, it is argued that (p. 118):

> but what we intend is the opposite of a soporific: it is not to fit children for their station in life in an ascriptive sense. It is to accept that many children must live out their lives in deprived areas and to inspire them to think boldly about it rather than lapse into resigned apathy.

The liberal ideology of community education in urban areas thus developed in *Educational Priority* has subsequently been transposed, particularly in the writings of Eric Midwinter (1973, 1975), into its curricula and policy implications. Notions of 'urban curriculum' and 'EPA curriculum' are constructed in relation to concepts of 'relevance' and the socially regenerative functions of community schools. A community-orientated curriculum, it is argued, will improve performance in traditional basic skills through its closer articulation with the pupils' experience, while at the same time providing the basis for a social and political consciousness which will change traditional inner-city 'apathy'.

The ideological battle on these issues is now a central feature of urban education both in Britain and America. In a strong attack on the Halsey (1972, 1976)–Midwinter (1973, 1975) formulations, Merson and Campbell (1974) assert that 'the defining characteristics of the people living in inner-cities is the fact of their political oppression' and argue that the 'socially relevant' curriculum when coupled with criticisms of 'middle-class knowledge and language' will result in 'the probability that community education will disqualify these children from entering the realms of political discourse at all'. Merson and Campbell (1974) underline what they regard as 'the dangerous pessimism of community education' and insist that 'genuine radicalism lies in ensuring that no child shall be cut off from the mainstream of social and political discourse by the accident of inner urban residence'.

85

The 'Problem' of the Urban School

The teacher in the contemporary inner-city school, is, as his predecessor was, at the focus of an ideological struggle concerned immediately with conflicting notions of appropriate educational experience for urban working-class children and more widely with socio-political issues. A conservative critique calls for the restoration of 'standards', 'discipline' and 'structure' and insists that the central activity of schools and teachers is the advancement of learning, not socialization, community regeneration or political consciousness. Such a critique articulates well with a popular tendency to believe that the patterning of educational experience can be and should be separate from social and political implications and that, in particular, forms of knowledge and rationality have an entirely absolute, universal and 'pure' character. *By appealing to this sociologically naïve myth; by reserving the label 'political' for the formulations of radicalism and Marxism and by astute use of publicity and mass communication, the conservative critique makes itself a powerful ideological force.*

The most powerful countervailing messages, in the sense of official legitimations at government and local authority level, are the various ideologies of liberalism. In their advocation of a wide spectrum of reforms for inner-city schools, from higher expectations and improved organization, pastoral care and 'efficiency with humanity', integration and progressive pedagogy to community education and community curriculum, they seek to resolve the dilemmas of the Victorian legacy of popular education. At their most ambitious the ideologies of liberalism are attempting to transform an urban educational system which was historically concerned with social control and 'socialization to type' into an agency for social democracy and self-realization. But this, from the viewpoint of various radical and Marxist critiques is nothing more than rhetoric or liberal gloss upon the realities of power and control and their relationship with the system of mental and material production.

These ideologies carry other messages for teachers in urban schools which suggest the necessity for more radical action.

Chapter 5

The 'Problem' of the Urban School: radical and Marxist formulations

The radical tradition

Against conservative and liberal reforms for urban schools, there has always existed an alternative and radical tradition of theorizing and ideology, which has advanced different constructions of the problem of urban working-class schools, raised alternative problematics and outlined radical different courses of action to those currently accepted in the conventional wisdom of the time. Thus the Chartist leader, William Lovett, argued against state provision of education and for an independent working-class system (Simon, 1972, p. 248–50):

> too many of those who stand in the list of education promoters are but state-tricksters seeking to make it an instrument of party or faction. We perceive that one is for moulding the infant mind upon the principles of Church and State, another is for basing its morals on their own sectarianism and another is for an amalgamation of both; in fact, the great principles of human natures, social morality and political justice are disregarded, in the desire of promoting their own selfish views and party interests . . . hence we have addressed ourselves to you, working men of Britain . . . and we think we have said sufficient to convince you of the necessity of guarding against those state and party schemes some persons are intent on establishing, as well as to induce you to commence the great work of education yourselves.

The recognition that officially provided elementary education would be more concerned with the controlling rather than the liberating of an urban working-class was continued in later socialist attacks on the content of education provided by the Board schools. Brian Simon (1965, p. 145) quotes a typical example; 'the elementary education given today in our Board Schools does no more than prepare the minds of children for the patient obedience to the domination of a proud and haughty middle and upper class.' A tradition of socialist opposition to state education was based on the notion that control of the state and of education *was in the wrong hands*. Another tradition of opposition was based on objection to *state control as such*, of whatever ideological character. As Joel Spring (*Libertarian Teacher*, no. 9, p. 7) has shown, 'anarchism as a social and political philosophy concerned with the role and nature of authority in a society has since the eighteenth century raised serious and important questions about the very existence of state systems of schooling and the possibility of non-authoritarian forms of education'.

The radical tradition has been derived from diverse ideological origins – from working-class movements in the nineteenth century, from socialism and Marxism, from anarchism and libertarianism. As a consequence of these diverse origins and of a tendency to radical sectarianism, this tradition has been and is, as much characterized by conflict within itself as by conflict with 'the system'. At the same time it has been united by a common perception of the school system designed for an urban working class. This common perception has emphasized that what is being provided for working-class children is *schooling rather than education*; that the process of schooling is oppressive and manipulative in character; that this manipulative process is being carried on in institutions which are dominating in their bureaucracy, authoritarianism and hierarchy; that the total effect of the schooling process is to control, to domesticate, to make passive and exploitable; that in the schooling process the person is regarded as 'object' rather than as a creatively conscious subject. *The central problem of all schools, though most clearly manifested in urban working-class schools, is the problem of liberation.* United in this common view of the problem of school, the radical tradition is divided in its understandings of what 'liberation' might mean and what programmes or courses of action are necessary for its realization. Among contemporary radical formulations a broad dichotomy exists between those derived from anarchism, libertarian philosophy and forms of critical sociology and those derived from the varieties of Marxism. Whereas the former tend to locate a notion of liberation in the achievement of states of critical consciousness and personal autonomy without commitment to explicit political solutions, the latter locate liberation in terms of the overthrow of an oppressive capitalist system of production and social relations by the action of the proletariat.

Ideologies of education derived from these sources have a growing influence particularly among young teachers who see the 'crisis of the urban school' as but one manifestation of a wider social and political crisis in industrial society. A new variety of the 'teacher missionary' is thus to be found in some inner-city schools – a missionary concerned not with the control and gentling of an urban working class, but with its liberation from authoritarianism, cultural and political domination and the exploitation of capitalism. The 'missionaries of liberation' although representing only a small section of urban teachers have the potential for considerable influence in contemporary schools where staff participation and democracy and autonomy in curriculum and pedagogy have any substantive reality. An attempt will be made in the following pages to examine some of the ideologies of liberation which focus particularly on contemporary urban schools.

Anarchism and libertarianism: 'the death of school'

Writers such as Paul Goodman (1966), Ivan Illich (1973) and Paulo Freire (1972a, b, 1974) provide much of the inspiration for the contemporary anarchist libertarian critique of schooling and this critique is popularly diffused in publications such as *Libertarian Education* (formerly *Libertarian Teacher*) and the *Great Brain Robbery*. With the recognition that 'there will be no libertarian revolution in society unless and until our education system is liberated', the problem of liberation is posed in these terms (*Libertarian Teacher*, no. 9, p. 16):

> The problem before us is enormous: we live in an unfree
> society; our schools are unfree; our teachers are unfree; our
> students are unfree. Somehow we must break into this vicious
> circle. It is important to stress that as anarchists we reject
> authoritarian concepts of education, however they might be
> used. The educator who sees himself as the possessor of superior

knowledge or skills which he 'passes on' to more or less willing
disciples, whether this is in the name of a liberal/democratic
outlook or a socialist/revolutionary analysis is part of an
authoritarian, or at best, paternalistic culture. The libertarian
will see education as a sharing of knowledge, skills and
experiences and will emphasise the importance of study aimed
at understanding the participants' place in society and the
nature of the forces acting upon them – with the object of
helping to equip the participants to counter oppressive aspects
of that society.

The problem of the urban school in a libertarian perspective is a
problem of human freedom and dignity, both of which are seen to be
denied by the 'custodial' school. This in turn generates a problem for
the libertarian teacher who faces the dilemma of working within the
state system 'where the kids are . . . and where the most oppressed of
them are likely to remain' or of seeking to establish alternatives in
free schools and other non-authoritarian contexts. Thus some
teachers committed to this position accept the compromise of
working within state schools in order to encourage learning situations
which are egalitarian, critical and based upon dialogue and
participation, while others unable to accept a framework of compulsory schooling, work to provide 'alternatives' for urban children.
Free schools are only one expression of the possible educational alternatives to the 'authoritarian' urban school but they are valued
because they 'tend to be firmly rooted in a neighbourhood so that
poor, working-class children have access to their liberating influence'
(*Libertarian Teacher,* no. 9, pp. 17–19).

The libertarian critique seeks to avoid explanations of the authoritarianism of teachers which locates this in terms of personal characteristics. The problem of authoritarianism is one of role and
structure not of 'personality' and 'attitudes' and therefore the
liberation of schools can only be found in changes at the level of role
and structure and not in the search for 'better' teachers. This thesis is
central to the critique (Paton, 1973, p. 19):

Ultimately, the authoritarian attitudes of teachers are *not*
something to moralise about. They should be *understood* as the
only way teachers are able to protect themselves in a hopeless
situation. It is the authority relationship not its by-product
(authoritarianism) that should be the target. . . . The social
forces, the *wear and tear* suffered by class teachers daily, these

are what are decisive in determining teachers' attitudes in the long run. These forces are inseparable from the teacher's role as such. . . . Authoritarianism is not an accident that can be disconnected and eliminated with courses in Ethics for Teachers. It is *structurally generated*. It is not "better teachers" that we should be talking about therefore, but the complete abolition of the teacher role itself as we know it.

Urban schools for the working class were founded as bulwarks against the 'anarchy' seen to be incipient in the social and political consequences of industrialization and teachers in such schools were socialized to become agents of authority (epistemological and political) and agents of imposed social control. *Libertarian ideology stands as the antithesis to this enterprise* in its rejection of a distorted notion of order, of the need for external control and of the need for the teacher role. Thus it is argued (Paton, 1973, p. 21) that:

In the blackboard jungle situation, the teacher is really enforcing chaos, conflict and wear and tear, not order. To promote order he would have to let go of his authority completely. In the short term this would just lead to intensified chaos which every one would just have to ride out. But gradually the chaos would turn into spontaneous order. From being out of another's control (chaos) the children would come to control themselves (anarchy).

In such situations of spontaneous social control it is envisaged that *true education and humanity could be realized without reference to categories such as 'school' or 'teacher'* – the whole community becomes the context for education and every member becomes potentially a 'teacher'. The doctrines of libertarian education reformation are clearly reminiscent of the doctrines of earlier religious reformation. In both cases an attack is made on what are seen to be alienating, oppressive and distorting institutions and upon unnecessary priestly roles of mediation. In both cases *authenticity* is sought among the people in notions such as 'the Church is the people' and 'the priesthood of all believers', which find their educational expression as 'school is the community' and 'all members are teachers'. The religious metaphor is particularly clear in the writings of Illich (1973) and in his attack upon 'the universal church of school' which teaches the need to be taught.

The libertarian critique (and also other radical-Marxist critiques)

91

draws upon the work of Paulo Freire (1972a,b, 1974) particularly in his advocation of 'conscientization' as an end for education rather than 'domestication'; of 'critical literacy'[1] as one of the means for its realization; of dialogue rather than direction as the necessary pedagogic mode and of a non-hierarchic context (the culture circle) in which 'teacher' and 'student' distinctions are fused in the common identity of participating member.

The messages of libertarianism, regarded by many established teachers as utopian, impractical or suitable only for non-industrialized and non-urbanized contexts, have nevertheless captured the imagination of some young teachers both in Britain and America who have been repelled by urban schools which they perceive as custodial, authoritarian and alienating. Those who seek to work for 'liberation' within the school system are vulnerable not only to charges of compromise but also to ideological attack from both establishment and left-wing sources. Regarded officially as subversive and irresponsible, libertarian teachers and writers are accused from a Marxist perspective of taking a romantic and apolitical view of the person and of society. Thus Gintis (1972, p. 95) argues that Illich 'rejects politics in favour of individual liberation' and claims that he fails to locate his analysis in the sphere of social relations and the mode of production. The libertarian response to such attacks has been to advance different interpretations of both politics and liberation to those characteristically employed by Marxist writers.[2] In arguing for solidarity with the young 'as the proletariat of the school system' and identifying with the 'genuinely popular idiom of revolt' which is seen to exist in some urban schools, libertarian ideology claims to be distinctive, as Paton (1973, p. 57) puts it, 'willingness to ally themselves with their pupils is probably the best touchstone for separating left-libertarians from left-authoritarians and liberals'.

While it is difficult to imagine that libertarian ideology can make a very general impact on bureaucratized urban school systems which are firmly entrnched,[3] it remains an active, fertile and provocative source of alternatives to the conventional wisdom, both in terms of the nature of the educational experience and social relations which it envisages and the contexts within which these might be realized. In its advocacy of 'learning networks', 'culture circles', 'free schools', 'de-centralization' and 'micro-schools', libertarian ideology and its mediators construct an alternative social reality for urban education. If, as many libertarians believe, the urban system and its associated schooling is 'cracking apart at the centre', then this alternative may become a significant reality in the future.

Critical sociology: 'the transformation of school'

In comparing positivist, interpretative and critical sociologies, Brian Fay (1975) suggests that what is distinctive about the latter is an explicit recognition that social theory is interconnected with social practice. Thus in its educative role, critical social theory tries (Fay, 1975, p. 103) 'to enlighten the social actors, so that, coming to see themselves and their social situation in a new way, they themselves can decide to alter the conditions which they find repressive. In other words, the social scientist tries to "raise the consciousness" of the actors whose situation he is studying'.

Such a description, it can be claimed, would hold true for a 'critical' sociology of education which has been developed in this country since the publication of Michael Young's *Knowledge and Control: New Directions for the Sociology of Education* in 1971. Powerfully diffused (and to some extent institutionalized) through publications of the Open University and the widely read *Tinker, Tailor: The Myth of Cultural Deprivation* (Keddie, 1973), this critique has attempted to 'raise the consciousness' of teachers and to encourage them to develop a praxis based upon radically different formulations to those of conventional academic and pedagogic wisdom. [4]

The essential message to urban teachers and to all teachers has been that they should adopt a stance of 'radical doubt' regarding the familiar and taken for granted characteristics of their pedagogic world. That rather than accepting as problems, the official formulations and definitions of educational authorities and experts, teachers and others should formulate their own constructions of problems. Such a stance it is argued might well locate the problem of the urban school, for instance, more in the practices and assumptions of educational authorities and experts than in supposed deficiencies in urban working-class pupils and their parents. In its encouragement to teachers 'to be their own theorists', the critique celebrates the liberating possibilities which arise from the practice of 'making the taken-for-granted world problematic' and in engaging in 'the subversion of absolutism'. Thus Young (1971, p. 6) suggests as fruitful, the conceiving of societies, 'as products of competing definitions and claims to cognitive and moral legitimacy rather than as integrated around a core set of absolute values'.

93

The 'Problem' of the Urban School

Within a framework of competing definitions, a critical sociology of education has generated a host of issues which many see to be particularly relevant to the problems of urban education. *Among these, questions of control and autonomy, the social organization of knowledge and the politics of the curriculum are salient.*

If questions of control in education are conceived in terms of 'the imposition of meaning' as Young (1971, p. 15) suggests, then it becomes legitimate to ask whose meanings dominate in any given context and time and *whether such domination is the result of the intrinsic superiority of such meanings or the result of an historical tradition or association with a dominant social group.* From the perspective of a radical sociology of knowledge many provocative questions are raised concerning academic and school curricula – questions which earlier generations of urban school teachers were unlikely ever to have considered. Was Marx right in his assertion that 'the ideas of the ruling class are in every epoch the ruling ideas, i.e. the class which is the ruling material force of society is at the same time its ruling intellectual force. The class which has the means of material production at its disposal has control at the same time over the means of mental production' (see Marx and Engels, 1965, pp. 60–5).

How true is the claim 'that some people's common sense becomes formally recognised as philosophy and other people's does not, depending on their access to certain institutional contexts'? (A. Gramsci quoted in Young, 1971, p. 28.) If knowledge is viewed not as an absolute but as 'available sets of meanings' and if rationality is understood as 'that which is understandable to the participants', what are the implications for educational practice? If academic and school curricula are viewed as 'no more than the socio-historical constructs of a particular time' (Young, 1971, p. 23) what conclusions might be drawn about their emphasis upon written as opposed to oral presentation, their individualism, their abstractness and unrelatedness to daily life and experience and their separation of knowledge from action?

The potential impact of such questions upon the consciousness of teachers has been powerfully enhanced by their juxtaposition with anthropological and linguistic inquiries which insist upon the validity and cognitive complexity of the thought and language systems of supposedly 'simple' or low-status cultures. Thus in presenting the work of Frake and Gladwin, Keddie (1973, p. 17) argues that their researches 'provide good grounds for supposing that Western formal

94

logic is not absolute but, like other logics, culture-bound or socially situated'. The linguistic researches of Labov (1973, pp. 21–2) are presented to rebut the notion that negro children in inner-city areas in America are 'verbally deprived':

> The concept of verbal deprivation has no basis in social reality: in fact, Negro children in the urban ghettos receive a great deal of verbal stimulation, hear more well-formed sentences than middle-class children, and participate fully in a highly verbal culture; they have the same basic vocabulary, possess the same capacity for conceptual learning. . . . The notion of 'verbal deprivation' is a part of the modern mythology of educational psychology. . . .

The simultaneous appearance in English translation of Paulo Freire's books, *Pedagogy of the Oppressed* (1972), *Cultural Action for Freedom* (1972) and *Education for Critical Consciousness* (1974) has added a powerful impetus to the critique of conventional schooling raised by critical sociologists of education. In the condemnation of processes of cultural invasion and domination in the third world and the 'culture of science' which this engenders; in its celebration of the possibilities of 'the people' to achieve a critical consciousness and a critical literacy and in its indications of the means to that end, the work of Freire has provided a world view which some urban teachers see to be as relevant to their world – that of working-class inner-city schools – as to the world of an oppressed peasantry in Chile.

From the perspective of a critical sociology of education, the problem of the urban school is to be located in its historic function of *transmission* of elements of mainstream culture to a population viewed as essentially devoid of its own culture and understandings and perceived to be deficient in many ways in its capacity to absorb and learn the culture offered to it. Within such an enterprise the consciousness of the teacher becomes preoccupied with questions of transmission, with new strategies (known as curriculum development) for the more effective transmission of 'old' knowledge in new pedagogic forms, none of which challenge the status, social determinations or social stratification of existing knowledge forms.

The exponents of critical sociology of education are concerned to change this historic function of the school and its associated assumptions and states of consciousness. This change would involve a conception of the urban school (and all schools) as an arena in which would be realized a variety of cultural traditions and cognitive styles; an appreciation of the various ways in which people 'make sense of the world'; a concern with learning as dialogue-participation rather than as transmission-reception and the recognition of all as 'learners' and 'teachers'. Crucial to such a transformation would be changed approaches to the language of urban working-class pupils, white and black, which would involve a full recognition of both the cognitive power and the aesthetic of these forms and the rejection of notions of any necessary superiority in white middle-class elaborated English. *In this sense, teachers of English especially in inner-city schools, would be the strategic agents to begin such a transformation.* [5]

The extent to which such critical sociology mediated through initial preparatory courses and courses of further study has changed the consciousness and the practice of urban school teachers cannot at present be fully known. The evidence of the comprehensive school headmaster, quoted by Bantock (1975) as numbering among 'teachers who cause difficulties' those who had come from the colleges 'with Knowledge and Control in the bloodstream', would suggest that in some contexts, critical sociology has achieved a measure of praxis and that this is seen to be a problem by school administrators. [6] On the other hand, it has been suggested that its emphasis on 'the politics of everyday life at the expense of more conventional forms of political confrontation' (Whitty, 1974, p. 132) and its tendency to under-estimate 'the power of circumstances' and the constraints which teachers face, reduce its potential as a means for the transformation of school. Such criticisms have been accepted by Young (1974) in later formulations: 'the "new sociology of education" has perhaps gone too far in its celebration of the possibilities which exist for teachers to redefine their own realities. We have paid too little attention to the vast range of practices which serve to maintain prevailing assumptions about knowledge and education.'

The contemporary thrust of critical sociology of education is now towards a notion of 'radical unity' and a more explicit location of the transformation of educational practice within wider action for the transformation of society. Thus Young (1974, p. 9) argues that:

> the struggle to change the ways in which knowledge production
> is organised must be carried on in a whole variety of
> contexts. . . . We would want to stress that teachers' efforts to
> change the nature of classroom relationships, attempts like
> those of Centreprise to return the means of knowledge

production to the community and the activities of groups like
'Rank & File' within the unions, are all part of a common
struggle to transform our everyday lives and create an
alternative future. . . . Wherever we begin our struggle to
change reality, we must be prepared to enter any other context
and link up with any other struggle which might help radical
experiments in education to become more than isolated and
short-lived ventures;

and (Young, 1975, p. 136)

if questions about our assumptions about curriculum are to be
more than just questions, political problems will inevitably be
raised for teachers and anyone involved in education. This
suggests that prevailing notions about curricula, though
sustained by those in formal education are not sustained by
them alone. A more adequate theory of curriculum as *practice*
would not restrict practice to that of teachers, nor of teachers'
practice to their activities in the school and classroom.

Re-conceptualized in this way, critical sociology of education may
provide a crucial link between the concerns of radical teachers in
urban schools and the concerns of other radical groups in the urban
context. Within urban education it provides a model of
transformation which is appealing and persuasive in its liberating
vision of cultural variety and in the enhanced dignity which it
accords to the poor and the powerless. Whether this vision can be
realized in contemporary urban schools is a question for the future.

Critical sociology: 'the problem of autonomy'

Writers within a critical sociology of education have sought to make
problematic the widely accepted notion that teachers in Britain enjoy
a high degree of autonomy in their educational activities. As has
been shown in earlier chapters, questions of control and of autonomy
have always been central preoccupations in the ideological struggles
of urban education. Concerned that the teachers of the urban proletariat might become 'active emissaries of mis-rule', the Victorian
middle class created an apparatus of control which encompassed
selection and socialization of teachers and effective monitoring of
curriculum and pedagogy. The contemporary urban teacher in
Britain within the same tradition of popular education, *appears in*

comparison with his American and European colleagues, to have attained a degree of autonomy which is unprecedented among professional workers.

This notion of autonomy – the relatively unimpeded right to select appropriate knowledge and skills and to transmit them in a teaching style judged to be appropriate to the situation – is celebrated in the rhetoric of the occupational group; is strong in the consciousness of many teachers; and is seen to be the glorious culmination of the long struggle waged by teacher groups against 'obnoxious interference', 'payment by results' and the prescriptions of an official curriculum code. But this in itself creates an interesting paradox and a whole host of further questions about the reality of teacher autonomy. *How has it come about that the teachers of the urban working class once so closely controlled as the strategic agents of social and cultural formation should, in the context of a modern capitalist Britain, enjoy so much freedom?* Is it to be explained in terms of evolutionary progress, the triumph of liberalism and of progressive education? Is it to be seen as the accomplishment of organized teacher power against both the constraints of official prescription and the hostilities of working-class parents, or is it to be explained, rather, in terms of an illusion of freedom?

Detailed consideration of all these questions goes beyond our present scope at this point but it is necessary to examine two provocative explanations of the paradox of the apparent autonomy of urban teachers.

John White (1975) has suggested that the change from a relatively high degree of control to a relatively high degree of autonomy in curriculum selection might be interpreted as *essentially a political decision at a time of perceived ideological crisis*, rather than as the steady progress of evolutionary liberalism, or as the triumph of progressive education. Pointing out that 1926 was the year in which the Board of Education, in an unprecedented manner, eliminated all mention of the subjects (except practical instruction) which were expected to be taught in elementary schools and, in effect, established the modern principle of curriculum autonomy in popular education, White suggests that such action was the result of an initiative by the then Conservative President of the Board of Education, Lord Eustace Percy, who was motivated by the fear of socialist domination in Britain. The notion of autonomy in popular education could in these circumstances become one of the bulwarks against such domination. White (1975) has shown how seriously the

President took the resolutions of the 1926 Labour Conference calling for investigation into 'how far, under a workers' administration . . . a proletarian attitude and outlook on life might be cultivated' (see Chapter 2, p. 49) in the schools, and has argued (1975, p. 28) that there is evidence 'of his [Percy's] fear that curricula might become infected with socialist ideas'.

All this, as White (1975) argues, *pointed to the need to establish a principle of school and teacher autonomy in respect of curriculum to act as a countervailing force against central socialist direction,*

> If Parliament still controlled the content of education, the Socialists would change the regulations . . . they would be able to introduce curricula more in line with socialist ideas. To forestall this, it was no longer in the interests of the anti-Socialists, including Conservatives, to keep curriculum policy in the hands of the State. . . . If they could devise a workable system of non-statutory controls, the Conservatives had everything to gain and nothing to lose from taking curricula out of the politicians' hands.

If this perceptive and persuasive account of the origins of the notion of autonomy is accepted, then *the question of the 'non-statutory controls' which remained is crucial to an understanding of the contemporary nature of teacher autonomy.* It seems clear that Conservative action was based upon an implicit faith in the essential conservatism of local educational administration and the essential conservatism of the majority of the teaching occupational group, taken together with a system of relatively 'invisible' controls over the occupational group.

The writings of Michael Young (1971, 1977), within critical sociology, have been concerned to make these 'invisible' controls visible to teachers, and to show the ways in which their consciousness of autonomy is in important respects a false consciousness. Thus Young (1971, p. 22) argues that the autonomy of the teacher 'is in practice extremely limited' (in secondary schools) 'by the control of VIth form (and therefore lower form) curricula by the universities, both through their entrance requirements and their domination of all but one of the school examination boards'. The constraints of examination boards and syllabus appear relatively invisible as constraints because many teachers take them to be a 'natural' and taken-for-granted part of the pedagogic world. They are also reassured by innovations such as Mode 3 examinations which suggest greater teacher control over knowledge definitions and evaluation.[7]

Young suggests that these prevailing notions obscure the reality of control in the crucial area of knowledge evaluation – the real power component of autonomy – any attempt to challenge in a radical sense 'existing notions of "what education is" will reveal the limitations of autonomy' (see Whitty and Young, 1976, pp. 191–9).

Within this perspective, the autonomy of the urban teacher is seen to attain some reality at the level of primary education and some reality in respect of teaching style at all levels, but in the strategic area of knowledge definition and evaluation in the secondary school it is seen to be largely rhetoric. Innovations may be permitted in low-status knowledge areas and with pupils who are seen to have 'failed' in conventional academic courses, but this does not seriously affect the central function of the school in celebrating received knowledge.

The problem of autonomy has been most sharply realized in urban working-class schools, particularly in inner-city areas. The reasons for this have already been indicated and are obviously related among other things, to the distribution of radical teachers in the school system. In recent history the problem has been dramatically exemplified within inner-London, both at secondary level (Risinghill Comprehensive School, Islington) and at primary level (William Tyndale Junior School, Islington). It is clearly an issue that will occur again, particularly if a critical sociology of education becomes a real force in the transformation of the consciousness and practice of urban teachers.

The Varieties of Marxism

Peter Worsely (1975, p. 499) has reminded us that Marxism is a body of social and political theory and practice which has been realized in a variety of ways:

> Sociologically Marxism does not exist 'in itself: it is embodied
> in and used by differing groups and milieux, from classes and
> coteries, with different social characteristics and cultural
> heritages, different locations in history and society, and is
> carried by a variety of 'bearers' and mediators.

It seems possible to detect two ways in which the varieties of Marxist thought are mediated to contemporary urban teachers in Britain. The first would be through the writings of academics and theorists who have analysed educational practice from an explicitly

Marxist position and whose writings feature prominently in some courses of further study for teachers. Significant at the present time would be the work of Hoare (1967), Althusser (1972) and of Bowles and Gintis (1976), writers essentially located outside the praxis of urban education in school systems.

A second set of mediators may be found among practising teachers within the urban school system (especially in London) who individually or collectively have made available their constructions of the problem of the urban school from an explicitly Marxist position. In the publications of Teachers' Action Collective of the Rank and File and Radical Education organizations, analysis of problems in education and prescriptions for action are advanced, which, while differing in emphasis, share a common ideological stance. This may be said, also, of the widely read work of one particular inner-city teacher, Chris Searle. Such teachers continue (albeit from an explicitly Marxist stance) the historic tradition of 'resistance from within' which, as was shown in earlier chapters, was always the characteristic of a minority of urban school teachers.

What are the contemporary messages of Marxism to the urban school teacher? Hoare (1967, p. 42) points out the essentially political nature of education:

> it is a fundamental component of the power structure in any society – the means whereby assent is secured to the values and privileges of the dominant class. Education, in fact, is the point at which vital needs and power structure immediately intersect. It is thus never neutral or 'innocent' as the other social services can sometimes be. Houses are houses and the more of them the better, but education is never just 'education' – it is the assimilation of a social order.

In arguing for a socialist theory and practice of education which would contribute to the transformation of capitalist society, Hoare (1967) indicates that its central concerns must be the development of critical reason; full acceptance of the social character of man; insistence on the active nature of participation in learning and a dialectical mode of pedagogy. To the achievement of these ends the position of the teacher in terms of consciousness and practice is strategic (Hoare, 1967, p. 52):

> a central problem is that of the transformation of the teaching body. For the teachers in Britain are overwhelmingly

conservative, not merely politically but educationally too.[8] To think in terms of a socialist alternative in education is purely illusory unless this alternative includes the liberation of teachers.

From this perspective the problem of the urban school is *located crucially in the presence of a largely apolitical or conservative teachers' group whose level of critical consciousness is low and which is not integrated with other workers in the struggle to transform both education and society.* The task for socialist teachers is, therefore, to work to increase such consciousness among their colleagues and to increase integration with other workers.

Althusser (1972, p. 259) identifies the school as 'the dominant Ideological State Apparatus' and schooling as 'the reproduction of the relations of production, i.e. of capitalist relations of exploitation'. The majority of teachers thus act in the role of 'professional ideologists' who transmit as 'normal' or even desirable the essentially exploitive social relations of capitalism. Only a few are as yet aware that this is the central problem of the school (Althusser, 1972, p. 261):

> I ask the pardon of those teachers who, in dreadful conditions, attempt to turn the few weapons they can find in the history and learning they 'teach' against the ideology, the system and the practices in which they are trapped. They are a kind of hero. But they are rare and how many (the majority) do not even begin to suspect the 'work' the system . . . forces them to do.

Bowles and Gintis (1976) call for a socialist strategy for education which involves 'the long march through the institutions', the capture of positions of strength; the democratization of schools and colleges; the undermining of 'the correspondence between the social relations of education and the social relations of production in capitalist economic life'. Teachers, they argue, should abandon their pretensions as professionals, 'pretensions which lead only to a defeatist quietism and isolation'.

In these ways the 'academic Marxists' following the imperative of their ideological position present not merely an analysis of the problem of the world of the urban school, but proposals for action to change that world. It seems likely, however, that while their work is significant within academic and non-school contexts, only a minority of hard-pressed urban school teachers will have had the time to study it closely.[9]

Potentially a more active element in the day-to-day world of contemporary urban teachers are the productions and activities of the 'teacher Marxists'. The *Teachers' Action Collective*, a group of Marxist teachers working in London schools, has explicitly set out to provide an analysis of schooling in a capitalist society and to locate the position of the teacher in this process. Made available in a series of collectively produced pamphlets are articles which 'speak directly' to teachers under such titles as 'Teachers as workers'; 'The exercise of teacher power'; 'The battle of the working day' and 'Teachers and the economy'.[10] In essence, the argument of the Collective is that the problems of urban education and of urban schools are derived from the system of economic production in which they are located: a system which requires teachers to shape, grade and discipline the next generation of the industrial proletariat. From this fundamental understanding comes the recognition that urban schools are 'factories'; that teachers are workers and that pupils are apprentice workers and that, together, they should consolidate their power within the work place to oppose an economic system (and its manifestations in schools) which is based upon an exploitive and dehumanizing set of social relations.

From the beginnings of state provision of schools for the urban working class there have always been group of teachers who have recognized in one way or another the controlling and skilling functions of that enterprise. The Teachers' Action Collective represent a contemporary example of such a group which seeks to make clear to other urban teachers the 'real' nature of the enterprise in which they are engaged (*Teachers' Action*, no. 3, pp. 1–2):

> We do not accept that compulsory state education is in any way
> an expression of the benevolence of capitalism towards the
> working-class. We do not see schools as being malfunctioning
> machines of enlightenment, institutions in which knowledge is
> magnanimously presented to the young masses for their
> intellectual betterment. . . . Schools are manufactories of
> labour power.

The Rank and File organization within the National Union of Teachers is another group of largely urban-based teachers which draws its ideological inspiration from the varieties of Marxism but which expresses both its analysis and its prescriptions for action in

103

terms which distinguish it from groups such as the Teachers' Action Collective or Radical Education.[11] One of the central problems of the school from a Rank and File standpoint is the poverty of, and constraints upon working-class education which arise both out of lack of adequate resources and lack of understanding by teachers of working-class consciousness. These deficiencies, it is argued, could be overcome through the agency of militant union action which would compel the provision of better facilities for urban working-class children and, *through the praxis of the struggle, change the consciousness of the teachers.*

As the Rank and File pamphlet *Education and Society* presents it (Rosenberg, p. 22):

> (Teachers) are in no way fitted to understand what makes working-class children tick and what makes them so rebellious. They have not personally experienced the insults and indignities suffered by those who fail to make it – and their special position in the classroom does not encourage them to make up their deficiency in knowledge. On the contrary, they are expected to crush rebellion. Consequently any feeling of solidarity with pupils is completely absent. . . . Their way round the problem, socially conscious pedagogues as they are, is to find justification for the pupils' deviance and antagonism to learning, in the sociology and psychology of maladjustment. . . .

It is envisaged that greater understanding of the working class would be forged in the context of militant union action (Rosenberg, p. 22):

> Through fighting with the Union against the poor pay, the large classes, the crowded conditions and rotten buildings and the bureaucratic yoke weighing on them, they . . . gain experience of the class struggle. Teachers' strikes, demonstrations and other protest actions show that they are learning fast. This lines them up directly with other rank and file workers whose problems are surprisingly similar.

While the various groups of 'teacher-workers' differ in the particular emphasis which they give to the analysis of oppression and in the specific focus which they give in prescriptions for action, *they are united in their common rejection of a conventional wisdom which suggests that teachers can be and ought to be impartial and neutral transmitters of knowledge and skills.* In the words of Chris Searle (1975a), 'these hypocritical and shallow dogmas are being challenged by classroom teachers throughout the country, particularly in the urban working-class areas where in every area of public service . . . people face systematic underdevelopment and attack'.

Teachers, it is suggested (Searle, 1975a), have to answer the question, 'whose side are we on?' The answer for urban teachers, from this perspective, is 'with the working class' and a 'committed syllabus' which will help their working-class pupils to develop 'a certain thinking power or consciousness – an ideology of resistance' (Searle, 1975b). In this sense we come full circle from the founding ideologies of the urban school with their concern for order, stability, religion and 'sweetness and light' to the contemporary challenge of Marxism and to the call for an ideology of resistance.

But while the ideological struggle is clear, *its impact upon the majority of urban school teachers has been generally unexamined.* We know relatively little about how contemporary teachers experience their work situation; what constructs they hold of knowledge, ability and the educational process; what professional perspectives or ideologies inform their practice; how they accept, resist or negotiate the prevailing order of the school; of their consciousness of autonomy and of constraint; or how they view the activity of teaching in an urban working-class school. It is to some empirical examination of these questions that we now turn.

Part Two

Fieldwork

Chapter 6

Situating the Inquiry

The previous chapters have provided some description of the social world of the teachers of the urban working class in terms of the historical, pedagogical and ideological contexts in which they can be located. At the same time, a tendency in some studies to treat teachers as 'social puppets' within those contexts has been resisted. Attempts have been made to reconstruct 'the experience of being a teacher' through the use of autobiographical and historical accounts which give some understanding of teacher consciousness[1] related to given school situations and of the 'solutions' and strategies which teachers devised, or were forced to make, to deal with the problems of their working world. Such attempts are clearly needed in relation to the contemporary world of the urban school and of urban school teachers. For inner-city classrooms in particular, the works of Becker (1952) and Smith and Geoffrey (1968) are among the few which address these sorts of issues directly.[2] In more general terms, the work of Jackson (1968) has attempted to describe the 'busyness' of classroom situations and teachers' reaction to this, while Stebbins (1975) has investigated the ways in which teachers define disorderly behaviour. Recent work in this country has pointed to the need to distinguish between teacher ideology and perspectives as realized in non-classroom settings (Educationist Context) and the actual practice of teachers within classroom settings (Teacher Context). Keddie (1971) has shown the inconsistencies and contradictions which exist between these two: the gap between 'doctrine' and 'commitment', in common-sense terms, that teachers say one thing

109

and do another. However, as Sharp and Green (1975) point out we are left with no explanation as to why this should occur other than (in this particular case) the continued pervasiveness of hierarchical categories of ability and knowledge in teacher consciousness, despite organizational changes in the direction of an undifferentiated curriculum. Keddie's study is valuable in pointing out the dangers of interpreting teachers' ideology as an indicator of their practice, but the question which this in turn generates is: why does this discrepancy exist? It may be, as Keddie suggests, that pervasive hierarchical categories in teacher consciousness operate to negate commitments to more egalitarian developments in education, whether in the form of comprehensive schools, mixed-ability classes or undifferentiated curriculum. It may be that teachers engage in liberal 'presentation of self' in the context of research interviews and discussions, which bears little relationship to their day-to-day practice.[3] While both of these explanations must be taken seriously, a third explanation also commands attention. This is, that the realization of teachers' ideologies and intentions is *frustrated* in important respects by the physical and social constraints of their work situation. The question then becomes, as Sharp and Green (1975, p. 13) express it, 'not merely to describe such instances and illustrate inconsistencies in the teacher's view of her role . . . but to ask at the level of teacher consciousness: "To what problems are these viable solutions for the teacher?"'.

With these considerations in mind, we turn now to some examination of the focus of the research.

The present inquiry

The following chapters give an account of a research project undertaken between 1975 and 1977 involving the co-operation of 105 teachers in ten inner-city comprehensive schools in London.[4] The concerns of the project were various and its emphasis changed and developed over time as a consequence of the activity of doing research. Nevertheless, its essential commitment remained the same: to gain a greater understanding of the social and pedagogic situation of some contemporary teachers of the urban working class, a group of teachers already shown to be historically, the strategic agents of social and symbolic control. It was hoped that this might be achieved by making explicit the ways in which the social world of the urban working-class school was constituted in the consciousness of teachers and to relate these social constructions to characteristics of their immediate work situation and to their location at the nexus of conflicting ideological formulations.

Specifically among questions to be investigated were the teachers' perceptions of the nature of inner-city teaching and of their pupils and the local area; of their construction of the problems of inner-city schools and of questions of pedagogic and curriculum change and of their experiences of the nature of autonomy and constraint in their work situation. In addition, contemporary social constructions of the 'good' teacher and of the 'good' school in such contexts were to be investigated with reference to the understandings of teachers, head-teachers, pupils and parents.[5] Overall, it was intended to relate these questions, where appropriate, to the characteristics of earlier urban schools and their teachers, in order to illuminate issues of continuity and change.

Approach and methodology

Initially the headteachers of the ten co operating schools were asked to designate those teachers whom they regarded as 'outstanding' within the context of an inner-city comprehensive school.[6] Apart from the initial suggestion that there might be such a category of teachers, *the interpretation of the category was left entirely to the social construction of the headteachers and their deputies.* The intention here was twofold. In the first place, such a procedure would provide some insights into the social mechanisms whereby exceptional or outstanding teachers were defined as such by their immediate superiors and in the second place, it would provide, for the purposes of interview and discussion, a sample of teachers who would represent some sort of epitome of what was taken to be 'good' in inner-city education.

The definitions in themselves were regarded as highly significant in terms of the light which they would throw upon notions of dominant models or categories of teacher activity in inner-city schools and the conceptions of the educational process which they would make explicit. It was felt that while there had been some socio-logical investigation of the 'good pupil role' in the consciousness of teachers, the investigation of the 'good teacher role' in the conscious-ness of headteachers, had been relatively neglected.[7] Such a construct would provide an important dimension of a teacher's work situation, in some cases providing a legitimation for action; in other

111

cases, providing a source of constraint and, in all cases, having implications for the teacher's own career and status and potential power within the institution.

The headteachers designated seventy-five teachers as 'outstanding' according to criteria which they made explicit in subsequent interviews.[8] The co-operation of the teachers was sought with respect to interviews and discussions and seventy agreed to participate in the project. Semi-structured interviews were conducted with these teachers, each interview lasting on average for one and a half hours. Fifteen deputy headteachers and the ten headteachers of the co-operating schools were also interviewed. In an attempt to minimize the imposition of research categories upon members of a particular social world, the co-operative nature of the inquiry was stressed and the teachers were asked to introduce issues which seemed to them to represent real concerns in an urban school, and were generally invited to take a critical attitude to any of the questions and to dismiss them entirely if they were regarded as irrelevant. The interviews were, in most cases, tape-recorded and completed transcripts were returned to the teachers in order to provide a further opportunity for them to reflect upon what they had said during the course of the interviews and to invite them to make positive suggestions for the focus of the inquiry. By these means it was hoped that some notion of the authenticity of the teachers' accounts could be established.

In addition to the formally designated sample, research activity within the schools and within other contexts such as teachers' centres, provided opportunities for interviews and discussion with other teachers not selected by their supervisors. These teachers constituted a small 'informal' sample, arrived at by other methods which provided some useful perspectives for comparative purposes.[9]

All this activity generated a considerable number of 'accounts' of various aspects of contemporary inner-city schools and education. The problem of how these accounts might be interpreted now had to be faced.

The value of accounts (of the person's subjective understanding of the social world as constituted and made explicit in discourse) has been widely recognized in a phenomenologically oriented sociology, in post-positivistic psychology and in recent applied research in education.[10] While attention has been directed to the conditions necessary for the eliciting of accounts and for approaches to the difficult question of validation, the processes whereby the actors' accounts are edited and interpreted by the researcher remain problematic. Bernstein (1977, p. 148) has pointed to the dangers of 'invisible control' in such editing and interpretation: 'the methods of this transformation must be made public so that its assumptions may be criticized. In the case of the new methodology, the principles used to restrict the vast amount of information and the number of channels are often implicit.' The problem is also recognized by Young (1976) in a commentary upon collaborative research with teachers, when he notes that frequently 'the practice of the researched – teachers and pupils – is appropriated into the theoretical framework of the researcher'.

The possibility of joint accounts, of measures of 'triangulation' or of returning interpretations of accounts to those in the social world being described could not be realized within the context of the inquiry.[11] Interpretation was thus finally based on the following principles and procedures:

1. *Theoretical saturation*[12]

From a starting premise that the teachers involved were in their accounts being 'theorists' of their social world, the attempt to understand their theory required as a necessary preliminary, close and repeated reading of all the accounts in order to reach some state of 'theoretical saturation' in relation to them.

In other words, this was an attempt, subject to the problematics of inter-subjectivity, to make some form of empathetic entry into the social world of another, through close acquaintance with the content and texture of their discourse.

2. *Central meanings and categories*

It was hoped that this initial theoretical saturation would assist in the elucidation of the social meanings and categories used by the teachers to describe and explain their immediate working world. While the research was clearly not an exercise in phenomenological analysis, since the categories of the researcher were in many ways obtrusive, a constant attempt was made to realize at least a phenomenological sensitivity in relation to the meanings and categories generated by the teachers in the process of the research activity. At the point of editing and interpretation the procedure adopted was to derive what appeared to be within each teacher's account, the

113

central meanings and categories in their discourse.

Central meanings and categories were taken to be those aspects of their discourse to which they devoted most time; to which they frequently returned as a point of reference and in relation to which they exhibited particular engagement in terms of emphasis in delivery and greater animation during the interview.

3. *Ideological articulation*

From the analysis of central meanings and categories an attempt was made to articulate the teachers' accounts with the ideological positions presented in ideal-type form in chapter 3. The problematic nature of this exercise was fully recognized, both in relation to possible imposition of the researcher's categories and in relation to the sheer difficulty of characterizing each teacher's account. Attempts were made to minimize the former and to achieve some authenticity in relation to the latter.

A tentative classification of teacher accounts was made in the first instance on the basis of an overall assessment of the teachers' perspectives in relation to the ideological positions. A general assessment across a range of diverse issues raised problems. While some teachers' accounts exhibited a high degree of internal consistency and coherence (which facilitated ideological articulation), other teachers' accounts were much more eclectic and various and revealed states of indecision, uncertainty and of change of consciousness.[13] Problematic as it was, this first overall assessment permitted some crude quantification of the ideological articulation of the group of seventy inner-city teachers, designated by their headteachers as 'outstanding'.[14]

While a tentative articulation of the teachers' positions in relation to certain ideologies of education could be attempted, it was apparent that a more specific classification of teacher perspectives was necessary, based upon each of the major issues and concerns of the inquiry (issues originated either by the researcher or the teachers). Thus analysis was also undertaken at this level. The location of a teacher as broadly within (or related to) a given ideological position did not predict the teachers' position on any one issue, e.g. curriculum, and different coalitions of positions could and did arise. By these means an attempt was made to achieve both a general and a specific location of teacher perspectives. The analysis attempted to achieve authenticity in relation to the understandings of the teachers, while at the same time locating this analysis within a wider socio-historical and theoretical framework.

The schools and their context[15]

The ten schools involved in the research activity constituted in some senses a social unity and in other senses a social diversity. All were maintained comprehensive schools, situated in comparatively close proximity in two adjacent inner-London boroughs. All were in a competitive situation with local grammar schools for the allocation of 'top ability' or 'Band 1' pupils and all, in the opinion of the head-teachers, suffered from this competition. All were essentially schools of the urban working class, both in relation to the composition of their pupils and the schools' physical locations in, or on, the boun-daries of inner-city working-class localities.

The continuity of some of these schools with an earlier tradition of working-class education was visibly proclaimed in buildings which had been established by the London School Board and which retained the imprint of the 'citadel school'. None of the schools drew their pupils exclusively from any definable working-class local community; all recruited from wide catchment areas involving anything from thirty to sixty 'feeder' primary schools.

All the schools had experienced, in varying degrees, what are taken to be the characteristic problems of working-class inner-city schools: problems of pupil poverty and of social and emotional insecurity; problems of response to racial and cultural diversity; problems of pupil achievement; problems of organization and stability in situations of high teacher mobility; problems of school image and reputation exacerbated by the activities of a largely hostile national press. While all of the schools had experienced these problems, a number of factors crucially affected *the degree of their realization in any given situation and the types of strategies evolved to deal with them.* These mediating factors included the historical origins and recent histories of the schools; their geographical loca-tions; the reputations they had acquired and the policies (or lack of policies) pursued by the headteachers.

The range of 'top ability' pupils represented in the schools varied from 5 per cent of the intake in School E to 20 per cent of the intake in School D. Representation of the lowest band of ability ranged from 22 per cent in School D to 41 per cent in School F. Indications of pupil poverty as defined by entitlement to free school lunches varied from 15 per cent of the school's population in School D to 56 per cent in School F. Local authority figures for the proportion of 'immigrant' pupils (according to the DES definition) showed a range varying from 11 per cent in School D to 56 per cent in School G. *Seven of the ten schools were formally designated as Social Priority schools, according to the local authority's index of relative school deprivations.*

The historical origins and recent histories of the schools were an important source of differentiation among them. This was most apparent in the cases of Schools D and F. School D, which had evolved from a girls' grammar school was in many senses atypical of the other schools. It retained a detectable grammar school ethos (albeit, a working-class grammar school), despite a comparatively long history as a comprehensive school. This, taken together with an attractive and impressive physical location and the school's retention of a powerful 'old guard' from the former grammar school staff, helped to set this school apart. Its 'privileged' position among the other schools was reflected in its comparatively high proportions of 'top ability' pupils and of pupils from middle-class homes (24 per cent) and a low proportion of pupils 'in poverty' (15 per cent). It also had the lowest representation of 'immigrant' pupils (11 per cent). Nevertheless, changes in local authority policy were producing changes in the school which were bringing it more into line with the pupil compositions of the other schools.

While School D enjoyed a certain privilege from its past, School F was actively engaged in fighting off the legacy of its past. School F had been formed from the amalgamation of two 'tough' secondary modern schools. It had later received an influx of boys from a neighbouring secondary modern school which had been 'reorganized'. This inauspicious start was further compounded by the fact that, as a comprehensive school, School F was organized on co-educational lines in a working-class area where such organization was viewed with the deepest suspicion and where a marked preference existed for single-sex schools. The social creation of a 'sink school' reputation was not long in developing and the then headteacher proved to be unequal to the challenge which this presented. At the time of the research the current headteacher and the staff were attempting to regenerate the school and to change its image.

Schools D and F marked the extremes on the scale of 'social legacy from the past', but the majority of schools were nearer to F than to D, in the sense that they derived from secondary modern schools, that their past was not an asset to them and that they had been the victims of unfavourable publicity and of organizational discontinuities caused by relatively high mobility of both teachers and headteachers. School A, a boys' school of 1,200 pupils, had suffered particularly from the latter and was characterized at the time of the research by a sense of fragmentation and disillusionment, partly engendered by high teacher turnover and partly by changes in educational policies introduced by various headteachers involving moves from formal/traditional to liberal/progressive and back again to a middle ground pedagogical position. School B, a co-educational school of 1,250 pupils and School C, of similar size and organization, were both located at the boundaries of working-class inner-city localities and of middle-class residential areas. These latter areas were very representative of those whom Bernstein has described as 'the new middle class'[16] and although both Schools B and C were designated Social Priority schools, there was evidence of an increasing middle-class entry. Both schools remained essentially working-class in composition, however, although School B was very cosmopolitan (with forty different nationalities) and constituted something of a local success story having moved in the space of five years, from a sink school image to being an over-subscribed school.

School E, unlike all the other schools (except School D) had originated from a grammar school and it is now a comparatively long-established boys' comprehensive school of 1,200 pupils. Unlike School D, however, it had no apparent 'privileges' derived from these origins: there was no detectable grammar school ethos and no remaining old guard (except one) from the former grammar school staff. The school had Social Priority status. The headteacher estimated that 70 per cent of the pupils came from semi-skilled and unskilled manual working-class homes and a considerable number of these came from families with four or more children. A third of the school's population was in poverty as defined by entitlement to free school lunches.

A distinctive feature of School E was its radical and militant image. Some of the teachers at the school had been among the most militant in London in their vigorous resistance to local authority proposals for part-time schooling or re-timetabling as a response to shortages of teachers in the early 1970s. Such proposals had been seen as a covert attack (especially re-timetabling or 'coping') on both the teachers' working conditions and the quality of working-class education, and the teachers had taken action to make these attacks

117

publicly visible and embarrassing to the authority. School E showed, among all the schools, the most obvious manifestations of an active radical and political consciousness among the teachers and, although 'the radical presence' constituted a minority of all the teachers there was evidence that it was influential in the activities of the Staff Council within the school and, more widely, in the general affairs of the division and of the local authority.

Of the remaining four schools, G, I and J had Social Priority status and occupied Victorian 'citadel school' buildings, established by the London School Board. The 'citadel school' image of G was emphasized by the fact that it stood in the middle of a redevelopment area in which all the immediate houses in the vicinity had been demolished. The atmosphere within the school, however, belied this grim image: in various ways an impression was created of cheerful and cooperative enterprise between the teachers and the pupils. School G is a co-educational school of 800 pupils, representing forty-eight different nationalities. It had been associated with a sink school image derived from its origins in tough secondary modern schools, but at the time of the research there was evidence that this image was fading rapidly and the headteacher reported the beginnings of a small middle-class entry.

The traditions of urban working-class schooling were most visible in School I, in its cramped premises in the heart of the inner city. A boys' school of 500 pupils, it had about it something of the ethos of Victorian popular education, compounded variously from the head-teacher's declared conservatism in educational, social and political matters; a tradition of emphasis upon artisan and craft skills in which the school had achieved some distinction and relatively clear-cut prescriptions on discipline. The school was not cosmopolitan: the great majority of its population being drawn from local white working-class communities (although there had been an important Cypriot presence in the late 1960s). In terms of poverty, 50 per cent of the pupils had entitlement to free lunches.

Although in similar buildings to I and derived from a secondary modern tradition, School J, of 800 girls, can be contrasted with it in terms of its cosmopolitan entry and in terms of its educational leadership. The headteacher saw her work as responding to the 'challenge' of a previously 'broken-down school' (now over-subscribed) and was forthright in her comments upon the need for educational change and the response which these required from teachers and from the local authority. A general impression of vigorous activism was created, coupled with a diagnosis that the problems of urban education stemmed largely from the inefficiency and incompetence of too many teachers, headteachers and administration.

School H of 1,250 girls was located in what appeared to be an old established and definable working-class community. The school, however, drew from a wide area and its population was cosmopolitan. Its background, like that of most of the schools, was chequered in that it had (according to the current headteacher) to live down an image of a turbulent past, but it had been greatly helped in this by the activities of a former headteacher, widely esteemed for her quality of social relations and her patronage of educational innovation. The school was not a Social Priority school and, in general, seemed to be less associated with poverty than some of its immediate neighbours. It had the advantage of a pleasant modern building and it drew a higher percentage of its pupils from skilled manual homes (40 per cent) than was usual in the division.[17]

In socio-historical perspective, aspects of continuity and change in urban working-class education were exemplified in these ten inner-city schools. The municipal grammar school tradition, although weakening, could still be discovered in School D. The elementary school tradition remained physically enshrined in many of the buildings of the other schools and something of the elementary school ethos was still detectable in School I. Almost all the schools were associated with relatively high levels of pupil poverty and almost all of them had been, or currently were, the objects of a social imagery which stressed their toughness and turbulence and their constitution of a 'pedagogic challenge' to any group of teachers. Both the poverty and the notion of challenge would have been familiar to a Victorian teacher of the urban working-class.

What would have been unfamiliar, however, was the type and quality of the response to this challenge provided by (among other factors) a local education authority widely regarded as both liberal and generous. The characteristics of liberal educational reform were apparent in policies of positive discrimination in favour of the poorest schools, in the provision of modern and well-equipped specialist rooms, in a high level of physical resources, in wide and comprehensive curricula, in pastoral care systems, in expressed concerns for community education and for wider participation in educational decision-making. Such evidence of change could be quickly established: they were seen and experienced during visits to the schools. What needed to be explicit was the 'invisible' social

119

Situating the Inquiry

world of the schools: the evaluations, categories, ideologies and constructs of the headteachers and the teachers. Only if these were made explicit could the contemporary reality of urban working-class education as realized in these schools become available for examination.

Chapter 7

The Social Construction of the 'Good' Teacher: a study in one school

'Good' teachers and basic principles

Constructs of the good teacher, along with constructs of the good pupil, make visible and explicit something of the underlying principles and ideologies which shape the educational process in particular historical periods and in particular social contexts. Specifically, models of the good teacher can be said to be enshrined in conflicting ideologies of education and the emergence of any dominant model is dependent partly upon a particular ideology attaining a position of legitimacy and partly upon the immediate exigencies and imperatives of the teacher's work situation. The good teacher is thus socially constituted in two senses: at the level of ideology and at the level of 'what the situation requires'.[1] The extent to which these two constitutions are the same will depend upon a variety of factors and the work of Keddie (1971) provides an example of the ways in which divergence can occur.

The constitution of a good teacher of urban working-class pupils, as embodied in the conflicting ideological positions of different fractions of the Victorian middle class, has already been outlined. At the level of ideology, emphasis was placed variously upon religious and moral character; extent of culture and refinement; efficiency in management and good order and skill in achieving measurable outcomes in elementary skills. The imperatives of the work situation, however, tended to increase the salience of management and results as crucial determinants, although enlightened inspectors could

121

always modify and mediate this situation in their advocation of intelligent teaching. In many ways the good teacher of the urban working class *epitomized a social and cultural antithesis to the imputed characteristics of the class among which he worked.* Against volatility and impulsiveness the good teacher counterposed steadiness and perseverance; against religious or political enthusiasms, an ideological blandness; against lawlessness and rebellion, an aspiration to respectability; against native wit and unsocialized intelligence, an embodiment of disciplined study. The good teacher of the urban working class was, thus, seen to be the efficient agent and countervailing influence against anarchy in all its forms.

Forms of integration

In what ways have these constitutions and these functions of the good teacher changed in contemporary urban settings? A major focus of the present inquiry was to try to make explicit some answers to this question, with especial reference to inner-city working-class schools. At the level of ideology, the existence of conflicting models of the good teacher has already been demonstrated and it is clear that the range of contemporary typifications is far more extensive than in an earlier period of working-class education. Whereas familiar associations of management and results are still mediated in contemporary settings by conservative/traditionalist and liberal pragmatic ideologies of education, associations new in their degree of explicitness are to be found in other liberal ideologies and in radical and Marxist formulations. Innovations are most apparent in the sphere of what are thought to be the necessary social relations of the pedagogic process. Whereas the good teacher in the past was distanced from his pupils in personal, cultural and pedagogic senses, the emphasis of many contemporary ideologies is upon a pattern of social relations which celebrates variously, notions of rapport, egalitarian dialogue, weakened hierarchy and role definition, mutual knowledge exchange or solidarity with the working class and its struggle. *In the rapport of liberalism the mutual knowledge exchange suggested in some radical formulations and the explicit Marxist identification with the working class in a political struggle, are to be found constitutions of what it is to be a good teacher which are very far removed from those envisaged by the founding fathers of State elementary education for the urban masses.* The good teacher of urban working-class pupils is now, from a number of perspectives, seen to be *integrated* with his

122

pupils in various senses and no longer in a situation of antithesis to them. Radical changes in the social relations of pedagogy have, at the level of theory, replaced notions of cultural antithesis and of social distance, with those of cultural engagement, of the importance of 'relating' and of the need for rapport. The good teacher no longer stands over and against his pupils but is in important respects 'with' them. The nature and extent of this relationship is, however, variously constituted in the conflicting ideologies of urban education. Only the conservative/traditionalist position, with its emphasis upon 'respect' and upon what are seen to be the functionally necessary boundaries of role and hierarchy, resists this tendency. Other ideologies celebrate integration, but at different levels of realization; at the personal and social level (rapport); at the cultural level (dialogue); and at the political level (solidarity).

But while associations of integration replace those of antithesis at the level of teacher–pupil relationships, a sense of continuity in the social construction of the good teacher remains. This is to be found in the continuing association of ideas of the good teacher with ideas of a countervailing influence. No longer conceived of in explicit terms as a countervailing influence to the anarchy and political threat seen to be incipient *in an urban working class*, contemporary versions relate to various characterizations of *the problems of an urban society*. The good teacher is, therefore, socially constituted in relation to a diagnosed problem or set of problems located either in the urban context or in the urban school. As already shown (in chapters 4 and 5), conflicting ideologies of education carry different messages as to what are seen to be the crucial problems of the urban context and the urban school and, thus they project different models of the good teacher as countervailing influence. What is to be explored is the way in which these ideologies, problems and models are constituted within schools and, particularly, within the consciousness of the headteachers and teachers of the ten inner-city schools involved in this inquiry.

The politics of research

It is important that before the accounts of the headteachers (or their deputies) are read as evidence about teachers in inner-city schools, the problematics of the research situation in which they were generated should be appreciated. The research situation could not be a pure context for the evoking of a 'pure' manifestation of social consciousness; it had its own situational, ideological and political correlates which were bound to affect the understandings and typifications realized within it. It is clear that when the headteachers were asked to characterize the best of their teachers, various considerations were implicated in their answers. In the first place it was unlikely that any of them would deny that they had *some* outstandingly good teachers, since to admit this would be to project an unflattering image of their schools and by implication, of their own capacity to select suitable staff.[2] In the event, eleven teachers were designated as outstandingly good at School A (out of seventy full-time staff); seven at School B (out of 84); nine at School C (out of 73); nine at School D (out of 75); seven at School E (out of 65); six at School F (out of 58); eight at School G (out of 50); seven at School H (out of 70); five at School I (out of 29); and six at School J (out of 48).

Other aspects of the research situation have also to be considered in reading the headteachers' characterizations. While the headteachers could claim a significant amount of autonomy *vis-à-vis* the local educational authority, they could hardly ignore the prevailing climate of political sensitivity at the time of the research concerning the local authority's schools and those teaching within them. Neither was it likely that they could altogether ignore and remain unaffected by the local education authority's powerfully diffused ideology of liberal school reform with its emphasis upon efficient management, the pastoral and welfare functions of schools and the importance of closer school–community relations. The internal politics of each school also would be implicated in the designations of the outstandingly good teachers. Although, at the time of the research, the teachers involved did not know the criteria upon which they had been selected, the headteachers would obviously have to consider the long-term implications of the research and its effect upon their relationships with their staff. These considerations are *not* taken to suggest a deterministic thesis: that the headteachers' designations and characterizations were finally nothing more than reflections of the ideological and political situations in which they found themselves. A continuing theme within this study has been to oppose a view of teachers as 'social puppets', whether this view arises from within functionalist role theory or from within a structuralist Marxism. These considerations are mentioned in order to context the research situation and in order to avoid any unduly naïve interpretations of the headteachers' accounts.

On the other hand, it must be asserted that the headteachers responded to the objective of trying to locate exceptionally good teachers with considerable interest. They saw this to be an important and neglected area for social inquiry and the researcher found that they were prepared to give generously of their time in order to try to make explicit the correlates of the good teacher within an inner-city comprehensive school. There are good reasons, therefore, to believe that their designations and characterizations represent a serious and thoughtful attempt to define crucial issues, and to make explicit the nature of 'good teaching' as they perceived it within their immediate school situations.

School G: constructions of the 'good' teacher

In all the schools the designation of the exceptionally good teachers made explicit a range of criteria which can be grouped in two areas: those relating to notions of excellence in the teaching and learning of a particular area or subject of the curriculum (*pedagogic competence*); and those relating to notions of excellence in social relationships and general organizational contribution (*interpersonal and organizational competence*). It was clear from the accounts that the ideal teacher was taken to be one who performed highly in both of these areas. The assertion was frequently made that the two areas were closely interconnected and that a particular characteristic of inner-city schools was that good social relationships had to be established *before* pedagogic excellence could be realized. While, therefore, there existed at a general level an abstract 'ideal type' of the perfect teacher and some of the designated teachers were seen to approximate to this position, in practice the headteachers' accounts tended to emphasize one or other dimension of this structure of competence.

The fullest and most detailed characterization of good teachers was given at School G. Of the eight teachers designated (out of fifty), one was seen to approximate to the 'ideal type', three were selected primarily for pedagogic excellence and four were characterized in terms of the excellence of their relationships, pastoral work or contribution to general organization.

Mrs I.: 'efficiency, punctuality and "busyness"'

Mrs I., an English teacher, was characterized as efficient in administration, skilled in achieving consensus, strongly work-orientated and

125

successful in the work socialization of her classes, liked by the pupils and concerned about their social and personal problems. The deputy headteacher of School G described her in the following terms:

> I admire someone who is an efficient administrator and, as part of her function she helps me with exams and I am always impressed with the speed, accuracy and volume of her work. . . . She appears to be one to whom most of the younger teachers and the other teachers go if there are any matters needing to be resolved. She virtually has the way of giving a consensus. . . . She is always punctual with lessons. When she isn't there her classes are in excellent control – not in as much as they are quiet, but there is always a hub of activity and they are working. They miss her when she is not there. She appears to have them working at maximum pressure throughout the whole of the teaching period. . . . She is very rarely sitting in the staffroom without having essays around her, text-books, exercise books, marking. She appears to be working the whole of the time that she is in school. . . . They [pupils] think very highly of her and will work for her. It sounds rather silly to say this, but one criterion of a good teacher is if a teacher has to leave the room then the class immediately carry on working, they never stop. So she has got them in an atmosphere that when they are in the room they know it is a working situation. . . . When she is away sick they will get their books out and start working as if she was there. That *is* the criterion of an outstanding teacher.

Mrs I.'s efficiency, punctuality and 'busyness'[3] were key elements in her constitution as an outstanding teacher and in particular the concept of 'busyness' was seen to relate both to her personally and to work situations with which she was involved. The precise ways in which she achieved such 'busyness' among her pupils were not specified in the account, other than the observation that 'she is concerned about standards'. It was implied, however, that qualities of personality and social relationships were involved:

> Personality wise, she is very calm, doesn't get into a flap – because she is organized. She never has any discipline problems, even with the most disruptive pupil. She is well liked by the sixth form [she also held the 'pastoral' position of sixth form tutor], yet at the same time she doesn't have to be 'one of them'

to be liked. She is liked as an adult, mature personality. . . . All the children speak highly of her because she is concerned with their total academic and personal life.

These comments highlight themes which ran through the accounts of most of the headteachers and deputies. These had to do with notions of 'mature', 'responsible', or 'positive' personalities; notions of commitment and professionalism and notions of rapport and involvement. In relation to the latter, and in a revealing comment on time and teacher mobility in an inner-city school, the established nature of Mrs I. was indicated: 'She has been here a very long while – I think eight or nine years.' (In fact it was ten years.)

Miss L.: 'an outstanding impact'

Of the three teachers designated as outstandingly good on primarily pedagogic grounds, one was a young teacher of drama (in her first year of appointment); one the head of the geography department (six years in the school) and the other the head of the art department (ten years in the school). Miss L. was seen to have made 'an outstanding impact' on work in drama because of her confidence, energy and enthusiasm:

'Outstanding in the sense that she never appears to be a young teacher . . . brought lots of new ideas, innovations . . . has in her first year offered to take children out to theatrical entertainments in the evening and done so quite successfully (after being guided as to how to do it).

For all her charisma and confidence, Miss L. was seen to relate well to her superiors:

The thing I like about her is that if she has problems from time to time with particular classes, she is always willing to come to seek advice, she is always willing to take advice. She always has the decency afterwards (which most young teachers don't) when you give some advice, to come to tell you how it's worked.

Miss Y.: 'meticulous and highly organized'

Miss Y., the head of the geography department, characterized as 'a rather prim Victorian' was seen to embody a timeless model of pedagogic excellence associated with organization, strictness and 'structure', a model to which it was felt the pupils responded well:

127

I think I put her down mainly for efficiency and control of an order which is relatively missing nowadays. She seems to be a throwback to efficient schoolmistresses twenty or thirty years ago. I'll give you one example: if a child requires a pencil there is a little pad on her desk, 'Pencil given to X'. At the end of the lesson when a pencil is given back it is crossed. Meticulous, highly organized, strict, but with her forms – an almost motherly, loving relationship. . . . The children respond and like her structure – every now and then, as it were. A school would be dreadful if it was run by fifty Miss Ys., but the fact that she is so meticulous, so prim, so strict, so organized, the children (funnily enough) rather like her lessons. Everyone will strive for her, work like mad and everyone she has (there are no failures not good enough for CSE for her) sits an exam. She will put everyone in, because she has everybody working. Why she is an outstanding teacher, to me, is that if everyone had that same dedication to their subject we'd never get children leaving school who have only sat one (or at the most two) CSEs.

Mr H.: 'goals, objectives and a likeable personality'

Mr H., the head of art department, had been offered an inspectorship and was characterized as 'probably one of the most outstanding teachers (of art) in London'. He was seen to combine high pedagogic excellence with high interpersonal and organizational excellence:

An exceptional relationship with pupils, an exceptional understanding of his art . . . extremely high standards . . . organized (which I like to see in heads of department) and a quality which is very important: is able to think and plan the way ahead for his subject and his department. There is a philosophy of teaching, of art, of the way he runs his department which you have the feeling is being translated into practical action. . . . He has a goal and an objective. In this sense he has the confidence of anyone who works with him. . . . Most of us feel that he would have done well as an art inspector in London because of his tremendous breadth of view in the subject . . . he could create a philosophy, an attitude of work which could be independent of the school, but nevertheless, emanates out through the school. All Mr H.'s attitudes and ideas are coming off on other subjects. He's able to create in children the desire to create – which is the business.

He is a likeable personality again. One with whom we can be totally honest, not be devious when dealing with him. You can say exactly what you feel. The sort of man you could reach a compromise with, he sees angles from both sides.

Personality and the 'good' teacher

From these three accounts it is apparent that the constitution of a good teacher within School G involved not only a recognition of notions of pedagogic competence and enthusiasm as such, but also, crucially, their relationship with organizationally approved behaviour. In other words, *pedagogic competence had to be realized in what was judged to be situationally appropriate modes.* Mr H. represented an epitome of this position. In some ways potentially very disturbing to the established order of the school because of his radical innovations in art education, Mr H. was legitimized in terms of his organizational style, 'likeable personality' and ability to compromise. There was evidence, from a subsequent interview with Mr H., that he had consciously worked toward such a situation of accommodation with the institution.

In the social construction of the good teacher constructs of personality feature largely. In this case 'likeable personality' was equated with 'one with whom we can be totally honest, not be devious when dealing with him'. *Does this imply that 'likeable personality' is a typification which stands for an acceptable organizational style with avoidance of conflict as its central characteristic?* Such an interpretation would seem to be supported by the deputy headteacher's designation of all the good teachers:

All these people I'm speaking of are well-liked by the staffroom. None of the people I've mentioned are extreme radicals in the staffroom, they are middle of the road people, veering a little towards the Left, as most teachers are generally in these sorts of areas. Nevertheless, they are prepared to look at individual instances, rather than be worried about rank and file. That makes them contribute very, very much to staff discussions.

If this interpretation, linking personality typification with organizational and political style, has any validity, then it would seem that teachers associated with overt conflict over school policies *might well become characterized in derogatory personality terms* and find themselves subject to a more devious strategy from their superiors. The nature of personality typification and its correlates has been the subject of recent sociological investigations at the level of pupils (see, for instance, Hargreaves and Hester, 1975). Its crucial nature at the level of teachers is here underlined.

Pastoral care teachers

In almost all the schools the designation of good teachers included a strong representation of pastoral care staff. At School G four of the eight teachers designated were pastoral care teachers.

Mrs R., a certificated teacher with eighteen years' experience at School G, had started her career as an assistant teacher of physical education, had subsequently been promoted head of department and then transferred to pastoral care work. At the time of the research she was the head of year with pastoral responsibility for the fifth form and in addition was the teacher in charge of biology. She was characterized in the following way:

> Very down to earth . . . has plenty of courage . . . will go out of her way to help a child outside the school in various ways. . . . Tends to take larger classes than she needs to because she offers to help those who have difficulty with particular children. . . . Fifth year pastoral role is a very difficult one. It is the year in which the children have a lot of problems at home, the year in which they are becoming more adult, mature and worldly. They seem to be able to talk with Mrs R. and discuss their problems with her in a completely free, open and easy way. That is a rare quality because a lot of teachers find it very difficult to discuss with teenagers. She is also very cheerful in the staffroom . . . and has a very steadying influence upon staff and pupils.

Mrs R.'s constitution as an exceptionally good teacher was grounded upon her perceived strengths in interpersonal relations and in general control – 'the children both like her and respect her . . . they never take liberties with her'. Her eighteen years' experience in the school gave her an established position and her down-to-earth, matter-of-fact 'steadying' influence was seen to be important at both pupil and staff levels.

Mr W.: 'rapport with difficult pupils'

The emphasis upon relationships was a main theme in the typification of Mr W., a young, certificated pastoral care teacher (head of year and teacher of science) with five years' experience at the school:

> He is someone who will give much more of his time to the school than the normal nine to four teacher. He is a year head who really gets to know every single member of his year and, getting to know them, develops a very close relationship – so much so that if they've done something wrong they will tell him quite cheerfully and honestly . . . and yet, at the same time, feel they have let him down personally . . . he's extremely active locally – a tower of strength in the formation of the PTA, he knows a lot of the parents. Why I think he is exceptional is that we've had some very, very difficult children in the third year and because he has worked and worked and worked away at them, he's actually been able to change their behaviour. This is unique in a way because he just hasn't bothered about their behaviour in his classes, but he's been working away at them before school, after school, on Saturdays and so on. For instance, sporting activities: he stays behind, arranges football matches and has developed this relationship with his more difficult class of children and, in developing a special relationship out of normal school hours, he seems to have developed a good rapport with them.

Mr W., described as 'a very fine, well-balanced, sensible young man' was seen to be the model of a good pastoral care teacher in an inner-city school: involved in the locality, highly committed to developing good relationships with difficult pupils and very successful in doing so. In a subsequent interview with Mr W. he was to acknowledge how much he had learned about relationships and discipline from Mrs R.

Mr C.: 'concern, commitment and mediation'

Concern, commitment and skill in mediating the social, organizational and personal problems to be found in an inner-city school, were seen to be epitomized in Mr C. who was typified as 'without doubt, the most outstanding pastoral care man in the school'. Mr C. had worked in the school for twelve years. He was characterized in the following way:

131

An excellent teacher, good control throughout the years. But moderate, calm, well-respected by the rest of the staff, a sense of humour, a good mixer. . . . Makes himself totally available at any time, to any pupil and to any parent, to help in any way he possibly can. As Chairman of the Staff Association, he is forceful, clever (in the sense that I'm sure there are times when he gets things done on their behalf by the way he arranges it, rather than the actual merit of the case), fearless and honest. A man in whom you can have the utmost confidence. And he is very useful (especially as far as I'm concerned) in the sense that if you want to get the tenor of what is going on he will be fair and honest and one can always anticipate that personal relationship you get with men you respect.

In a subsequent interview, Mr C., acknowledged the force of certain radical and Marxist criticisms of pastoral care work in inner-city schools, but justified at a personal level what he recognized to be the dilemmas and contradictions of a liberal interventionist strategy in education.[4]

Mr A.: 'creating unity'

The emphasis upon *integrating functions* to be found in the typifications of Mrs R.'s 'steadying' influence, Mr W.'s rapport with difficult pupils and Mr C.'s skilful mediations, was made particularly explicit in the designation of Mr A. Mr A., who had worked in the school for ten years, was an assistant head of year and responsible for teaching in handicraft and technical drawing. He was seen to perform a key integration role within the school:

Calm, quietly spoken, has the ability to be more valuable to the school and his colleagues than necessarily to individual children. He seems to be able . . . where there is a diversity of individuals, some of whom can be at times rather departmentalish . . . to link them together and create unity where there is apparently not.
I nominate him as someone who is necessary in the school, has exceptional qualities of knitting people together.

In summing up the eight designated teachers, it was observed that all of them possessed 'a likeable personality which makes them acceptable not only to the pupils but to their fellows'. They were willing to put in more time than the average' and to 'talk, talk, talk . . . to try to get the child to look at himself and his behaviour'.

School G: the imperatives of integration

School G could be taken as typical of the other schools in the inquiry, in terms of its secondary modern origins, its Social Priority status and its multi-cultural population. It was, however, smaller (800 pupils) than most of the other schools and atypical in the relatively low teacher mobility it had experienced. In terms of social climate, the headteacher and the deputies emphasized strongly that in a school which had the potential for many conflicts arising partly out of its cosmopolitan population, the predominant quality of the school was one of harmony, co-operation and team spirit.

It is against this background and this immediate situational context that the constructs of the good teacher must be examined. The accounts show that good teachers in this particular inner-city school were characterized primarily in *organizational* terms (efficiency, control, busyness); in *inter personal* terms (rapport, consensus, understanding) and in *welfare* terms (concern for pupil problems, commitment of time and energy). Good teachers were associated with *the defusing of potential conflict situations*, either at pupil or staff levels: they were the agents of integration. Specific pedagogic excellence in curriculum areas was emphasized only in English, drama, geography, and art, and only in connection with the latter was there any substantial indication of radical innovations in the contents and categories of knowledge or the modes of its transmission. Widely disseminated notions that inner-city schools have been over-exposed to the disturbing effects of radical curricula innovation could not be substantiated at School G.

Locating the 'good' teachers

Three characteristics are often taken to typify the teaching group in inner-city schools and in comparative terms to distinguish it from teaching groups in other locations and settings. These are the relatively high proportion of young teachers in inner-city schools; the relatively high levels of teacher mobility in inner-city areas, resulting in low average levels of teaching experience within each school and, often seen to be implicated with the first two characteristics, a relatively high level of radical cultural and political consciousness.

133

The designated teachers at School G ranged in age terms from twenty-three to fifty-nine: (Miss L. 23; Miss Y. 27; Mr W. 27; Mrs I. 31; Mr H. 32; Mr C. 39; Mrs R. 41 and Mr A. 59), and in years of teaching experience from one (Miss L.) to thirty-one (Mr A.) years. They were atypical of inner-city teachers as a whole in relation to the static nature of their teaching careers. With the exception of the teacher of one year's experience, Miss L., none of the teachers had less than five years' teaching experience within School G and their average level of teaching experience within the school was ten years. Of the seven 'established' teachers, five had taught only in School G; and one had three years' experience in another type of school at the start of her career twenty years ago. Of the eight designated teachers, only Mr A. had taught in a range of schools and had full-time teaching experience outside of London.

The biographies of the teachers were comparatively uniform in relation to social origins and occupational socialization. Six originated from middle-class or lower middle-class backgrounds, mostly outside of London; two (both Catholics), from lower working-class backgrounds in London and within the general locality of the school. Mr C. had qualified by virtue of his university degree (having had no professional preparation) and the other teachers had between one and four years' preparation in colleges of education, art or drama. None were currently undertaking further courses of study except Mr H. [5] In political terms, five identified themselves as Labour voters; 'moderate socialist' or 'generally Labour'; one as Liberal; one as 'strong Conservative' and one as apolitical. Asked if they were consciously aware of any sort of relationship between their political beliefs and their work, most claimed that the two were completely separate. Only Miss L. suggested a tentative relation:

> My socialist leanings have no conscious connection with my teaching in this area, but I suppose the reason I'm teaching in a school like this is that I feel I might be able to do something for kids who didn't have as good an up-bringing as I did; it's as simple as that.

All the teachers were members of the National Union of Teachers except Mr C. and Mrs R., the latter having left the union 'because they started to strike'.

In general, therefore, the designated teachers were characterized by relatively long service within one school (and narrow range of teaching experience); relatively low levels of academic qualification;

moderate Labour politics and an ethic of strict separation of politics from work. All the teachers were characterized by what might be called *immersion: a total involvement in the life of the school and concern for its pupils which made heavy demands upon their time and energy and which tended to produce a very school-centred consciousness which gave low salience to the wider structural location of the educational process or to its social and political correlates.*

Ideology and the teachers

In terms of the ideological positions outlined in chapters 3 to 5, discussion with the teachers on a range of school issues made explicit that four of them took up predominantly conservative/traditionalist positions and four of them broadly liberal positions. The conservative stance tended to become explicit in an emphasis upon notions of 'structure' and discipline; in ambivalent attitudes to increased staff participation in decision making; in attitudes to knowledge and pedagogy and in attitudes to structural change in education, particularly the abolition of grammar schools. The liberal stance, which was largely, although not entirely, of a pragmatic character, manifested itself particularly in attitudes to curriculum and structural change and welfare issues.

On the need for structure

Mrs R. epitomized the conservative position within School G in her emphasis upon the 'need for structure' when teaching inner-city pupils. She accounted for her own success ('It sounds conceited to say so, but I know I'm a very good disciplinarian and a good teacher.') in terms of effective socialization from a senior colleague at the start of her career and in terms of personality:

> *Mrs R.:* I went to an all-girls' school where it was disciplined. That was a more gentle introduction. I had a very good introduction. I didn't like the school but certainly I was taught the right way to do things. I was helped a great deal by the senior mistress there. . . . The personality of the teacher is by far the most important thing. All the preparation in the world, if you haven't got the personality and real interest in the job, then you might as well go out and do something else.
> *Q.:* What then does personality mean?

> *Mrs R.:*   I only know that the children here tend to respect the
> teachers who discipline them. They like to know that this is
> right and this is wrong. They like a structured classroom. They
> don't really like it if a teacher lets them do what they like
> . . . they respect and get on best with those who've got a
> structured classroom set-up. . . . They certainly don't like the
> teachers who try to be one of them. The younger teachers who
> like to dress like the sixth years in all the modern gear. They
> don't like that. They still like their teachers to be that bit
> different. Younger teachers think that the more familiar you
> are, the more like them you are, the easier it is. But it is not at
> all. It works quite the opposite. There must be a distance. . . .
> But they can bridge that gap once they know you – they can
> come to you with any problem and you will sit down and listen
> to them. . . .

The use of 'structure' as a term was to occur repeatedly in the discourse of many teachers and headteachers, as did the term 'personality'. Both of these notions signalled a variety of meanings which can
only be examined in detail in later chapters. For the present it can be
observed that Mrs R.'s utilization of these terms embodied the notion
of *functional boundaries* and was grounded upon a particular model
of social order and relationships and upon the teacher's role in
creating this.

Mrs R. was ambivalent about the increase in staff participation in
decision-making within the school. While she supported the idea in
principle, she was alarmed by its manifestations in practice:

> There are quite a few teachers in the school at the moment
> who are young and quite gifted in persuading other teachers.
> Some of them, I think, tend to want to destroy things, and it's
> very hard for those of us who have been a long time here and
> are trying to build things up, to see them being destroyed.
> (Perhaps that's being old-fashioned!) Like – we have a speech
> day (not like when we went to grammar school, but it is some
> sort of speech day). Now they want to drop that. . . . They
> think that at this type of school you shouldn't have this sort of
> thing, it's too much of the old grammar school image. . . . It's
> a bit of tradition in the school and I get a bit upset about
> people trying to destroy it. . . . The end of prize-day is in sight.

Mrs R.'s support for tradition and hierarchy placed her in opposition to the local authority's policy of abolishing its remaining grammar schools. Although teaching in a comprehensive school, *she did not endorse the basic concept of such a school:* [6] 'I think the more able children on the whole, tend to be dragged down. They are dragged down more than them pulling up the lower end of the school. I don't think it works.'

As a teacher of science, Mrs R. was involved in a curriculum area which has been subject to a considerable amount of debate and innovation. She felt that despite some changes, examination successes in science (particularly biology) required 'repetition, repetition, repetition – more homework, more homework'. She justified this doctrine by pointing out that 'this is what the Examination Board wants'. [7] Her attitude to 'Nuffield science' was cautious:

> For your average child it's very good, for your less able child, no. It is too difficult because it relies very much on logic and reasoning power. This sort of thing takes intelligence. The less able child cannot work it out. The less able child can't reason things out logically for itself. . . . They can't get approximations, they can't deduce things. Nuffield is very much doing the thing yourself and deducing something from what you've done. The less able child finds it very difficult. . . . They really need more formal teaching.

In general, Mrs R. saw her work in an inner-city school as essentially concerned with providing a stable and disciplined environment for children, many of whom she believed had backgrounds of 'emotional stress and disturbance' and, within that environment, through a strongly teacher-directed pedagogy, seeking to maximize the examination successes of her pupils at CSE level. Although her major role was a pastoral one, as head of year, she regretted the existence of a system of reward which has caused her to look for promotion outside of classroom teaching:

> With so many free periods given to heads of department and people in pastoral care . . . your most experienced teachers (who are often your best teachers) are not in the classroom very much. . . . The only way you can get promotion . . . is by leaving the classroom. . . . The best teachers are only in the classroom for two-thirds of their time and that's where they do their best work . . . you should reward your good classroom teacher with allowances, not make them leave the classroom.

The Social Construction of the 'Good' Teacher

The conservative position within School G was constituted in varying degrees of explicitness in the attitudes, discourse and 'vocabulary of motive' of Mrs R., Mr W., Mrs I. and Miss Y. These teachers accepted particular constructs of structure, boundary and hierarchy as necessary features of the educational process, particularly in inner-city areas. They took the forms of knowledge and their valid realizations in examination performances as largely given and sought to achieve success through hard work and a strongly framed pedagogy. They recognized the necessity for teachers of 'positive' personality in inner-schools. They stressed the need for consensus and happy co-operation among a teaching staff and deplored the existence of any 'political' element in school life. In many of these characteristics they were the heirs of an earlier age of urban teachers.

The ideologies of liberalism

Broadly liberal positions within School G were associated with Mr H., Mr C., Miss L. and Mr A. This liberalism expressed itself largely in curricula and pedagogic terms, welfare ideology and in attitudes to various structural changes in education. There was no explicit political emphasis even of a social democratic nature and there was little mention of social class or of the wider socio-economic implications of schooling. Their liberalism was almost entirely school-centred.

Mr H.: 'working within the system'. Curricula liberalism and reformism was most associated with Mr H. and Miss L. Mr H., as already indicated, had successfully negotiated and institutionalized wide-ranging innovations in the field of creative studies, involving the integration of art, design, and technology. Recognizing the difficulties and institutional resistances to such a change, and the disturbance of existing categories and power relations within the school which were implicated, *Mr H. had pursued a consciously worked-out strategy of acquiring institutional power in order to facilitate change:*

> I'm interested in the curriculum; I've got very strong ideas
> about it. I believe that it's extremely difficult to change
> anything at all unless you're in a position of power. It's for that
> reason that I wanted to be head of the faculty. I saw this
> authority as being the place that would allow one to expand

one's ideas on curriculum more quickly than other places. You can quite easily and quickly get into a position of power – power in the sense that you can have some finance to work with. I've found with my efforts here that unless you've got some purchasing power to change things you can only go so far . . . and the power to influence the appointment of your staff is another important thing. . . .

The strategy of acquiring institutional power had involved an initial accommodation to 'the system':

When I started here as head of art, I presented the Head with fifteen passes at 'A' level. That was bigger than all the other groups put together. For about four years we never had less than twelve people for 'A' level Art. At its best there were twenty 'A' level, thirty 'O' level and one hundred CSE entries in one year. I was using this as my way of asking for money. The head was delighted but I would say, 'I cannot do anything next year because I've used the surplus stock.' This was my way into power. I meet the system on its own terms until I get what I want. . . . I didn't feel I was compromising my ideas at all. For 'A' level I did London but not for 'O' level because that was too traditional. . . . We worked very hard at it. It was super to see the looks on the faces of three kids who had no other 'A' level in another subject.

Curricula liberalism. By these means, involving the use of much personal initiative, Mr H. had succeeded in making a significant curriculum change within School G.[8] He saw the integration of art, design and technology as providing a more meaningful educational experience for his pupils; making more efficient and flexible use of time, physical resources and teacher competence and going a considerable way towards overcoming the 'tremendously strong sexist arrangement of the time-table in this school'.

Mr H. acknowledged the 'stress' of teaching in an inner-city school but also its particular satisfactions and stimulation:

I get a lot of personal satisfaction from seeing kids who come from, quite often, deprived backgrounds, still being able to be creative. That is a miracle in some cases – really it is. I particularly enjoy working in a multi-cultural set-up which you are only likely to find in an inner-city area. It's particularly

139

true if you're doing art and design, because they all bring their own particular culture to their art.

Sensitivity to the strengths of different cultures was also a characteristic of Miss L., the young teacher of English and drama. Aware of the importance of context in language realization[9] and aware of notions of cultural imposition, she was attempting to find some ways of mediating a difficult pedagogical situation, although she claimed to take a position of moderation. As part of her preparatory course in college she had undertaken a project on free schools, being particularly attracted by the way in which 'children are not viewed as passive receptacles waiting to be filled with knowledge, but participate actively in every respect of their learning'. Although only in her first year of appoinment at School G, she was optimistic about the possibilities of realizing something of this approach within the school, especially given its relatively small size and its 'good community feeling'.

Curriculum liberalism is necessarily premised upon the belief that accommodation with 'the system' is a real possibility, *given the appropriate situation and strategy*. Both Mr H. and Miss L. endorsed this position, the former claiming to have realized it in practice and the latter having an aspiration to do so. In the discourse of both of these teachers, however, curriculum was only tentatively related to wider features of society: Mr H.'s indictment of sexism being the most explicit statement in this area.

Welfare liberalism. Welfare liberalism within School G was epitomized by Mr C.:

> As a whole, I warm to the children very much and feel a great sympathy for them, especially those who are much less privileged. Sometimes one has to force oneself: there might be a child that one feels rather repugnant towards because of their personal habits, or the things they do, or their anti-social behaviour. But one gets into the habit of putting oneself in that kid's position and saying, 'well, what chance has he had?'
>
> In my present job as year teacher there's a lot of one-to-one helping of children, a pastoral role. The naughty ones get sent to me in my own year, but also children where there are social problems or personality problems, all sorts of things. I get involved in helping them, or their parents. Sometimes it's very distressing because the problems are so enormous that you feel

there is nothing you can do. But even the trying to do it, the talking over with the child or with the parents, can be satisfying. I'm aware that, both from my teaching and social experience, so often the most important role one can fulfil is that of listener.

Welfare liberalism as manifested in the pastoral care activities of many of the designated good teachers in inner-city schools was a predominant feature of this inquiry. It can be noted here, that Mr C.'s emphasis upon the essentially individualistic and caring orientation of pastoral work and upon the personal satisfactions that it could provide for teachers was a recurring theme.

The eight teachers designated as outstandingly good within School G thus represented either conservative/traditionalist or liberal ideological positions within urban education. Radicalism, as defined in this study, found only a muted expression in the curriculum areas of art and drama. None of the teachers, during the course of discussion, consciously related educational process with political process and none of them aligned themselves with anything left of 'moderate socialism'.

Labelling the teachers: definers of excellence and processes of selection

Teachers, as well as pupils, are labelled although the processes involved in this labelling are in some ways less visible than those relating to the pupils. The process of streaming by ability has, for instance, made the labelling process for pupils much more explicit.

In this case the research situation was artificial in the sense that the headteachers were specifically *asked* to apply to teachers the general category of 'outstanding in an inner-city school'. Thus it can be argued that the research activity itself created the labels. On the other hand, it can be argued that the research activity *provided an occasion for the making explicit in a specific form of evaluative categories which were already present in the situation*. It seems likely that headteachers do differentiate their teaching staff by some qualitative criteria, if only for the requirements of a formal promotion process. The research activity may, therefore, be looked upon as a context for the realization of a specific form of teacher labelling, not necessarily that which typifies the everyday world of school, but not necessarily a mere product of the research activity itself.

141

Headteachers make judgments about teachers and their judgments can have a variety of consequences, among which effects on promotion possibilities are an obvious example.[10] In making these judgments various factors are clearly implicated. These will include the headteachers' own ideological position in education; what are taken to be the imperatives of an immediate school situation; the headteachers' detailed knowledge of each teacher's activity and the general 'political' situation within the school and within the local authority. In this inquiry the designation of outstandingly good teachers was made by the headteachers in consultation with their deputies. In some schools, names were arrived at independently and collated into a final list and, in other schools the list was a co-operative project from the start. In School G the headteacher and the two deputies compiled lists which were, in the words of the headteacher, 'almost identical, there was one difference'. This was not thought to be surprising, 'Well, we work together and we are fortunate in having very much the same outlook – the three of us'.

Definers of excellence: the headteacher School G

Crucial to the understanding of the social construction of the good teacher in contemporary situations is some location of those who have the power to be the definers of excellence: in this case, the headteacher and the deputies of School G. The headteacher had received her professional preparation for teaching in a training college and had subsequently taught in primary, secondary modern and comprehensive schools in the London area. She had been head of School G for eleven years. During the course of discussion on a range of school issues, three recurring notions provided the core of her professional credo: the need for 'security', the need for 'structure' and the existence of 'harmony' within the school. She had diagnosed the need for 'security' as paramount on her first appointment to School G:

> When I first came here the thing that struck me most was the terrible insecurity of the children. . . . the children at that time, no matter who came to the school, always asked, 'Why do you want to come here?' – which seemed to me pathetic. The thing that we needed most to give these children was security. I have never seen any reason to change my view

because no matter whether the children come from so-called professional middle-class families or from children's homes or from anywhere, we are still, for many of them, the only predictable people. . . . These children need warmth. I don't mean soppiness but they particularly need sympathy. This is true anywhere, but I find particularly here because of the deeply disturbed backgrounds (whether politically disturbed from other countries, or whether socially disturbed, or whether they are intelligent people trying to live at the present time). . . . We are perhaps a little old-fashioned in that we are structured, but it is because the children rely on the structure, and I think the staff do too. I don't mean we are hide-bound, but there is a certain code of what is expected.

Central to the provision of 'security' was the pastoral care system within the school:

I think it is very important, again it comes down to security. If the children haven't got security when they need help, then they cannot work or achieve the academic standards of which they are capable. We must have relationships. We must know the parents and if there are difficulties with the parents. . . . One of the jobs of our pastoral care system is to establish contacts so that social service workers and educational welfare workers and teachers understand each other and don't get at cross purposes. That is very important in an inner-city area. We've heard so much of people not being able to work together, or the philosophies being so different that we ran a series of meetings here which have broken down many barriers.

The headteacher characterized her school in general in terms of this harmonizing impulse, regarding it as something of an epitome of a tolerant multi-racial community and a school with little ideological conflict.

Professionalism and the 'good' teacher

Of the various criteria which were utilized in designating outstandingly good teachers, 'professionalism' was to occur repeatedly in her discourse:

143

> *Headteacher: Professionalism* – that's important.
> *Q.:* What, precisely, might that mean?
> *Headteacher:* A sensitivity to the needs of their colleagues, so that they don't act with any child in such a way that it becomes embarrassing or divisive.
>
> Any professional act in relation to their colleagues. That's very important because if you don't have that you will not have a happy staff. When I say professionalism, I mean, too, an ability most of the time to care very much but without getting emotionally involved, because if you get emotionally involved you tear yourself to pieces and you can't be effective.

In the same way in which the notion of 'structure' served many purposes in teacher discourse throughout this inquiry, so, too, did the notion of 'professionalism'. Here it was used to indicate *an approved mode of social relationships between teachers and between teachers and their pupils*. Later the headteacher was to use it to indicate the *proper relationships of teachers to explicitly political issues*:

> It is interesting that at a time when a Marxist group (I had a couple of Marxists on my staff – professional people, but Marxist) wanted to come into the school to exercise influence . . . my staff just didn't want to know, they weren't interested. These people were invited in and came and conducted a meeting – with two people.
> *Q.:* So would you say your staff has little time for a political stance?
> *Headteacher:* I would say they are professionals. I've got left-wing people. I'm left wing myself (not *far* left: I vote Labour). I've been a socialist all my life and intend to remain so . . . but I like to think I'm an educationist rather than a doctrinaire politician. If the system is wrong and we teach people to think honestly, then nothing we do here is going to stop them seeing what is wrong and trying to put it right. It's not our job to push people one way or the other. It is our job

144

to turn out people who think to the maximum
of their capacity. That perhaps, is also what I
call professionalism.

Although the rhetoric of professionalism was in these senses
strongly represented in the headteacher's discourse, her account of
the process of selecting her good teachers was at a very general and
almost intuitive level:

Q.:   When you make judgments about the quality of
your staff, how are you able to do so? What
sorts of evidence do you get?

Headteacher: I don't know, frankly. I suppose . . . well, one
knows the effectiveness of the classroom
situation. A lot of it is: obviously you will know
if somebody is a good teacher by the results (not
only exams) and the reactions of children,
because children don't like people who they
don't think teach them well.

Also – the part they play in the school as a
whole. Their reaction to each other; their
relationship with myself (I don't mean crawlers –
God forbid!). When they're about the school,
not necessarily on duty and doing things, but
just by their being about, one gets the feeling.
More than that one can't say.

It is remarkable that, at the level of the headteacher, the criteria
for the evaluation of staff was of such a general and diffuse
character. Does such generality indicate lack of precise knowledge
about what teachers are actually doing? Does it, on the other hand,
indicate the inherent difficulties in being precise about complex
phenomena, or does it suggest that teacher evaluation may, in some
cases, be precariously grounded upon externals?

Definers of excellence: the deputy headteachers School G

It can be noted here that the detailed characterization of the
teachers in School G were given by the first deputy, Mr N., and his
criteria are also apparent in earlier sections of this chapter.[11] The
second deputy, Miss E., had taught at the school for less than three

years, but had nine years' experience in a neighbouring girls' comprehensive school. Miss E. had received her professional preparation in a training college in the Midlands. On coming to London she had been rapidly promoted, becoming a head of department after three years,[12] subsequently a head of house and then deputy at School G., by the age of thirty-three. Here experience in her previous school had led her to esteem a 'common-sense' and 'down-to-earth' approach to teaching:

> It is far more important (i.e. than preparation) that you get the right type of person. . . . That is a very out-going personality, sympathetic but very firm. . . . You also need bags of common sense, more than anything else. It doesn't matter how high your academic qualifications are, if you are the sort of airy-fairy waffly person who never gets anywhere, than you're not going to do anything in a city school. . . . At my previous school we had a lot of airy-fairy waffly people and you had a terrific pull. You had the common-sense, down-to-earth people who said you could teach a child even if she hates you, so long as you've got your discipline and personality you can go in and teach it and you will get good results. You had the other school who said you must love the little dears and you can't teach them unless they love you. It doesn't matter about uniform and whether they wear jewellery, the thing is to get your message over to them in the nicest possible way. There was a terrific struggle there for about four years. The common-sense band won eventually. Mainly because the other had to give up and leave: they couldn't cope, their philosophy didn't work. . . .

It seems clear that Miss E. was, herself, of the common-sense school and her observation of the 'failure' of alternative approaches in pedagogy and relationships had confirmed her in that position and this had become an important constituent in her evaluations of teachers.

School G: an overview

In these ways and by these definers, the designated good teachers of inner-city school G were characterized. Their typifications celebrate in many ways the virtues of an earlier generation of urban school teachers, although these virtues find their expression in a different vocabulary and in contemporary liberal forms. The college of education (training college) had provided the basic socialization for most of the teachers, as for their predecessors. Their characterization as positive personalities, organized, structured, energetic, committed and professional, repeats an earlier theme in the history of the teachers of the urban working class. So too, does the absence of strong ideological enthusiasms or radical questioning of the enterprise of which they are a part. The ameliorating activities of an earlier generation of urban teachers are still strongly exemplified in contemporary manifestations of liberalism, particularly in the highly regarded pastoral care system. These emerge as the constants of this specific urban education context. Changes were mainly to be found in cultural and relational areas. The beginnings of some form of cultural liberalism and a strong emphasis upon good social relationships between teachers and pupils mark some of the main discontinuities between Victorian principles and contemporary principles in urban education, as exemplified in School G.

Black Paper images of political teachers (i.e. socialists) and of subversive progressive pedagogies in inner-city schools could hardly be further removed from the actual social reality of School G. Far from being exponents of a critical radicalism (even in purely curriculum terms) the teachers were either conservative in orientation or exponents of forms of liberal pragmatism or welfare ideology.[13] They were in the headteacher's term, 'professionals'. The extent to which the situation at School G was representative of the other schools must now be examined.

Chapter 8

Defining 'Good' Teachers in Ten Schools

Those defined as outstandingly good teachers of inner-city pupils in School G had been characterized in terms of the quality of their relationships with pupils; their likeable and positive personalities; their organization and professionalism; their demonstrated involvement in the life of the school ('immersion') and their commitment to the welfare of its pupils. They were seen to perform important integrating functions within the school, both at teacher and pupil level. *Interpersonal and organizational competence had, in general, a greater salience in the judgments of the headteacher and the two deputies, than had pedagogic or academic competence.* In particular, Miss E.'s triumphant celebration of the victory in her previous school, of the 'common-sense, down-to-earth people' over the 'airy-fairy, waffly people' carried with it the implication that a tough, pragmatic, atheoretical stance was the necessary correlate of the effective inner-city teacher. It can be observed that none of the teachers designated (most of whom had qualified in colleges of education, art or drama) had been involved in advanced theoretical studies in education (other than Mr H.). Their 'professional knowledge'[1] was, therefore, very much empirically derived from their experiences within School G (or one other school) rather than from subsequent courses of study. This might be taken to explain the relatively unproblematic, school-centred and common-sense accounts of their teaching activities; an attitude of 'getting on with the job' rather than raising questions about how the job was constituted.[2]

The social construction of the good teacher within School G made explicit something of the underlying principles and ideology which shaped the educational process in that particular context. However, these principles were not merely context-specific phenomena. They were to be repeated with varying degrees of emphasis in the other schools in the inquiry. Variation occurred in so far as the headteachers of some schools (especially Schools C, F and H) placed more emphasis upon pedagogic competence and academic outcomes than was the case in School G: and in so far as some heads designated teachers who represented the radical and Marxist perspectives which had been entirely missing in the designations at School G.

School D: 'organization' and 'getting on with the job'

In three of the other schools (D, I and J) a predominantly conservative social and pedagogic ethos was discernible and the constitution of good teachers within these schools broadly (but not entirely) reflected this emphasis. The headteacher of School D, in designating nine of her staff as outstandingly good teachers in an inner-city school, characterized them as such primarily in terms of their organizing ability, leadership qualities, common sense and energy. Of the various criteria used, 'organization' and 'getting on with the job' featured very largely. Organization, in particular ('I would rate highly sheer organizing ability – this is still a rare quality') served as a crucial means for differentiating good teachers from poor teachers. Poor teachers had an inability to think ahead and lacked certain basics:

> really very simple and virtually trivial drills which it is
> extremely useful for a teacher to have, i.e. I will go into a
> classroom, say 'Good morning' and everybody is standing up.
> Possibly the instructions for what I want before they even sit
> down; otherwise, 'Sit down, I'll tell you exactly what I want
> you to do'. They have separate chairs and desks and as soon
> as they've sat down you've got to be ready to go into the
> lesson immediately (otherwise they take advantage). . . .
> Always the same drill: a margin, a date, a title. So there is a
> pattern and then you're ready to start in good order. Then
> you can relax and do something totally different from normal.

The headteacher's use of the notion 'organization' seemed to imply

149

a very precise and meticulous specification of detail in the activity of teaching and it was central to her characterization of five of the nine teachers as outstandingly good. Included in the typification of four of the teachers was a reference to the excellence of their subject teaching (the heads of history, science and physical education departments and a young teacher of science), but only in the case of science was specific mention made of curriculum innovation. Of the nine teachers designated, four were university graduates and five had qualified in colleges of education. With the exception of two young teachers (recent Bachelor of Education graduates) all the teachers had worked in the school for more than five years[3] and, as in the case of School G, their range of teaching experience was, in general, limited to one or two schools. Subsequent discussion with these teachers was to show that most of them adopted a broadly conservative stance in matters of curriculum, pedagogy, the internal government of schools and issues of structural change in education.

School I: 'discipline' and 'loyalty'

The conservative ethos of School I (which, at 500 pupils, was the smallest school in the sample) was made particularly explicit by the headmaster:

> I regard myself as a highly respectable Conservative: a
> supporter of privilege[4] and that is no secret to anybody.
> Those of my staff on the Left who like to snipe at it, do so
> occasionally . . . but they have got to put up with it.

However, despite its small size and the explicit conservatism of the head, the social and pedagogic situation at School I was not straightforward. The situation contained various contradictions and anomalies which affected the process of characterizing the good teachers and which, as a consequence, produced some unexpected results. The most obvious contradictions were to be found in the headteacher's own account of his educational ideology and practice. At the level of ideology the headteacher, on some occasions, seemed to imply that good teachers had come to accept a 'realistic' level of academic achievement from the pupils and that, in any case, objectives other than the academic were of more significance.[5] On other occasions the head spoke of the importance of high standards of work and typified two of his staff as outstandingly good in achieving such standards. These inconsistencies in the headteacher's account can probably be explained as arising out of differences in the criteria used by the head and his deputy (who was involved in the designations):

> The criteria are difficult to establish, they must vary from area to area. My deputy has other criteria to me, since he is concerned to push up academic standards. I remind people that we have largely non-academic kids and they have their needs.

The second major contradiction occurred in relation to the head's account of his practice within the school. This asserted a close knowledge of, and involvement in school affairs and a particular concern for staff relationships. In subsequent discussion with the five designated teachers in School I there was a *consensus in expressed dissatisfaction with the headteacher's practice in precisely these two areas.* One teacher expressed the general dissatisfaction in very explicit terms:

> At the end of last term there was quite an open rebellion at the headmaster's lack of interest in the school. . . . Why the hell should everybody else in the place flog themselves to death when he isn't interested in us. . . . We get upset when he thinks things are going reasonably, when they are not. He's not really involved – he doesn't know the kids, he doesn't teach the kids. He can't really, in that situation, understand the problems.

These contradictions may go some way to explaining the fact that included in the headteacher's designations was a young teacher of English of comparatively radical views. She was esteemed by the head in terms of her 'positive' style, but it seems clear he had no detailed knowledge of her critical attitudes towards the curriculum. [6] In characterizing his good teachers, the head of School I placed particular emphasis on their capacity to produce discipline and their capacity to relate to him in an appropriate mode:

> I always say that discipline and the behaviour of a place really counts. Exam results, of course, up to a point, but in this sort of area the majority of customers don't know what they're all about in any case, so it doesn't cut a lot of ice . . . the basic reason for a successful school in this sort of area,

151

I'm quite certain, is general reputation for discipline and behaviour.

Of the five teachers designated as outstandingly good, three held major pastoral positions as heads of year and two were heads of subject departments (English and mathematics). Although recognition was given to the pedagogic achievements of the latter (e.g. head of mathematics: 'expects and attains very high standards of work and behaviour'; head of English: 'good syllabus, develops new themes, is doing Mode 3 – the only one in the school'), there was a strong emphasis, also, on their being good disciplinarians:

> I tend to judge a member of staff primarily by the way he is able to manage the children: firmly and in a sympathetic manner. An iron arm type can maintain order by brute force but this finally does not count.

An appropriate mode of relationships to the head himself was also stressed:

> Despite the general political atmosphere, by and large some good, old-fashioned manners are desirable. I am old-fashioned enough to respect the person who puts his point of view politely.

Throughout the headteacher's discourse, notions of an appropriate style of relationship to superiors and notions of 'loyalty' recurred. They were particularly explicit in the characterization of the senior head of year (twenty-four years' experience in the school): 'He always relates to me in the right way – he has always been loyal' and in the headteacher's labelling of some of his staff as 'dissident': 'not extreme as we know them now, but people who were opposed to me, didn't like my methods'. The head observed that there had been comparatively little ideological conflict within School I and attributed this to *a careful policy of staff recruitment and institutional socialization*:

> I fill most of my vacancies by London First Appointments (LFAs) because I like to be able to train them up the way we want them to go. Therefore, unless you're very unlucky and you have a young person who is very politically motivated already, you can see they keep the right company.

In view of these criteria, it is not surprising that four of the five teachers designated as outstandingly good proved, in subsequent discussion, to hold predominantly conservative views on a range of educational issues. The one exception was the head of English, who although one of the headteacher's carefully selected LFAs, claimed to have become radicalized and politicized by the experience of teaching in a deprived inner-city school such as School I.[7] The strong association between designated good teachers and professional socialization in colleges of education, which had been apparent in Schools G and D was repeated in School I. In this case *all of the designated teachers had qualified in colleges of education*, although two had subsequently undertaken further studies.

School J: 'tough-mindedness'

School J (800 pupils) was a single-sex school which was locally well thought-of and as a consequence, was 'over-subscribed'.[8] Its popularity was explained by a number of its teachers as relating to a reputation for discipline and order: 'the parents of this area do think highly of the school, it's got a name for being very disciplinarian'. The headteacher saw staff evaluation as an important part of her function in the school: 'One of the chief roles of the head, and if the head is successful in this then the school is successful, is talent spotting'. In designating six of her teachers as outstandingly good, the head (and the deputy) stressed qualities of 'empathy with the pupils', 'rapport', 'good administration' and 'getting results'. By these criteria the heads of English, geography, home economics and remedial departments were selected; the acting head of mathematics department and a young teacher of home economics, who was also a tutor at the school's youth centre. Although the head of School J claimed to be very much concerned with curriculum innovation, *only in the case of the teachers of mathematics and home economics was reference made to innovatory activity* and this at a generalized level of having 'a lot of ideas'. In practice, the designated teachers were once more characterized largely in terms of their interpersonal and organization competence and despite the head's assertion of 'talent-spotting' as a central feature of her role, the typifications of the good teachers were in very general and diffuse terms – as was the process by which they were selected.

Unlike Schools G, D and I, School J had no strongly institutionalized pastoral care system and, consequently, pastoral care

153

teachers as such did not appear in the designations. Both the head and the deputy were hostile to what they regarded as soft middle-class welfare ideology in inner-city schools. As the deputy put it, 'teachers have definitely become soft by understanding them [pupils] too much and it is not doing the kids any good. I believe the kids need firm but kind handling. . . . The last thing these kids need is a middle-class 22-year-old best friend'.

School J presented a number of contradictions to the researchers. The head's emphasis in her discourse upon the importance of curriculum innovation *did not appear to feature significantly in her actual characterizations of her outstandingly good teachers.* Neither was her emphasis upon 'talent spotting' concretely exemplified in any very precise descriptions of the special qualities of the teachers she had chosen. In Keddie's (1971) terms, the gap between the 'Educationist Context' and the 'Teacher Context' appeared in these respects to be very wide. An unusual feature of the designations at School J was the relatively short length of experience within the school. Three of the teachers (English, mathematics, remedial) were in their first year at the school; one had two years' experience and two (home economics and geography) had five years' experience. Given that a general theme throughout the inquiry was that crucial to successful inner-city teaching was time and continuity (the essential correlates of rapport and of results), the designations at School J were surprising.

Four of the six teachers, in subsequent discussion, took up broadly conservative positions on questions of curriculum, pedagogic and structural change. In considering the process whereby good teachers were defined in School J the characterization of poor teachers may provide some implicit comparative criteria. They were typified by the headteacher in terms of:

> the absence of self-criticism; the fear of anything that could be labelled accountability; the resistance to it in some extreme cases; the immediate joining of way out and rather militant groups (i.e. Rank and File or International Socialist).

'Good' teachers and 'poor' teachers

The social construction of the good teacher in Schools D, I and J repeated in many respects the pattern in School G. Overall, a prevailing conservatism was apparent, constituted in the ideologies

of the heads and the deputies and made explicit in their typifications and evaluations. With the exception of School D (a former
grammar school) these schools were the smallest in size of the ten
institutions involved in the inquiry. This may suggest some connection between school size and ideological orientation, some
indication that smaller institutions tend towards higher levels of
consensus and conservatism. [9]

The good teachers within these schools were characterized in
terms of their 'organization', 'administration', 'rapport', 'positive
personality', 'hard work' and 'professionalism'. *Few teachers were
selected for the quality of their pedagogic work as such and very few
for introducing significant changes in either curriculum or
evaluation procedure.*

Poor teachers were seen to be 'lazy', 'of weak personality' and
'ineffective in classroom management'. They were also seen to be
associated with *conflict* within the institution. This association,
although expressed in a different vocabulary, was apparent in all of
the schools: as 'lacking professionalism' (School G); 'of a political
slant' (School D); 'dissident' (School I); and 'joining way out groups'
(School J).

The analysis also revealed that the process of typification (the
means whereby some teachers were designated good and others
poor), was, at the level of the headteachers, *frequently general and
diffuse in character* and necessarily raised questions about the
justice and reliability of the process. These questions were given
added significance in those schools where important contradictions
were revealed between a headteacher's account of his or her
priorities and practices and the indications derived from other
sources of evidence. [10]

Defining 'good' teachers: the liberal emphasis

As Sharp and Green (1975) point out, the notion of 'school ethos'
presents problems to the sociologist of education in that its use may
involve undue reification and undue simplification. At the same
time, its widespread use both in common-sense understandings of
schools and in formal sociological studies suggests that it has some
analytical utility despite these problematics. School ethos is taken
here to refer to *a matrix of history, biography, social relations and
ideologies, realized and made sensible within a given school*

155

context. As hierarchical institutions, the ideology and the practice of the current headteachers and deputies are taken to be important in the constitution of a school ethos at a particular time. However, it seems likely that these relationships are strongly influenced by the size of the institution and that, in general, notions of school ethos and of the headteacher's part in influencing this become more tangible and explicit, the smaller the school. Thus the conservative ethos of the relatively small schools (G, I and J) and the role of the heads and deputies in partly constituting this ethos, was relatively more accessible to the researchers than was the case with the other schools.

These schools (A, B, C, E, F, and H) were larger (950–1,250) and more complex institutions in relation to which a notion of school ethos was difficult to establish. The greatest variation with the previous schools was in terms of the relative influence which could be exercised by the current headteacher and deputies *vis-à-vis* the staff and *vis-à-vis* a pre-existing situation. Whereas the head-teachers of Schools G, D, and J were established by length of appointment within their institutions (eleven years; fourteen years; twelve years; nine years), the headteachers of the remaining schools were, with the exception of School B, relative newcomers (two years; six years; three years; two years; one year) and four of them were relatively young headteachers (under the age of forty). The attempt to categorize a school ethos in these circumstances was particularly problematic. The sense of liberalism which was discernible to the researcher could, in some schools, be located explicitly in the ideologies of the headteachers and the deputies, whereas in other schools a sense of liberalism or radicalism appeared to be essentially located in certain sections of a large and ideologically diverse teaching staff. The notion of 'liberal' as applied to these six schools is, therefore, used *in a relative, rather than absolute sense* (i.e. in relation to the ethos of Schools G, D, I and J) and its claimed existence is not necessarily thought to be attributable only to the ideologies and practices of the current headteachers.

School A: 'a sense of balance'

In terms of school ethos, the situation at School A was particularly fluid at the time of the research. A previous headmaster had attempted to liberalize the school but with only partial success. As one experienced teacher put it:

He had many liberal viewpoints but, unfortunately, lacked certain skills. He wanted mixed-ability teaching and informal structure. He wanted to break down the bureaucracy; have informal relationships with the staff and share the power. He wanted the school to revolve around the curriculum. But he didn't realize the full power of the bureaucratic set-up, or of the personalities he had to deal with, and he was too gentle a person.

The period of innovation had been a time of ideological conflict within the school and of increased uncertainty for the teachers. The current headteacher, who had been a member of staff during this period, saw his role in terms of consolidating a 'middle ground' position. A lack of identity in the school and a sense of alienation from it, at both staff and pupil level, he attributed to this time:

it was due to insecurity – the boys and staff didn't quite know from day to day what the atmosphere was going to be (I wouldn't like to go into the reasons). But lack of sureness, combined with a teacher shortage brought this about.

The headteacher of School A saw his role as that of facilitator[11]:

There's a pretty massive degree of talent in the school, with lots of ideas and lots of people who, in other ages, would have themselves been heads. They have a real contribution to make. It is my job to make it possible for those ideas to work, rationality, objectivity, compromise (if you like) are going to be the more dominant attitudes.

Within this context and with these declared orientations, the headteacher designated nine teachers as outstandingly good; a list to which the deputy added a further two. Despite the head's reference to a 'pretty massive degree of talent in the school, with lots of ideas', *in his actual designations and typifications of 'good' teachers, references to 'ideas' or to specific pedagogic excellence or innovation were, in fact, very sparse.* Two young teachers (English and mathematics) were selected for the quality of their subject teaching (and associated relational competence) and the current (and previous)[12] heads of humanities were also selected by these criteria. The main emphasis of the headteacher's characterizations

157

was, however, once more, *in the sphere of inter-personal and organizational competence* rather than in innovatory or pedagogic terms. Five of the nine teachers selected as outstandingly good in the context of an inner-city school were chosen primarily on these ground and were teachers centrally involved in the pastoral work of the school (two heads of year; two deputy heads of year and the school counsellor). They were characterized as having a high degree of rapport with the pupils and as being able to deal with stressful situations in a calm and mature way. The headteacher made these priorities explicit in his general typifications of 'highly effective teacher':

> Basically, energetic, enthusiastic people – with a sense of balance – being a level sort of person, not personalizing situations or difficulties. A person who can see he is in charge of the young, who cannot be expected to behave at all times with rationality and maturity.
> Someone secure in his own identity . . . and basically magnanimous – being able to understand what makes young people tick, but not in a sentimental way. . . . Obviously also an interest in what they are teaching – children like to know that what they are doing is seen by the teacher to be important to their development.

The two teachers designated additionally by the deputy head-master (without additional comment) appeared to represent the previous divisions within the school on questions of curriculum change. The current head of English proved in subsequent discussion to be a severe critic of many contemporary educational and institutional changes, while the (former) head of integrated studies[13] argued the case for curriculum reform.

Accordingly, the overall impression of School A was that a liberalizing period of curriculum and institutional change (perhaps incompetently handled) which had been associated with loss of identity, direction and security, was being abandoned in favour of a return to a state of certainty and equilibrium, and that good teachers were being designated and characterized primarily in relation to these aims. The question of bureaucracy within the school was still very much a live issue.[14] A strong division existed between those who argued the need for bureaucracy as an inevitable, necessary and functional element within a large school, and those who saw bureaucracy as an impediment to curricula and institutional change.

Of the total of eleven teachers designated, seven of them were subsequently to be associated with broadly liberal ideologies of education, one with an emergent radicalism and three with generally conservative positions. The majority of these teachers, unlike those in previous schools, were strongly in favour of comprehensive education and tended to relate this form of education to wider political-social changes. However, while a sense of 'commitment' was in this way apparent, only in the case of two of the teachers was a vocabulary of political consciousness explicitly used in relation to the comprehensive school and the general impression was of a group of teachers who saw the comprehensive schools as essentially being 'more fair' than a divided secondary school system.

School B: 'pastoral care, curriculum development and public relations'

While the liberalism of School A appeared to be receding, that of School B was in the ascendant. This large, co-educational school of 1,250 pupils had, in a period of six years, changed its image and reputation from that of a 'sink school' to a school which had become over-subscribed and increasingly favoured by a middle-class section of parents in the locality. The 'regeneration' of the school was widely believed to have resulted from the interrelated activities of a shrewd, experienced headteacher, skilled in public relations and the concerted action in support of the school by middle-class parents committed to state comprehensive education for their own children.[15] These parents were generally identified as being of 'the new middle class' and were typified by neighbouring headteachers as 'politically conscious'; 'left-wing intellectuals'; 'trendies' or 'media people'.

The headteacher of School B was explicit about his strategy in regenerating the school:

I carried out my own analysis of the school and looked at it positively to see what I could do in order to improve its reputation. I came with some success behind me and my union work had brought me into contact with a very large number of teachers and heads. So I had some personal credibility and I could build on that and, frankly, I used it. I had to sell a product, so I used these contacts. Perhaps, sometimes I was a little ahead of what was going on in the school. But if you don't do it that way, you'll never build up the image. . . . I had to release the tensions inside the school: there was a good deal of aggression amongst the pupils and a good deal of disillusion and disgruntlement amongst the staff. . . . With the staff, I democratized the whole process to give every member of staff the feeling that they were participating in the changes. So I organized a regular time-table of staff meetings and meetings for departmental and pastoral care staff. I got them to organize themselves and to think about curriculum development (because I felt some of the aggression might be coming from stereotyped arrangements in the school). . . . Also, I altered the pastoral side very rapidly from a superficial and competitive pastoral system to an involved, caring and real one: a house system with house staff. . . . I had to work subsequently on the primary schools. . . . I made a deliberate appearance on the circuit and sold the school.

The characterization of exceptionally good teachers at School B reflected these three priorities of the headteacher: the pastoral care system; curriculum development and public relations. Of the seven teachers designated as outstanding, three were heads of house and esteemed for the quality of their relationships with pupils, parents and colleagues; their organization and their 'immersion' in the total life of the school. Four of the teachers (head of home economics and community service, acting-head of mathematics, acting-head of drama and a young teacher of history and social studies) were esteemed for the quality of their classroom teaching and their contribution to curriculum development in the school. While it was clear that the pastoral care teachers were regarded as *key agents in the regeneration of the school* and crucial mediators between it and the local area, School B was one of the minority of the inner-city schools in which pedagogic competence and innovatory activity featured as a significant constituent of the good teacher.

School C: 'making the comprehensive idea work'

The emphasis upon curriculum development and the quality of classroom teaching, which was apparent in the typifications at

School B, might have been associated in some degree with the expectations and influence of its 'new middle-class' patrons. Such an explanation seemed to be less likely in the much more exclusively working-class schools, C, F and H and yet in these three schools such criteria were dominant in the characterization of good teachers.

At School C the headteacher diagnosed the problem of his school and that of many inner-city comprehensive schools, in terms of a serious under-estimation among teachers of what could be achieved with working-class pupils. This situation he partly attributed to the legacy of a secondary modern past: 'their old staff had stirling qualities, but not expectations of high academic attainment. I think this has tended to keep standards low'. The headteacher defined his outstandingly good teachers primarily in relation to their ability to produce 'high standards' in their particular curriculum area. In his view, such teachers were characterized by 'a profound belief that high standards are achievable, coupled with the sort of experience and realism which has enabled them to realize how it is achievable'. The headteacher saw this to be central to the comprehensive school idea: 'the chief function of any comprehensive school is to develop everybody's abilities to the maximum, working on the assumption that all can be developed and one cannot predict how far. . . .'

The headteacher of School C, a graduate historian, was unique among the ten heads interviewed in that *he explicitly located his school and its activity in an historical framework which utilized notions of class struggle and ideological struggle:*

Historically, education is a battle-field and always has been, because it is so much the main means of bolstering up and shaping society and levels of prestige in society – and levels of power and accessibility to wealth and position. Owenites, Chartists, etc. all established an educational institution for their people first of all. Trade unions have increasingly realized the importance of education, perhaps not enough, but it's always been a very burning issue. . . . Engels in 1844 talked about the bulk of books of importance being read by politically minded skilled artisans, not the middle class. They've [the working class] been fighting for weapons to improve their position. This is still the case: basically this is what 'comprehensive' is about. . . . It's another matter whether they're getting these weapons in these schools. . . .

On the criteria of high expectations and 'high standards', nine teachers were designated as outstandingly good by the headteacher and the deputies of School C; six heads of department (art, music, biology, home economics, physical education, religious education/humanities) and three assistant teachers (English, history, mathematics). Almost all the teachers were young (under the age of forty) but despite this, and despite the headteacher's own strong commitment to the comprehensive school as the necessary context for a more egalitarian educational process, *only three of the seven teachers subsequently interviewed, shared his commitments and articulated broadly liberal positions.* Four of the teachers were either sceptical about, or hostile to the concept of the comprehensive school (e.g. 'I think we need to keep the grammar schools because, finally someone has to run the country' – teacher of history). They were generally critical of the NUT as 'Communist-dominated' or because of its involvement in strike action and their views on curriculum and pedagogic issues were conservative. While these teachers did not share many of the headteacher's commitments, they 'produced results' which he (or his deputies) regarded as impressive. The notion of results was a constant theme in the discourse of the headteacher, and yet the way in which these were to be constituted and understood was rarely made explicit. *Thus, results and standards frequently used in the typification of good teachers remained at an essentially unexplicated and taken-for-granted level of meaning.*

School H: 'high expectations'

This was less true of Schools F and H. Here the emphasis in the characterization of good teachers was, once more, strongly upon 'expectations' and 'achievements' but in these cases, the headteachers made more explicit their understandings of these terms. The headteacher of School H was critical of one of her 'progressive' predecessors whom she saw as a liberal-romantic:

> he didn't really see that in the real world in which we live, academic qualifications have an ever-increasing emphasis being put upon them. He didn't see that in order to liberate working-class children from their backgrounds you had to give them the basic tools. The chances aren't there and the doors aren't open unless you've got basic qualifications.

The dominant ideology of School H, in so far as this was constituted by the headteacher, was a *tough-minded, pragmatic and meritocratic liberalism* which diagnosed problems of under-achievement in terms of low teacher expectation and saw its solutions in terms of higher expectations from teachers. In perceiving an important part of the activity of teachers in an inner-city school as being concerned 'to liberate working-class children from their backgrounds', the headteacher expressed, albeit in the vocabulary of contemporary educational liberalism, the essential imperatives of 'rescue' which characterized state-provided urban education from its origins. Whereas the ethic of rescue for an urban working class has been constituted by the Victorians in essentially moralistic terms: 'in rescuing that class from its misery of ignorance and attending vices', its constitution by the headteacher of School H was pragmatic and utilitarian:

> exam results matter terribly for all kids and in particular for these kids because the only way that they will have the opportunity to live a different life-style to that which they have at the moment will be with the qualifications that enable them to do so.[16]

The inner-city school from this perspective, provided the essential means for *individuals* in a competitive social structure to attain to what was seen to be a better future: an escape from the limited job opportunities of the area; an escape from its associated occupational and social role ascription and an escape from the 'limitations' of its cultural and intellectual horizons. Here was the epitome of a liberal meritocratic ideology.

The headteacher designated seven teachers as outstandingly good (the heads of department of modern languages, dance, English, mathematics, sociology; a head of house and a teacher of French) on criteria which stressed high expectations (for work and behaviour) and high outcomes as realized in good examination results or impressive performance (in the case of dance). These qualities were accounted for in terms of 'charisma' (in one case), teachers' biography (in three cases) and 'enthusiasm for their subject' in all cases. The fact that three of the heads of department were themselves of working-class origin was thought to be an important correlate of their success:[17] 'very definitely of working-class origins and they all share a certain resentment that people expect so little of the working class and they have each picked themselves up

163

by their bootlaces. This is an important factor for success in this area.'

The designated teachers at School H proved, subsequently, to have a political unity at the level of Labour Party support, but this in no way predicted the general ideological positions within education which they espoused. These ranged from a conservative/traditional stance which was sceptical about structural and pedagogic change, to a committed radicalism which took seriously the notion of knowledge as a social construct and which attempted to vary in important ways the social relations of pedagogy. The young teacher of sociology who held this latter view among the designated teachers, saw the work of her department as crucial in an inner-city school for its celebration of 'the idea of man as active participant in his world, of becoming *aware* of what is going on' and for the context which it provided for the potential generation of a critical consciousness and of the realization of mutual knowledge exchange: 'it's important for the children to feel that they can give knowledge to their teachers about this area.'

It was apparent from School H that, whereas for some teachers examination qualifications provided crucial outcomes of the educational process in terms of their potential for liberating inner-city pupils from the constraints of the locality, other teachers, while accepting the need for universalistic examination 'currency', saw the crucial outcomes of the educational process in terms of generating a critical consciousness which might in the long term contribute *towards changing the constraints of the locality, rather than encouraging escape from them.*[18]

School F: 'clarity, imagination and sensitivity'

At School F the headteacher was committed to making comprehensive education work in the following sense:

> I could work in a far easier school where there were far
> fewer disadvantaged pupils. But I think the real test of
> comprehensive education (this is a political statement) is how
> far it can successfully help children in a very deprived area to
> extend their levels of achievement and help those few children
> who are already very clever when they come to us at eleven
> and who are quite often (though not necessarily) from
> professional homes.

164

In designating six of her teachers as outstandingly good in realizing these ends (the heads of departments of English, art, science, technical studies, social projects; and a senior teacher of English), the head emphasized the importance of clarity, imagination and sensitivity: 'getting into the minds of the children', as crucial correlates of the effective teacher.

The headteacher of School F was exceptional in that she regularly taught classes within the school as a matter of principle. This direct pedagogic experience, it was claimed, not only kept her in touch with the realities of classroom teaching (and its exhausting nature) but provided, incidentally, some grounds for teacher evaluation:

I learn a great deal from the pupils themselves. That does *not* mean that I explicitly ask the pupils, but children talk about teachers, teaching and lessons incessantly. The way I teach, in my classes, there is time quite consciously for children to talk about all sorts of things apart from the subject.

Given the diffuse and almost intuitive way in which the processes of typification and labelling of good teachers had been constituted in some schools, the designations and typifications at School F appeared to be grounded much more firmly at the level of pupil evaluation and response.

In Schools C, H and F the dominant emphasis in the social construction of the good teacher was upon notions of high pedagogic competence which were realized in conventionally understood and socially approved results. The associated vocabulary of motive was, however, varied as between the schools. At School C, constituted at the level of the headteacher (although weakly constituted at the level of the teachers designated) was a notion which related educational achievements with a notion of increased power ('weapons') for inner-city pupils in a socio-economic and political struggle. At School H and again at the level of the headteacher, educational achievements ('qualifications') were perceived to be a necessary currency of liberation for individuals to escape from a context of inner-city constraints; while at School F they were regarded as the essential tests of validation of the comprehensive school idea and, in particular, necessary to reconstructing the image of a former sink school.

165

School E: 'consistency'

At the last of the ten schools, School E, the headteacher's criteria were more general and eclectic. In a school which had gained a reputation for teacher militancy against the 'coping strategies' suggested by the local authority at the time of staff shortage, the head initially designated four of his teachers as outstandingly good on the grounds of 'positive personality', 'commitment and professionalism', 'standards and *consistency*'. The responsibilities of two of the teachers designated were largely pastoral and administrative (year head and head of lower school); one was the head of geography and one a teacher of 'basic education'. While two of the teachers were subsequently to take up broadly liberal ideological positions, especially with reference to curriculum reform, nothing of the radicalism and militancy which had been imputed to the school became apparent in their discourse. Subsequent designations,[19] however, brought into the sample two young English teachers, one of whom adopted a broadly radical and libertarian stance on a range of educational issues and one of whom adopted an explicitly Marxist position. The headmaster was aware of the political and rank and file union commitments of the latter, but regarded them as not impinging directly upon the teacher's performance:

> He's an extremely good classroom manager, doesn't have
> discipline problems. I'm impressed by his work in English.
> . . . Certainly I'm very glad I've got him on my staff for his
> teaching (not always for other things – but that's not the
> point). Anyway, it doesn't do any harm for headmasters to be
> kept on their toes.

In these six designations of outstandingly good teachers at School H were constituted the full range of ideological positions within the urban education context, from the strong conservative/traditionalism of the head of lower school (later promoted deputy head of another inner-city school) to the explicit Marxism of the young English teacher. School H was unique in this comprehensive representation of educational world views among its good teachers.[20] While ideologically diverse, they were seen by the headteacher to have a unity in the quality of their relationships with pupils; in 'good classroom management' and in energy, enthusiasm and commitment ('professionalism'). The headteacher felt that he was able to say this with confidence: 'I know what is going on in most of my classrooms, either I actually go into them, or for the more formal subjects, I can see into them.' Despite this confident assertion, it must be noted that *dissatisfaction was encountered within the school on this very issue,* some teachers claiming that the head was too often out of the school 'at County Hall meetings'.

Defining the 'good' teacher: consciousness and situation

Analysis of accounts in ten inner-city comprehensive schools revealed that the dominant emphasis in the social construction of the good teacher of contemporary urban working-class pupils was upon *relational and organizational competence,* 'immersion' in the life of the school, and demonstration of an individualistic welfare commitment to the various distresses of inner-city pupils. The notion of professionalism served to encapsulate many of these qualities which, taken together, constituted the model of teacher excellence in such schools. Professionalism also served, in some schools, as an important discriminator between notions of appropriate teacher activity and 'being political'. *In only a minority of the schools was the emphasis in typification of good teachers strongly upon the quality of classroom teaching or pedagogic skill as such.* Innovatory activity related to curriculum, pedagogy or evaluation procedures was only rarely mentioned.

How are these characterizations to be interpreted and located in a situational sense? It seems clear that in relation to the historical origins and situations of urban working-class education, it is possible to see in the emphasis upon 'need for structure' a continuing preoccupation with social order and social control, with the containment and domestication of an urban population. In the emphasis upon teacher 'professionalism' it is possible to see a continuing preoccupation with the dangers of a potential politicizing of inner-city teachers. In the emphasis upon individualistic welfare liberalism can be discerned the continuance of former ameliorative activity and in the emphasis in some schools upon liberation through qualification can be seen a transmuted form of the 'ethic of rescue'. All such interpretations give support to radical and Marxist formulations of contemporary urban working-class schooling, particularly the assertion that the enterprise is basically unchanged in its ultimate social functions. On the other hand, the headteachers were defining good teachers in relation to what they

167

saw as the 'needs' of their immediate and contemporary school situations: what one of them explicitly referred to as *'the imperatives of the situation'*. These imperatives were constituted at a strictly instrumental and 'technical' level, not at a socio-political level.[21] For instance, the perceived needs for structure, continuity and stability were set against a diagnosis of the problem of the inner-city school which emphasized the detrimental effects of high teacher mobility, interrupted schooling and a general context of increased social and economic disorganization in inner-city areas. The imperatives of pastoral care commitment and of 'getting qualifications' can also be seen in this light. In other words, the headteachers could claim that they were making explicit in their typifications of the good teacher *the rationalities which the schools as constituted and the situation as constituted, necessarily required*. All of them strongly rejected particular radical or particular Marxist interpretations of the 'real' function of urban working-class schools as being either propaganda or caricature.[22]

These issues raise important questions concerning the relationship of consciousness to situation. It could be argued that the headteachers were, in many ways, the victims of their social situation and possessed of a 'false consciousness' of it. This would be a view similar to that of Althusser (1971):

> I ask the pardon of those teachers who, in dreadful
> conditions, attempt to turn the few weapons they can find in
> the history and learning they 'teach' against the ideology, the
> system and the practices in which they are trapped. They are
> a kind of hero. But they are rare and how many (the
> majority) do not even begin to suspect the 'work' the system
> (which is bigger than they are and crushes them) forces them
> to do or worse, put all their heart and ingenuity into per-
> forming it . . . so little do they suspect it that their own devo-
> tion contributes to the maintenance and nourishment of this
> ideological representation of the school. . . .'

The attribution of 'false consciousness', however, has its own problems in this context, not least of which is the indignant reaction of those so characterized, i.e. 'false consciousness' can become in itself a version of deficit theory and as such counter-productive. A more fruitful approach in interpretation would seem to be a position which accepts as 'true' the headteachers' diagnosis of the imperatives of their situation, but *which goes beyond this to ask what socio-economic and political processes have produced such imperatives in the first place.*[23] Such considerations generate a host of questions about inner-city schools and the teachers within them. For instance, *against what* are good schools and good teachers seen to be a countervailing influence? What socio-economic and political structures and processes have resulted in a situation whereby imperatives are socially constructed for inner-city schools which have to do with 'needs' for structure, stability and continuity; providing a ladder of escape or becoming immersed in individualistic welfare liberalism? Why has teacher shortage and teacher mobility been highest in inner-city areas – in other words, *why have those who are amongst the poorest and most powerless of the city encountered in their schools the greatest concentrations of problems?* Why have relational and organizational competence come to count for more in the constitution of the 'good' teacher of inner-city pupils than have pedagogical competence and some notion of the quality of classroom teaching?

In so far as the social construction of the good teacher and the good school makes explicit and visible what are taken to be the imperatives of the inner-city situation, *it necessarily raises more fundamental questions concerning the socio-political constitution of that situation.*

Chapter 9

Pupils, Localities and the Experience of Teaching

'Urban corruption'

The 'child-saving' and rescue imperatives of Victorian popular education in urban areas were legitimated by typifications of what city living did to children. As shown in chapter 2 the 'teachers of the people' frequently characterized working-class pupils, parents and localities in a vocabulary of social pathology.[1] The pupils were 'without one exception precocious'; the product of 'generations of moral and intellectual indiscipline'; 'coarse in speech and manners'; and having 'the fluid mind of the true barbarian'. At the same time, there was a recognition that many of the children were 'sharp' and 'acute' and possessed an unsocialized intelligence which resisted in various ways the categories and processes of formal schooling. Themes of the volatility, restlnessness and sharpness of inner-city working-class children can be traced in later 'sociological' accounts concerned with education. R. A. Bray in the *Town Child* (1907, p. 47) observed the deleterious effects of urban living:

> children who have acquired the habit of sharing the life of a crowd, find the routine existence of the individual insipid and distasteful; they become more noisy and uncontrolled in their ways, less tolerant of any restraint, less capable of finding any zest in pleasures of tranquil enjoyment. The crowd-influence is one of the most potent factors in the environment of a town.

The town child might possess 'a phenomenal sharpness and readi-

170

ness of resource' but he lacked the crucial qualities of self-control, concentration and application.[2]

Comparatively little is known about how contemporary teachers in inner-city areas characterize their pupils and to what extent these early typifications have been displaced by other constructs and yet, it is clear that such typifications will have important consequences for the social relations of schooling and for the outcomes of the educational process. Becker's (1952) well-known study has shown within the context of Chicago that teachers' 'moral sensibilities' were often violated by inner-city children and that these children were seen to diverge significantly from teacher images of the ideal pupil. Discussions with the teachers in the ten inner-city schools in the inquiry sought to make explicit the extent to which these reactions to and constructs of the pupils were repeated and, in general, sought to examine the ways in which the teachers characterized the immediate localities of the schools and the experience of teaching within an inner-city school.

Typifying pupils and their backgrounds

Both the ideology and the structural arrangements of Victorian popular education in urban areas predisposed teachers to characterize their pupils as social *types* rather than as individualistic *persons*.[3] The constitution of such social types occurred within a schooling enterprise which utilized a pedagogy based upon large instructional units. Contemporary urban teachers, on the other hand, have been exposed to forms of socialization and professional preparation which emphasize other objects and outcomes for the educational process and which celebrate pedagogies based upon the crucial importance of recognizing 'individual differences' among the pupils. Such as *individualistic* emphasis was apparent in the discourse of the majority of the teachers when making reference to their pupils and they insisted upon the need both to understand and to relate to pupils as *individual* personalities rather than seeing them as members of any particular social category, whether that category was based upon social class, race or locality. They, therefore, generally rejected the validity of discussions which attempted to utilize such categories as 'working-class children' or 'inner-city pupils' and such terms did not constitute a natural part of the vocabulary of their work situation. Indeed, many of the teachers showed a noticeable distaste when descriptions involving some form

171

of social-class location of their pupils were introduced in the discussions.[4] This hostility to and rejection of social-class locations for their pupils, as militating against the consideration of the individual, resulted frequently in the teachers giving only relatively brief and tentative characterizations of their pupils as 'children like other children'. A further reason for this tentativeness (as suggested by the teachers themselves), was the fact that a considerable number of them had teaching experience only in 'urban working-class schools' (utilizing the researcher's terms) and, therefore, they felt *unable* to make any valid comparative judgments as to how their pupils might be differentiated from pupils in other contexts.[5] This general unwillingness to socially typify their pupils raises many questions. Was this a real celebration of the importance of the individual pupil in the practice of these teachers and a rejection of any notion of class identity or was it, on the other hand, a rhetoric of individualism absorbed as part of a modern socialization for teaching? Was it an indication of a genuine disregard for social class, racial and locational factors (indeed, an assertion in a sense that they 'did not exist') in order to establish the basis for a morally higher order of human relations in the educational process, or was it an unwillingness to come to terms with these as facts of the social world implying domination, exploitation and conflict and raising questions about why inner-city areas and their schools were constituted in the way they were?[6]

Despite this inhibition on the part of many of the teachers to characterize their pupils in any general terms, a minority, for one reason or another, did so. In these typifications, three categories could be discerned: those which, in locating the pupils, utilized an 'attribution of blame' in relation to low educational achievements in the school (*judgmental*); those which, in locating the pupils, sought to show them as 'victims of circumstances' in all sorts of ways and wished to insist that in no way were the pupils innately ineducable (*explanatory/understanding*); and those which involved very positive evaluations of the pupils and which generally included explicit socio-political commentary upon their position (*fraternal*). It is not suggested, of course, that all the typifications given can be constituted within one or other of these three categories; in practice, many of the teachers' characterizations were eclectic, but some provided a clear epitome of these positions.

The language of judgment

One of the greatest changes that can be observed in what might be called the discourse of urban education, seen historically, is a move *away* from the use of moral absolutes, the language of moral judgment to the use of a situational morality and the language of 'accounting for', explaining and understanding. Very few of the teachers in this inquiry used forms of judgmental typification about their pupils, the parents or the locality. Among the few who did there was a distinct sense of social pessimism and a consciousness that standards both in society and in the school were in decline:

> There's pretty widespread educational apathy in the
> community here and this is reflected in the classroom. Many
> of the kids here are blasé, precocious and bored. They give
> the impression of having done everything by fourteen: being
> drunk, had intercourse and so on. . . . Too many parents
> expect the schools to do everything and are not prepared to
> take responsibility for ensuring that homework is done. Many
> seem unwilling to insist on regular hours, too many pupils are
> permitted to watch TV until it shuts down for the night. . . .
> Too many parents whose children are on free dinners and
> uniform grants have expensive material possessions (cars,
> colour TV). In short, the whole show is taken for granted.
> Finally, I believe there exists in the Cockney mentality the
> idea that school is not really beneficial, it is not seen as a
> means towards self-improvement. Truancy is condoned and
> there are always plenty of jobs in London when you leave
> school (head of lower school, School E).

The teacher whose views are quoted above was shortly afterwards appointed as the deputy headteacher of another inner-city school. His own biography embodied in many ways the values and the practices of the 'Protestant ethic' and he saw with alarm these values and practices as being increasingly and decisively rejected by both the pupils and the parents of this particular part of London.

A head of year with twenty years' experience within School A observed a 'brutalizing' and 'coarsening' of the pupils manifested in increased materialism and increased violence:[7] 'look at the soccer hooliganism and the violence to one another'. The 'coarsening' of the pupils he attributed to a loss of moral values and to the politicizing activities of some teachers:

173

We have thrown over a lot of the things that gave people moral values and found nothing to put in its place. The very fact that nowadays, to have a sense of duty towards society is terribly lacking in the kids. The only sense in which they seem to get anything like that is usually a certain amount of political theory put over to them in so-called social studies lessons. But the idea of their duty towards their fellow man seems to be going by the board. . . . We are breeding a political-materialistic animal (in the adult and the child) and so long as we've got materialistic and politically minded people we're going to get the kind of sour society which we are building up around us. . . .

In the discourse of teachers such as these, there were constructs of a *moral and spiritual crisis* (seen to be most clearly manifested in inner-city areas), which repeated in various ways the preoccupations of an earlier generation of urban school teachers. Against such constructs of moral and spiritual crisis was counterposed a view of inner-city teaching which involved a notion of 'holding the line' for established values and culture against what was seen to be the increasing resistance of pupils (and some teachers) and the general apathy and permissiveness of parents. Such an analysis caused the head of the English department at School A to see his role in very Arnoldian terms: *'I feel there's a certain sense of moral fulfilment, in that one is standing as a buffer against what often seems like a tide of barbarism.'* It is not possible to say how widespread such typifications may be among inner-city teachers in general. In a social climate in which moralistic judgments are eschewed for neutral or explanatory diagnosis and in school contexts in which a sense of social and pedagogical *optimism* was often formally defined as a necessity of the situation, the designations of good teachers were unlikely to include many who took up the Arnoldian stance. Most of the good teachers either refrained from all generalizations or social typifications by insisting upon the crucial nature of individualism in relation to their pupils, or where they did engage in any form of social accounting, they utilized models of inner-city children which emphasized their adverse circumstances in an understanding rather than a judgmental way.

Victims of circumstance

The adverse circumstances of inner-city children were constituted by the teachers in a variety of ways. The aggression of the pupils, their volatility and sharp irreverent style were seen to be the products of an inner-city environment:

> Among our pupils there is probably a higher proportion of emotionally disturbed children, children from one-parent families, and all kinds of problems like housing. Problems caused simply by the density of population and the pressure of people too tightly packed together. These kids tend to make a lot of noise. They tend to react to any sort of reprimand in an aggressive way, it's a sort of defence mechanism (head of geography, School E).

Vandalism was 'explained' in terms of the impermanence of their own environment:

> They live in a concrete world, as you can see from this window. They live in a world which is exploiting them far more than in rural areas. They live in a world where they see dirt and broken-down buildings, especially the demolition in the city centre. Much of the vandalism can be attributed to this . . . they see it everywhere in operation (head of science, School F).

In these sorts of ways teachers who characterized inner-city children as different in their relatively low achievements, their loudness and aggression and their volatility found explanations for these attributes in a host of social, economic, institutional and environmental handicaps to which the pupils were seen to be exposed. These included 'poverty', 'overcrowding', 'living in tower blocks', 'uncertain employment prospects', 'limited social-cultural horizons', 'culturally deprived homes', 'restricted language', 'disturbed family backgrounds', 'high teacher turnover in schools', 'poor primary education'. It is a truism of sociology of education to say that teachers in such areas as these characteristically find explanations for school failure in a 'social pathology' view of working-class homes. Such a view would be an *over-simplification* of the teachers' accounts in this case. While some undoubtedly utilized deficit socio-cultural models of working-class homes, involving notions of deprivation, restriction and disturbance, others pointed to deficiencies in the wider socio-economic framework and in the organization of schooling as crucial to the appreciation of the style and educational performance of inner-city children. However, while there was

175

no simple location of the problem of inner-city pupils in relation to imputed shortcomings of their home backgrounds and while institutional and social structural shortcomings were recognized by these teachers, the 'colour' of their discourse was essentially neutral. *The teachers largely eschewed 'blaming' working-class homes, but they also abstained from 'blaming' the wider constraints of the socioeconomic system within which they and their pupils were located.* Their stance was essentially one of *explaining* the contexts within which their pupils were formed, in order to arrive at a better *understanding* of the pupils.

This *neutral-explanatory* stance of many of the teachers stands in sharp contrast to the robust, judgmental categories utilized by an earlier generation of urban school teachers. Unlike their predecessors, this particular group of contemporary urban teachers showed little desire to blame the pupil and his upbringing for problems of behaviour and achievement in schools. On the other hand, while they observed problems of poverty, overcrowding and unemployment, they largely abstained from wider socio-political criticism. It can be argued, of course, that both of these areas are very problematic for overt criticism from contemporary urban teachers. The former can be attacked for its associations with 'social Darwinism' and 'deficit views of the working class' and the latter for 'being political'. Perhaps, therefore, it was *as a resolution to this dilemma* that such explicit criticism as there was, focused upon school deficiencies, particularly the detrimental effects of teacher mobility in inner-city secondary schools and of teaching conditions in inner-city junior schools.[8] Thus, in seeing many of their pupils as 'victims of circumstances' the teachers effectively countered geneticist theories of deficit, utilized to some extent socio-cultural models of deficit, but also pointed to institutional and socio-economic locations of their pupils' problems. In doing so, however, they were disinclined to make overt criticism of these factors (other than school focused) either, it would seem, because they had come to take for granted the constitution of that world as in some sense 'normal' or because they regarded such wider criticism and observations as infringing against a teacher imperative of not 'being political'. Within such a neutral explanatory framework *the teacher's role in an inner-city school became primarily concerned not with moral judgment or moral stances; not with social and political criticism or political stances, but with the attainment of a state of empathetic understanding which would enable the teacher to act within the school as some sort of counter-*

vailing influence against the complex of adverse circumstances in the lives of the pupils. These attitudes and orientations constituted a pragmatic liberalism which had as its object the amelioration of the visible symptoms of disadvantage as they were daily realized in school situations. It was a liberalism preoccupied with the 'vivid present' of adversity and with the school-based action which this seemed to require. A liberalism which celebrated the teacherly virtue of 'getting on with the job' and which thereby avoided (or had no time to consider) why the job involved amelioration.

Fraternal images

A small group of generally younger teachers involved in this inquiry, employed a vocabulary when typifying their pupils, which was significantly different from the neutral-explanatory categories of a pragmatic liberalism. Characteristically, their typifications involved either a strong assertion of the capabilities and abilities of their pupils (and a location of their problems in *radical*, as opposed to surface deficiencies of the school system) or an explicit assertion that the problem of the inner-city pupil was, in actuality, the problem of a rotten society. These teachers, working in the curriculum areas of English, history, sociology, art and science broke through in various ways the conventional explanations used in accounting for inner-city schools and their pupils and they espoused other sorts of actions to those conventionally adopted. There was an emphasis upon the acuity, resilience and vitality of inner-city children: qualities seen to be partly generated by their environment; seen to have considerable potential for educational progress and yet, at the same time, to be potentially threatening to many teachers. One young teacher in noting that her pupils had 'the intelligence of defence' and were 'very quick at sussing people out – very quick to find arguments to say why they shouldn't do something', typified the lower stream pupils for whom she had responsibility, in these terms:

> They can be incredibly bright, very witty and very observant,
> but they are so used to being attacked, picked up by the fuzz
> (mostly rightly), that their first discussion with you is
> aggressive. They will pick holes in any argument you come up
> with. If you aren't entirely convincing or convinced yourself in
> an argument, they will find a hole in it. If you're being

177

slightly pretentious (as we all are) they'll find out where and why (teacher of English, School A).

A lack of inhibition and a lack of deference in inner-city children were seen to be positive virtues by some of these teachers. An art teacher at School C observed, 'in my own subject these children have a lot to say. Pretty exciting, rough and tough, but their work shows a lot of punch . . . they are courageous to try things out, prepared to have a go'. A young teacher of history at School B noted among her pupils,

> far less willingness just to bow to the authority of the teacher and to accept and do what the teacher says. . . . They will rebel against that. They question the relevance of something as well, . . . but it is very encouraging that they do question what we say because very often I say things without thinking, just because that is what a teacher says.

The failure of urban schools

That the problem of the inner-city pupil was really a conventional gloss upon the real problem of the inner-city school, i.e. *the failure of the schools as constituted to utilize and take seriously the abilities of the pupils*, was strongly argued by a number of the teachers:

> I think for many teachers, the inner-city school is very different from situations they have encountered before; therefore, it has a quality of strangeness. There's a kind of energy there, physical, linguistic, manifested in all sorts of ways. An energy which has to be used in some sort of way. There's no consensus among the kids as to why they're in school. A lot of the kids' philosophy is 'having a laugh': they're going to be a scaffolder or a barrow boy and they know that. This provides a threat to all teachers. But, on the other hand, they do have a sense of what the teacher should be doing for them. Many have played truant because the school is doing nothing for them. They talk very lucidly about the faults of the system, they are aware of the dishonesty (head of history/humanities, School A).

This account from a teacher with seven years' experience in a tough school, stressed that inner-city schools were failing their pupils because of undue preoccupation with administration, irrelevant curriculum content and a generally dull and boring pedagogy. Thus he interpreted the resistance of the pupils as entirely natural and 'to be expected': 'the one thing that used to impress me with a lot of kids at [School A] is the entirely rational reasons as to why they opted out of the system.'

The head of science at School A whose work was widely esteemed,[9] saw failure to take seriously the abilities of inner-city pupils as virtually institutionalized within the local authority:

> In explaining problems, the major analysis of the
> establishment is the difficulty of the pupils. The minute you
> look upon your pupils as difficult you start thinking of them
> as unteachable. If administrators were forced into the
> classroom this would change. To be involved in the classroom
> is to understand that our pupils are teachable and highly
> intelligent. At the moment, however, there is *no* belief in the
> ability of our pupils at all. I have put in forty-five pupils for
> 'O' level Physics and the deputy head said 'It was a bit of a
> shock, it's going to cost the Authority quite a lot of money'.
> This is a sign of the malaise, an attitude to the pupils. There
> is a lack of confidence in the pupils. I'm sure it's general in
> London.

The discourse of these teachers both in its content and in its colour, involved a fraternal identification with inner-city pupils which was different in kind from the sympathetic understandings of liberalism. Images of the pupil as 'victim' were not utilized: on the contrary, the many positive attributes of inner-city pupils were stressed and problems were located not at the level of the pupil but in radical deficiencies of the school system. *Classrooms, teacher roles, pedagogy, authority relations, curriculum and schools as constituted, provided for this group of teachers the true source of an urban education problem.* There was a sense, realized in various degrees of explicitness, that what urban schools were there to do, or what they were, in fact, doing, had little articulation with any serious notion of the process of education as a critical and possibly stimulating experience. These 'radical' accounts, however, did not draw upon a specifically political vocabulary or a specific theoretical framework in typifying pupils and school situations.

179

The failure of the capitalist system

A different analysis and a different kind of fraternity was signalled by those few teachers who did adopt a specifically Marxist stance. Their accounts, while stressing that deficit images of inner-city children were 'part of capitalist mythology' and while asserting that inner-city children should be provided with an education capable of generating a critical literacy and a critical consciousness, also involved the view that the real issues of crisis were located elsewhere and that real action would have to be taken in arenas other than the school. Such a recognition – 'that schools of this kind cannot be instrumental in radicalizing society' (teacher of sociology, School E), or that 'if kids come from backgrounds of poverty, under-nourishment, badly housed, badly clothed, there is nothing schools can do about it. You've got to change the social and economic basis of society to put that right' (teacher of English, School E) – produced for some teachers an *ambivalent attitude to the activity of teaching* and resulted, also, in the experience of contradiction and dilemma over questions of what would be the most valid form of commitment to the interests of the pupils.[10]

The experience of teaching

Any understanding of teachers' typifications of their pupils, of their constructs of what 'teaching' and 'education' implies, or of their pedagogic and other actions, must be situated *within some view of their work situations*. It is possible for an observer to note some of the crucial features of those situations: the constraints of time, space, numbers, and resources; the organizational arrangements and the division of labour; the distribution of power; the constant interactive demand of inner-city classrooms and of school 'busyness'. In this way, some notion of the school and the classroom as an objective social reality can be created and located within a wider socio-historical frame of reference. On the other hand, the school and the classroom also have a subjective social reality within which the teachers and the pupils live and which constitutes for them the experienced and 'real' world of their day-to-day existence. How is the 'real' world experienced and how does this experience affect the constitution of contemporary teacher perspectives and consciousness?

'Initiation by ordeal': 'challenge' and 'being tired'

Most of the accounts given by the teachers of their experience of teaching in an inner-city school repeated themes which were apparent in the accounts of some of their nineteenth-century predecessors. Despite the apparently changed physical, social and pedagogic contexts of modern classrooms and schools, the experience of teaching still had its apparently timeless associations with notions of initiatory ordeal, challenge and of high interactive demand. This account by the young and outstanding head of English in School I is typical of many:

> Yes, I had a shock – I was physically frightened. Maybe a
> large man might not be, though I saw pretty large men
> getting pretty damn scared at the school. It's a combination
> of coping with one's own dignity and self-respect in a
> situation where one is apparently rejected. Of course, in a
> sense one never is as a private individual – it's what you
> represent that is rejected. That is the first thing most teachers
> have to come to terms with. Also, the shock of what is
> demanded from you on a physical level. Good teaching is
> extremely hard work physically, quite apart from mentally.
> Where you've got kids who, because they don't actually see a
> great deal of value in the education you are trying to give
> them, resist it – then you take on a tremendous amount of
> responsibility to stimulate, to get things going. It's exhausting
> both physically and mentally. Then, of course, there are the
> sorts of personal crises which crop up because, if you're a
> teacher, you've gone through some sort of received standard
> of education, you have certain notions of what it is to be a
> man or a woman – a good man or a good woman   you have
> certain notions of what's right or wrong and how you should
> treat people – and this isn't necessarily the criteria which the
> kids adopt at all. Crazy things (like a teacher who refuses to
> chastise a child) will very often lose the respect of the class
> because, for them, physical chastisement is what they're used
> to.

The reactions of the teachers to what was frequently experienced as the 'shock', 'challenge' and 'demand' of inner-city teaching were constituted in different forms and at different levels. Some young men teachers claimed that they had been forced to use direct

181

physical means to maintain some notion of order or some notion of teacher authority (or even personal self-respect).[11] Some of the more charismatic teachers found such situations exciting and stimulating and at a personal and, in a sense *artistic level*, seemed to enjoy the tempo and style which they associated with inner-city schools and with the experience of teaching within them. Some, less charismatic and more pessimistic, felt that they were holding the line against 'a tide of barbarism'. Most, however, responded by looking for ways in which they could develop relationships with the pupils: relationships which would help to generate greater inter-personal understanding and which would help to facilitate the work in hand. This search for some 'basis for understanding' and for a working relationship with their pupils became a central and time-consuming preoccupation for many teachers and was constituted by them as a central challenge of teaching in an inner-city school. It was widely believed that 'being accepted' by the pupils was a crucial state for the teacher to attain and that the state of 'being accepted' required, in an inner-city school more than any other, a consider-able amount of self-investment from the teacher. This self-invest-ment might involve a variety of actions designed to help the teacher 'to get to know' the pupils, their culture and home backgrounds and the general socio-economic features of the locality. It might involve participation in sport, youth centres and youth activities, community festivals, and educational visits both at home and abroad. In short, the ideal of teacher involvement implied a visible demonstration of liking to be with the pupils and caring about them, in addition to taking the formal aspects of their education seriously (e.g. detailed lesson preparation; regular marking, etc.).

Attempting to meet all these expectations for the good teacher resulted in the process of *'immersion'* in school and school-related life and in the frequent experience of exhaustion.[12] It is clear that 'immersion' and 'being tired' have important implications for the teachers' activity in other contexts, whether this concerns taking a critical and reflexive stance to curriculum and pedagogy; taking an active part in shared decision-making in schools or in union activi-ties, or in locating school activities within a wider socio-political framework. Some teachers were explicitly conscious of this as an occupational hazard:[13]

> The worst thing about teaching, in a way, is that it stops you thinking and reading. We're caught up in the here and now

activity. What I resent the most is the fact that I am not
thinking deeply. I know I'm intelligent, but I don't act in an
intelligent way anymore – as a teacher. . . . The school
demands so much of me . . . (teacher of history School B).

In addition to the experience of 'immersion', the accounts
revealed that constructs of the challenge of inner-city teaching were
very much bound up with notions of a Protestant-ethic, i.e. with
notions that teachers had to find their *individual salvations*.
Teachers had been left to find their own salvation with difficult
classes and some took the view that this was an intrinsic and necessary feature (ordeal) of the teaching situation. There was little consciousness in most of the schools of any reality of team or collective
action and support in relation to difficulties and there was a sense
in which the *individual teacher-survivor* still provided the norm of
the work situation.[14] The crucial characteristics of inner-city
teaching were, therefore, constituted in these ways by many of the
teachers. For them the 'paramount reality' of the work situation was
a search for, and understanding of, a relationship with their pupils
and as a consequence of this, the making of a considerable investment of self in the busyness of school life. This reality was contexted
within an essentially individualistic and Protestant-ethic stance to
questions of success and failure in teaching. Such a reality can in
itself be seen to be the product of the particular socio-historical and
cultural locations of the schools in question; of the physical, pedagogic and curricula arrangements within them and of the dominant
mode of socialization of the teachers.

The school and the activity of teaching experienced in these ways
seems to be crucially related to a teacher consciousness which
emphasized the pupil as disadvantaged, but de-emphasized social
and political criticism; which emphasized activism or 'getting on
with the job' but de-emphasized critical reflection and which
emphasized individualistic perspectives rather than social structural
perspectives of both pupils and of the activity of teaching. If the
experience of inner-city teaching is associated with initiation by
ordeal, 'challenge' and 'being tired' then it is clear that any calls for
teachers to consider the wider socio-political implications of schools;
to engage in acts of critical reflection of their practice or to take
seriously notions of group solidarity and group decision-making are
working *against the occupational grain*. The mode of socialization for teaching; the constructs of the good teacher and the

organization and experience of the work situation all militate against such activity. If these are regarded as valuable and important activities in which teachers should engage, then there is a very real sense in which not only inner-city pupils, but also their teachers may be viewed as 'victims of circumstances'. In this case, questions are raised concerning how such circumstances arose in the first place and whether they should not be changed?

The school as obstruction

While for many of the teachers the salient experiences of their work situation were associated with those of challenge from the pupils and from the demands of school busyness, for others the salient experiences were associated with the challenge of institutional rather than pupil obstructions, i.e. *that they had a real sense of having to fight against 'the school' as constituted*, in order to achieve their pedagogic ends.[15] It would be misleading to suggest that this sense of institutional obstruction was very general among the teachers, it was, in fact, a minority phenomenon and was made explicit in only three of the ten schools involved. On the other hand, it can be argued that a sense of institutional obstruction is most likely to be realized where *radical innovations* in curriculum, pedagogy or evaluation are attempted and that, in general, there were few instances of this throughout the research.

For the head of humanities department in School A, the experience of teaching was one of 'struggle' against administration 'as an objectified task'; against a failure within the school to utilize the full abilities and interests of teachers and against the tyranny of the time-table:

> All the time various impediments were put in the way of
> people's energies. . . . It seemed to be this business of not
> looking for the positive advantages of certain things that were
> going on in the school, not drawing upon people's talents, not
> even encouraging people (I don't mean that horrible
> avuncular patronage of senior hierarchs), but a genuine
> interest which means that you actually make things available:
> time, space or money.

This particular teacher had, in fact, been able to 'carve out great blocks of time because I had the political weight to do that in the school' and he saw this as having had advantageous educational outcomes:

> Within that time I had a much more enjoyable experience with kids, much more potent learning experience with them than would ever have been possible in the little hour of demarcation. . . . What it did do, quite definitely, was break down all the very instant pressures of classroom teaching in which you are really restrained and constrained by the time allocated in as much as you've never really got time to work through situations with kids, which is quite a valuable thing to be able to do. Not time even to enjoy it, because of the 'must-get-on-with-it' syndrome.

Although this had been achieved, the achievement in itself had about it a 'special arrangement' association, *yielded* to a powerful individual teacher, rather than endorsed as the natural and desirable way of organizing time generally within the school. Thus it was seen to be a precarious achievement against the norm of school arrangements and as such dangerously dependent upon the charisma of a single innovator. The teacher involved retained the conviction that the experience of teaching and learning in urban schools could not be radically transformed until such structural changes had become the norm rather than the exception.

It may be the case that the majority of inner-city teachers have become so immersed in questions of system maintenance through a crisis period that questions of radical innovation in school procedures have been marginal to their concerns. It may be the case, that institutional obstruction (defined in these senses) is particular to a few inner-city schools where the hierarchy 'lacks imagination'. The possibility has to be faced, however, that a sense of institutional obstruction may be more widespread among inner-city teachers than this study has indicated and that it may be a common occupational experience among those teachers who attempt radical transformations of practice. [16]

Resisting immersion

The tendency for inner-city teachers to become immersed in school busyness (accentuated by the particular problems faced by their schools) and the constitution of immersion as a central characteristic of the good teacher, has already been made clear in this analysis. Some of the teachers, as already indicated, were conscious of the dangers of such immersion and of the need to resist it. For some this resistance was essentially for individualistic and personal reasons: 'to keep alive intellectually'; 'to have a wide range of interests'; 'to remain sane'. For those teachers who were Marxists it was necessary to resist the immersion and incorporation that was latent in the experience of teaching in order to be free to take action in other areas. This was experienced as an acute dilemma by a young teacher of sociology at School H, caught between a recognition of what 'being a good teacher' involved and a recognition that action within the school could not produce significant social change:

> A good teacher in this school expects very high standards of the kids because in general you tend to get what you expect from kids. He/she attempts to be as efficient as possible, not to let the kids down. Kids are very canny – they know the teachers who really have their best interests at heart and really want them to do well. . . . This is the great problem for me, because if I was going to teach well, in the way that I've sorted out that I should teach, with *very* good preparation, good relevant materials, good back-up with visits and films, etc., then that would take twenty-four hours of seven days a week and I haven't got that time. Neither am I prepared to devote that time to it because my political activities are very important. Therefore, there is a conflict for me.

Although this teacher was regarded as a 'good' teacher by her immediate head of department, the headteacher, while esteeming her work, did not designate her as one of the outstandingly good teachers in the school because commitment to school work was seen to be delimited by her other commitments.[17] Thus, in resisting immersion in these terms, she had failed to measure up to the specifications for the ideal teacher in School H.

A young English teacher in School E argued that resisting immersion was necessary for real commitment to the best interests of the pupils·

> I've always been mainly involved in teacher politics but largely outside school, so my attention to curriculum and lesson preparation has always been very minimal. I don't prepare

any lessons (I'm not proud of that, I just don't have time). I'm not using that as an excuse, but it's a very accurate description of the way I lead my life. I recognize that it's far more important (if you're interested in defending education from massive cutbacks in expenditure) to do it through trade union action, school-based union action in which union members get together and say they're not prepared to accept this or that, or that they want these conditions. You're not going to do it by spending hours preparing lessons and making life more interesting for the kids because all the time you're turning in on yourself in the classroom/school, the whole ground is being cut from underneath you by wider political activities. Basically what decides what goes on in schools is not from inside the school, but outside political considerations.

Thus, for some teachers a central experience of teaching within an inner-city school was that of resisting immersion. Total immersion in the life of the school (and the many problems associated with inner-city schools seemed to demand this of concerned teachers) involved for some a threat to their intellectual and social vitality and wholeness and for others, a threat of incorporation into welfare liberalism. *For the former, to become the ideal teacher was to place at risk 'being a person' and for the latter, it was to place at risk 'changing the world'.*

On being a 'good' teacher

Many of the teachers in making explicit their experience of inner-city teaching, stressed that after an initiation by ordeal and after negotiating successfully the process of 'being accepted', they received considerable satisfactions from their relationships with pupils. This high interpersonal satisfaction arose because inner-city pupils were seen to be generally friendly, forthright, honest,[18] uninhibited, lively and witty and, given that their powers of 'sussing out' people were widely esteemed, to be accepted was a personal and professional accolade. At the same time, a sense of satisfaction at the level of interpersonal relationships was not widely paralleled in academic or pedagogic satisfactions. Most of the teachers found explanations for their pupils' academic under-achievements in a 'victim of circumstances' theory. Avoiding attribution of blame in either cultural or social structural terms, they effectively constituted their role as countervailing influence to the adverse circumstances in the lives of their pupils and accepted immersion in school and school-related activities as *a necessary and moral consequence*. Nevertheless, the pupils continued to be, for many, a constant source of challenge and demand, particularly in relation to formal curriculum work. A minority of radical teachers attempting innovation in curriculum or pedagogy experienced, not the pupils, but their schools as constituted, as the essential challenge and saw massive under-utilization of both teachers' and pupils' abilities. From this viewpoint, *the good teacher had to find ways of resisting the established order of the school in order to facilitate real educational experiences.*

Those teachers who had explicit Marxist commitments insisted that the good teacher, who had the interests of urban working-class pupils at heart, must resist school immersion in order to fight in the wider union and political arenas.

Pupils, teaching and the work situation

An attempt has been made in this chapter to show how some inner-city teachers in London comprehensive schools characterized their pupils and the experience of teaching. The crucial features of this analysis, it is suggested, are the *socio-historical continuities which it demonstrates*, particularly typifications of the inner-city pupil as victim; constructs of the teacher as ameliorator and the experienced busyness of the school as immersing, exhausting and, in some senses, neutralizing. The social and ideological contexts which 'produce' such features have been indicated.

While these features remain dominant, it seems unlikely that contemporary urban teachers, any more than their nineteenth-century predecessors, will become 'active emissaries of misrule' or even that they can easily bring about radical transformations of educational experience for their pupils.

Nevertheless, it has been shown also that some teachers are working to establish what they regard as *radical alternatives to the given order of school curriculum and pedagogy*. However, even when such alternatives have been formally achieved, they seem to occur as isolated and precarious enclaves within the 'normal' structure of the school. In schools where administration may have become historically preoccupied with system order, and the

188

minimizing of change, and in schools where notions of individualism and a Protestant-ethic stance towards teaching are strong, it seems unlikely that wider transformation can occur. Some would clearly regard this as being in the best interests of the pupils.[19] Others would see in this the continuing and unacceptable face of social control in urban education.

Chapter 10

Curriculum and Pedagogy

The dominant principles upon which the curriculum and pedagogy of working-class schooling in the nineteenth century was based were those of 'civilizing', 'gentling' and 'making competent' an increasingly urban population. Civilizing involved the transmission of appropriate selections of secular and religious culture from those *with* civilization to those without it; gentling involved socialization in acceptance of the given social order and of the forms of its relationships; and making competent involved the production of a range of skills required by an expanding industrial economy. As indicated in earlier chapters, these principles were in some tension in so far as different fractions of the Victorian middle class gave different emphases to them. However, despite such intra-class struggle as to which principle should be accorded priority and, while the contents of the curriculum might vary, its *structure* and the *mode* and *social relations* of pedagogy remained constant for long periods. A sense of order derived from the apparent certainties of the time. The superiority of the forms of knowledge to be transmitted; the logical necessity of the structure of the curriculum; the self-evident requirement for a strongly teacher-directed pedagogy and the clear need for 'discipline of mind and body' gave to this schooling enterprise a self-confidence which is physically manifest in the assertive architecture of the London Board schools.

Such certainty and such self-confidence at both societal and at school level is hardly a feature of the contemporary situation. A pervasive sense of order at both levels has been replaced by a pervasive sense of crisis, particularly tangible in the centres of metropolitan cities.

At school level, the superiority of the forms of knowledge to be transmitted no longer goes unchallenged. Yesterday's work of civilization has become today's work of cultural domination. The socio-historical relativity of knowledge is asserted and claims are made for the inclusion of other cultural traditions, other languages, logics and understandings, including those of an indigenous working class. The conventional structure of the curriculum, far from being regarded as a logical necessity derived from the given boundaries of knowledge, is frequently seen to be an alienating and meaningless collection of arbitrarily defined contents. A pedagogy based essentially upon teacher transmission within ordered hierarchies of subject groupings and pupil groupings is criticized for generating intellectual and social *passivity* for the majority.

If, following Bernstein (1977, p. 85), we say that 'curriculum defines what counts as valid knowledge, pedagogy defines what counts as a valid transmission of knowledge and evaluation defines what counts as a valid realization of this knowledge on the part of the taught' then it is apparent that *in contemporary urban working-class schools in particular, there exists a crisis of validity in all of these areas.* Uncertainty and disagreement exist over what is to be considered an appropriate curriculum, pedagogy and mode of evaluation. In the face of existing low levels of educational achievement by inner-city children, of rising truancy and of a general sense of crisis and malaise in the schools, the structure and content of the curriculum, the forms of pedagogy, of pupil grouping and of evaluation. In the face of existing low levels of educational achieveof certainty and purpose in urban education is but one manifestation of a wider loss of certainty within society. Bernstein (1977, p. 111) reminds us that Durkheim saw changes in pedagogy as indicators of a moral crisis and has himself suggested that a move away from traditional 'collection' curriculum towards integrated forms 'symbolizes that there is a crisis in society's basic classifications and frames and therefore a crisis in its structures of power and principles of control'.

While these issues are clearly constituted at the level of theory and also at the level of conflicting educational ideologies, their constitution *at the level of the cultural transmitters in the situation of crisis* (i.e. inner-city teachers) has been relatively unexamined. What constructs of crisis exist at this level? What curricula and

191

Curriculum and Pedagogy

pedagogic forms are advocated as solutions to crises? What are the underlying principles and intentionalities of such solutions? What is the reality of autonomy and constraint within present curricula and evaluation procedures?

Contemporary teachers in urban working-class schools, unlike their nineteenth-century predecessors are at least active (or potentially active) partners in processes of curriculum formation and change and they have a wider area of pedagogic discretion than was previously the case. It becomes crucial, therefore, to know what kinds of epistemological and pedagogical models are salient for such teachers and what principles guide their day-to-day activities. Discussion with the teachers sought to make explicit some of these questions.

Defending traditional disciplines

While the majority of teachers designated by their headteachers as outstanding were committed in theory (or in the educationist context) to various measures of curricula and pedagogic change, a minority of generally senior teachers saw their role as that of defenders of traditional disciplines and excellencies against the attacks of an educational progressivism which utilized relevance as a central notion for change which appeared to them to be most strongly located in departments of English in inner-city schools. The general position adopted by this group of teachers was that the traditional curriculum enshrined 'the best that has been thought and known'; that it made available to the pupils a richness and width of cultural experience which would not otherwise be available to them; that its essential disciplines were concerned with the inculcation of rationality, order and precision and that such experiences and such disciplines were as necessary for the pupils of the inner-city as for any other group of pupils. These teachers were hostile to a contemporary emphasis upon relevant curriculum or community curriculum because they read in this the provision of a special (sub-standard) curriculum for urban working-class pupils. They were hostile to discussions concerned with notions of middle-class imposition of values, meanings and knowledge, claiming that such argument was either 'merely political' or analytically unclear.[1] *For such teachers the crisis of the urban school was that these ideas had gained so much ground*, particularly among younger teachers and especially in English departments.

192

A senior teacher at School E epitomized this position:

The arguments at the moment about knowledge and the curriculum being remote from the pupils and not sufficiently relevant, I would reject. The curriculum in my view is relevant enough . . . we will soon be teaching only about the immediate environment of the child. German, for instance, is being abandoned next year as a second language, on the grounds that it is irrelevant.

I think the danger of reducing the curriculum to the immediate world about the child is that you can produce no inspiration for the child. I think English departments in comprehensive schools must bear the blame for much of the ambivalence about the curriculum at present. They are totally absorbed with the immediate environment – the idea of teaching Shakespeare, for instance, is out. This has the effect of rubbing kids' noses in their environment.

English departments are the most trendy and progressive. They seem to have, almost a policy (or, at least a unified approach) to these questions. There is more liaison between English departments and they have a very active professional group. I think it is true to say that there is *an alternative form of education* being espoused by English departments in London. They see themselves as the van of educational innovation. Invariably the largest department, they can exert a powerful influence, yet they are unwilling to accept responsibility for declining standards of competence in the basic language skills, especially reading.

It may be remembered that in an earlier period of urban working-class schooling the special mission of the teacher of English had been recognized by various writers. Teachers of English constituted as 'preachers of culture' and purveyors of sweetness and light had been seen to be the crucial agents of harmony, of social integration, of anti-urbanism and of the uplifting work of civilization. Now, by a number of teachers in this inquiry, English teachers were seen to have adopted a very different special mission: a mission which appeared to them to be generally *subversive* of standards and dangerously focused upon the grimness of the urban environment and the pervasiveness of conflict and exploitation within it.

Such views were made explicit by senior teachers at Schools A, D, E, F and J. At School D the head of history, in criticizing 'English departments which seem obsessive about curriculum being rooted in class tradition', saw the provision of literature concerned with contemporary working-class urban living as 'incestuous . . . I am sure that it perpetuates class divisiveness and imprisons the child instead of freeing it'.

The notion that the contents of the traditional curriculum could 'free' the working-class child from a world of cultural, social and economic limitations ran through the discourse of such teachers. The traditional contents of the curriculum were seen to provide 'windows to other worlds' and to provide the means whereby pupils could *escape* both imaginatively and (for a minority) actually, from the grimness of inner-city living. Constructs of the curriculum as ultimately *a path to individual freedom through escape* had their own biographical locations. Those who most strongly maintained this position and were most critical of progressive English departments had personal biographies of scholarship success from working-class origins. For them the curriculum as path to individual freedom had a real and personal validity and they saw their work in an inner-city school as essentially concerned with *reproducing* their own biographical experience in as many children as possible. Progressivism was seen to be a threat to this possibility and a betrayal of working-class children. Some suggested that this could be explained by the class location of such an ideology and by 'this peculiar tendency in our time for very middle-class teachers to react against the educational systems of the past and to attempt to change them in our time' (head of English, School A).

The 'need' for structure

Defence of the traditional curriculum and of traditional forms of pedagogy was often associated with a diagnosis of need for structure in inner-city schools. It has been observed in earlier chapters that notions of structure feature significantly in teacher discourse but carry a variety of meanings. The notion can stand for a particular framework of social relations; a sequence of prepared material for lessons; the existence of indicators demarcating 'right' and 'wrong' (morally and academically) or a particular organization of curriculum and pedagogy. The central meanings, however, appear to be those of *'boundary'* and *'certainty'*. That the educational experience of inner-city children should be such as to provide both a sense of boundary and a sense of certainty, was thought to be crucial by a number of teachers. Boundary features and features of certainty were seen to be in dissolution as a consequence of social and economic change in inner-city areas and, also, as a consequence of more frequent family 'breakdown' in those areas. Thus, some teachers argued against curriculum and pedagogic change on the grounds that change was already *a too frequent occurrence* in the lives of the pupils and that a countervailing experience of the familiar and the structural should be provided by inner-city schools. The school was thus cast as some form of *sanctuary against the world* and not to be merged with it in forms of community education or in being more relevant.

In general, this group of teachers provided realizations of the principle of 'things must be kept apart' which Bernstein (1977) has suggested as a fundamental feature of traditional curricula and pedagogic arrangements. They also provided realizations of a strongly individualistic ethic, in terms of notions of individual freedom, liberation or escape for working-class children, as made possible by existing curricula arrangements. They rejected the validity of alternative curricula models and particularly the view whereby curriculum became the means for a *social group* to become conscious of its situation of oppression and exploitation. This was 'political'.

'Being relevant' and 'being interesting'

Many teachers saw the problem of the urban school as essentially one of boredom with and alienation from the traditional contents and structure of the curriculum and traditional modes of pedagogy. Such boredom and such alienation was most visible among the less able pupils who formed the most challenging and resisting section of the school population. Concern about such pupils was a salient but not exclusive feature of liberal reformist thinking among the teachers. Notions of *relevance* and notions of *interest*[2] were utilized frequently in the teachers' discourse but were accompanied by uncertainty as to the principles being invoked or the means of their realization. In particular, many teachers appeared to be convinced that the curriculum was not sufficiently relevant, without being very explicit as to what being more relevant would involve. They appeared to register an *intuitive sense of disjuncture* between the curriculum and their pupils' present and future lives, a sense which they encapsulated as 'not relevant'. Such an intuition was registered by a young and outstanding teacher of modern languages at School H:

> I think education is the way by which the working class can one day be made more active in the democracy. That's why I teach in a school in this area and not in a middle-class area. I make active decisions about my teaching because of these ideas. But I often question the validity of teaching modern languages to those with needs in other directions. I'm sceptical about teaching languages to inner-city children, it seems somehow irrelevant to their experience when they have far more basic problems that we should be considering.

Some teachers were uncertain of the relevance of modern languages, of algebra or of Shakespeare in an inner-city school and yet, at the same time, they were reluctant to advocate what they intuited as an inferior curriculum for their pupils in which these items would be absent. There were various manifestations of curricula change in the ten schools which ranged from the addition of subjects such as sociology, economics and computer studies, through curriculum projects such as the humanities project, Nuffield science and new approaches in mathematics and modern languages, to the creation of new curriculum categories such as integrated studies, community education, social education and learning for urban living.

Community-, social- or locality-focused curricula were, for some teachers, one possible answer to the problems of relevance and interest, particularly for less able pupils. These studies characteristically involved work experience, placements in various community agencies, visiting speakers (from law centres, social services, housing departments, etc.) and small group discussion of salient local issues.[3] The intentionality of such courses varied widely, relative to their curricula origins. Where community education was an outgrowth of religious education or of home economics (as was the case in two schools), it tended towards objectives of responsible citizenship: 'an interest in the community where they live so they can see, maybe, how they could change things a little. I'm not a great believer in social change' (School B). Where its origins were in sociology, the emphasis was more upon community rights and development of a critical consciousness. While some teachers spoke enthusiastically of the levels of interest generated by community education, there was strong criticism of it from both conservative and radical teachers. Conservatives were sceptical of the relevance/interest arguments: 'community education is difficult to teach. The kids are often *not* interested in these subjects. There is a need for a good hard look at innovation which is often grounded in ideological reasons rather than in good practice,' (head of year, School H). Some radicals were suspicious of its 'soup-kitchen mentality', especially where notions of community service were involved and tended to regard it as a 'liberal trip'. In one school a group of teachers who thought in this way had successfully broken away from an existing community education department in order to establish a separate sociology department with other sorts of objectives.

In examining the ways in which the schools and the teachers had responded to ideas of 'being more relevant' and 'being more interesting' it is apparent that various and sometimes contradictory principles were implicated. These included the use of principles of relevance to the conditions of contemporary society and economy (which legitimized the inclusion of sociology, economics, computer studies, technology, etc.); relevance to a particular ability category of pupils, especially less able (which legitimated social education); relevance to being responsible and competent citizens (which legitimated forms of community service); relevance to a particular community or locality (which legitimated community education) and relevance to a particular social category of pupils: in this case inner-city working-class pupils (which legitimated for some teachers inclusion of 'working-class history' and 'working-class literature' as well as an emphasis upon community rights). For some teachers being relevant implied essentially curricula and pedagogic change designed to modernize and make more efficient the educational experience of the pupils. For others being relevant was a necessary response to a growing resistance from among the tougher elements of the school's population to the contents and mode of the traditional curriculum. For a minority of young radical teachers being relevant was finding connections with urban working-class life experience, both historically and contemporaneously, in order to facilitate the development of a group consciousness and sense of identity.[4]

If a central principle of the curriculum of urban working-class elementary schools in the nineteenth century was that of 'civilization', it can be argued that a central principle of their contemporary successors is that of 'relevance'. In the same way that

197

principles of civilization for an urban working-class population implied various selections of curriculum contents and various emphases in pedagogy, so, too, do contemporary principles of relevance. Their current realizations in urban schools provide an important area of inquiry for urban education.

Within the present study a dominant liberal ideology of relevance could be discerned in most of the schools, an ideology concerned with modernization, efficiency, overcoming boredom and producing responsible citizens. Such principles of relevance had affected the constitution of all the subjects of the curriculum and had, in some cases, found a particular institutionalized expression in forms of community and social studies. Against this dominant liberal emphasis was counterpoised in some schools an alternative principle of relevance. This principle implied that an understanding and appreciation of the socio-historical and cultural experience of working-class life should be a central preoccupation of the curriculum of urban schools. As such, it represented the *antithesis* of the founding purposes of such schools.

'Being integrated'

Older and more conservative teachers in this inquiry were concerned to preserve traditional curricula arrangements for, among other things, the sense of boundary which they implied.[5] Young teachers in at least five of the schools, were concerned, on the other hand, to promote notions of an integrated curriculum which would remove a sense of boundary in favour of a 'relational idea'. As with the notion of relevance, the notion of integration was a powerful constituent of liberal school reform, though signifying a variety of motives and intentions. At School A under a previous headteacher, integrated studies (including history, geography, religious education, English, mathematics and science) had been an important feature of the time-table and its position legitimized by the creation of a head of department status. At School B, C, E and F various forms of curriculum integration were in process. As a general pattern the idea of integration involved, in Bernstein's (1977, p. 93) terms 'the subordination of previously insulated subjects or courses to some relational idea'. This might be 'discovery', 'the Creation', 'London living' and so on. The logistics of integration required minimally a team of co-operating teachers, a continuous 'space' on the time-table, adequate physical space and resources for an active pedagogy, e.g. work sheets, audio-visual aids, reference books. These minimal requirements often presented in practice, *major* obstacles to those attempting to introduce measures of integration.[6]

The move to integration was justified from a variety of standpoints. At School A, the former head of department of integrated studies utilized a particularly wide range of arguments. These included suitability for London children

> (London kids are the type that need integrated studies, they are mature, they don't need chalk and talk, they need to inquire. They have so much thrust down their throats that to have the freedom to study their own thing is important as is, also, working at their own rate. It's an ideal thing for London kids.);

making a 'bridge' with the pedagogy of the junior school and helping to give 'security' to the child; producing a 'natural' approach to study 'because the child sees the world as a whole' and helping with secondary school order – 'what is very evident is that the system has facilitated administrative control and cemented quickly the important social contact between pupil and group leader'.

At School B a young history teacher's involvement in integrated studies had provided her with greater satisfactions than she had experienced previously:

> It is very hard work but very satisfying. I have built up an excellent relationship with the class because I see them seven hours a week and get lots of feedback from the kids. They enjoy it.
>
> I hope the scheme will extend, because the possible topics of curriculum and the approach seem to me to be the most relevant and effective method of teaching. Away with traditional subject barriers!

This call for 'revolution' in curriculum arrangements, 'away with traditional subject barriers', epitomized one approach to the introduction of integrated studies. There was in the discourse of teachers associated with this approach an emphasis upon the need for 'wholeness', 'naturalness', 'meaning', 'perceiving relationships' and obtaining greater 'freedom and enjoyment'. Problems of alienation in urban schools were seen to be related to a lack of meaning and involvement in the curriculum, arising out of the

199

distorting effects of arbitrary subject barriers. If these could be removed then an important part of the problem would be removed. A different quality of learning and a different quality of relationships would be realized. [7]

The strongest advocates of curriculum integration tended to be teachers from colleges of education, rather than university departments of education. In some senses, their own less strongly bounded subject identity was a crucial element in their involvement with the development of integrated studies and its institutionalization in the schools' time-tables. It must be noted, however, that those who most strongly advocated integration with its central notion of the 'relational idea' did not themselves characteristically engage in theorizing which related pedagogic forms to wider cultural or socio-political forms; or the constraints of the curriculum with any wider structure of constraints. However, at a more pragmatic level the pioneers of integration had experienced in their efforts for change, the reality of constraints arising within the school and it was such constraints which tended to preoccupy their thinking. Before considering these, it is necessary to examine some other approaches to integration which co-existed with the search for greater meaning and wholeness.

While integration found justifications in a language of educational principle, it also found justifications in a language concerned with notions of order. As already noted, the head of integrated studies at School A observed that 'the system has facilitated administrative control'. The value of the greater knowledge which a team of teachers working with first year pupils for consolidated periods of time could acquire about them, was commented upon in a number of schools. Motives here were various. There was an expressed concern to give first year pupils entering large urban comprehensive schools a sense of security by continuing a mode of pedagogy already familiar to them. At the same time, some teachers observed an increase in the difficulty of teaching first year pupils within a traditional curriculum structure: 'each year the first year are creating more and more problems. There are more maladjusted children, more children with really quite bad behavioural problems. They are beginning to come in unmanageable instead of developing into being unmanageable' (head of English, School J). There was a sense, therefore, in which the development of Integrated Studies appeared to be *necessitated* by an intake of pupils less tractable and amenable to traditional structures.

200

Integrated studies, from this viewpoint, provided a necessary 'space' within which socialization procedures for the secondary school could be undertaken. [8]

Teachers involved in the introduction of measures of integration had experienced a variety of problems in attempting change. Two of the most salient were seen to be 'the question of team cohesion and dealing with head of departments' territorial positions'. At School C the head of biology explained that these issues were made particularly explicit:

> If you entertain any major curriculum changes then it
> presupposes that there is a consensus ideology informing what
> you're doing, particularly . . . if you're breaking down the
> degrees of insulation that exist between each discipline. Now,
> if that's going to happen, you've got to have a pretty common
> ideological base on the part of the staff. They've got to know
> what they're doing. They've got to know what the aims of the
> school are, the policy. Here there are small cliques of people
> who may be doing what they collectively feel is a good thing
> but they will be frustrated at some point when they come up
> against the non-co-operation (either active or passive) of
> someone who is not of the same sympathies. How do you
> overcome that? Do you do it by appointing appropriate staff,
> in which case it's going to take decades; or do you do it by
> having a very strong dominating man at the top who says,
> 'this is how it's going to be done'?

Attempting integration raised many questions at the level of school politics: of the distribution of power in the existing curriculum structure; of the varieties of ideological conflict; of strategies for change; of the provision of resources and of the general possibilities of school arrangements being otherwise. While these questions were being considered initially at the level of the school, they carried with them, as Bernstein (1977, p. 145) has put it, 'the potential of making visible fundamental social contradictions'. The realization of such potential, however, seemed conditional upon radical changes in the consciousness of liberal curriculum reformers, changes which would link more explicitly curriculum structures with social structures.

Curriculum and Pedagogy

Developing alternatives

A small group of inner-city teachers in criticizing the curriculum and pedagogy of their schools and in advancing arguments for change, utilized a different vocabulary and pattern of discourse to that of the liberal majority. Although sharing with the liberal curriculum reformers the language of 'relevance', 'integration' and 'active pedagogy', these terms carried messages different from those of liberalism and were articulated within different theoretical frameworks. Characteristically they formed part of a much more radical critique of existing school procedures and, in some but not all cases, involved much more explicitly socio-political linkage.

The account of the former head of humanities at School A provides an example:

> The business of the imposition of middle-class knowledge is a nonsense because one of the real problems in our school was that none of the kids, in some sections, felt that they were receiving any goods at all, middle class, working class, or otherwise. Their basic descriptions were that they were absolutely bloody bored and that they were learning nothing . . . They were asking for a teacher who would interest them and make them work in a way which they thought was purposeful and valuable. They weren't getting it at all. What they were getting was all kinds of experiences which are something to do with them not being very good, being something of a failure and, often that was legitimated in all kinds of ways. . . . It's got something to do with establishment of hierarchies; with the dashing of anticipation and expectation; with the enuring of their feelings towards all kinds of things . . . with seeing society mirrored in what was happening to them. It's never as bald as that, one has to keep qualifying, but in the sense that the experience reinforced a lot of the political, social and economic experiences they were going to have or already had through their parents and families in society.

Against such a diagnosis, this teacher had attempted within the context of a humanities course (which provided legitimation for blocks of time and acquisition of resources) to create a purposeful learning situation which examined, among other things, aspects of British working-class history, trades unionism, Chartism, etc. While

202

providing an initially strong pedagogic 'frame', the intentions of the course were ultimately liberationist: 'to see kids who are critical, autonomous and generative of ideas'. Although a measure of success was claimed for this venture, the teacher involved was generally pessimistic about the possibilities of developing critical alternatives within urban schools as constituted. Their preoccupations appeared to him to be otherwise. This pessimism (or realism) had finally resulted in a decision to leave teaching and to find educational work in another situation concerned with urban problems. His reasons epitomize the dilemma of the radical working within state schools: 'I felt I had to get out of teaching because it had a *corrupting* influence. I started to take on the cant explanation of what was happening in schools'.

A similar diagnosis was given by a head of science within the same school:

> Teachers are not encouraged to take seriously their actual
> classroom work as opposed to their organizational and
> disciplinary responsibilities, so that any kind of optimism that
> one would feel is, I think, killed by the system, killed by what
> is required of a person. I think you have to have tremendous
> resilience in this Authority to stick by your desire to teach.
> . . . Your headmaster and your inspectors and the whole
> ILEA machine . . . you have a kind of theory about what is
> important to them. It may not be very correct but how do
> you get that theory? You get it by hearing what they say . . .
> you instinctively absorb that as 'that's what the headmaster
> thinks is important' . . . you begin to build up a picture of
> what you think the Authority thinks is important, the way in
> which the Authority works. You never catch this Authority
> being interested in real success in the classroom. . . . it's
> something to do with the pressure of day-to-day organization
> of these giant places.

The alternative which this teacher had worked to develop involved a science course which took seriously the need for scientific understanding and confidence for all pupils and which attempted to achieve this through a primarily experimental approach; an open access policy to laboratories (open during lunch-hours and in the evenings); the explicit relating of science to everyday life (electronics, discos, photography, cars, motor cycles) and the creation of an atmosphere of scientific dialogue rather than a 'culture of silence'. Crucial to this whole venture was the notion that understanding, as opposed to rote, took *time* and that if inner-city schools were in the serious business of promoting the understanding of their pupils, then ways would have to be found of opening up the schools and their facilities to the community outside of formal hours, for intellectual as well as for leisure recreation. *Thus a real, as opposed to a nominal concept of education might be brought into being for inner-city children.*

At School H two young teachers of sociology were attempting to develop alternatives to the 'liberal consensus' of the curriculum by providing courses designed to 'get kids to begin to construct their own knowledge; to view the world critically; to become socially aware and to become active in terms of changing their position if they want to'. Both saw such activity as a necessary and legitimate *countervailing influence* to the many conditions within their pupils' environment which tended towards the production of either social and political passivity, or the acceptance of conservative and even 'reactionary' views on a wide range of subjects.

The principle of *change of consciousness* was a central feature of such thinking about the curriculum and its possibilities were celebrated both at pupil and teacher level. Thus, in referring to her colleagues, one teacher observed:

> I suppose the majority are middle-of-the-roaders. I wish they would all read the first part of Bowles and Gintis's *Schooling in Capitalist America* and that would certainly change their view. Schools *are* centres of cultural domination, they are custodial and repressive and they are reproducing the social relations for a capitalist mode of production, but in a subtle liberal way, so that it is not obvious to most of the teachers involved that this is what they are in fact doing.
>
> Basically, I put my faith in the encounter with a critical literature as being a means of changing the consciousness of teachers (this reflects my own experience). Also as teachers get to work together more to discuss the *real issues* of the curriculum and of teaching (without petty subject status divisions), that would be the beginning of a new form of consciousness and solidarity.

Those inner-city teachers who saw themselves as developing alternative educational experiences for their pupils in the ways described, were united in their rejection of what they took to be the

204

principles of *schooling* for an urban working-class population and in their advocacy of what they took to be the necessary principles of *education*. In their view, *principles of schooling were essentially concerned with hierarchy, individualism, passivity and acceptance. The necessary principles of education on the other hand, were concerned with fraternity, understanding, criticism and changing the world.* Urban schools (and all schools) had to be changed; such change to be in the direction of a greater collective realization of the intellectual and political power of 'ordinary people'. Such a revolution had hardly begun.

English departments

Although English departments had been cast by conservative defenders of the traditional curriculum as centres for the subversion of standards, there was little in the *discourse* of the eighteen teachers of English involved in this study to give support to this view. On the other hand, it must be recognized that no close examination of classroom practice or of the pupils' work was undertaken and it must also be remembered that the sample of teachers was largely *selected* by the headteachers and the deputies. Nevertheless, discussions with eight heads of department (six current and two former) and with ten assistant teachers provided an important part of the research activity and constitutes some basis (although admittedly an incomplete one) for considering such claims. Whether an examination of the practice of such teachers would have produced a radically different account to that given here must remain an open question.

English teachers represented a complete spectrum of ideological positions in education, from the Arnoldian to the Marxist stance. If they differed significantly from other groups of teachers it was not in respect of a thorough-going radicalism designed to subvert the conventions of English usage (in fact, approximately half of them articulated conservative positions on many subjects), but as a group they contained more teachers who exhibited 'radical doubt' and critical reflection about the curriculum, than was the case with many of their colleagues. English departments in the study did not appear, as had been asserted by some senior teachers, to be espousing 'an alternative form of education', but in certain schools their members showed a *distinctive awareness of recent theoretical criticisms of the assumptions of traditional curricula and of the*

205

dilemmas and possibilities which these posed. While their responses to
these dilemmas and possibilities were naturally varied, they constituted in the main the endorsement of a principle of *'cultural comprehensiveness* rather than a principle of subversion or of class conflict.

This position was exemplified by two young (former) heads of
department:

> There is an element of condescension in talking about
> 'working-class culture'. I'm not very convinced about Chris
> Searle, quite honestly (though I suppose I should be). I like to
> use both possibilities. With all children there is great
> relevance in teaching them things like Shakespeare . . . or
> certain of the classical poets. Working-class children would
> find the vocabulary very demanding, but they can cope. One
> of the great dangers of saying 'Oh, they are working-class
> children, let them do projects on the Bay City Rollers or the
> football club' is that that can be as condescending as saying,
> 'We've got to bring them "great culture" and teach
> Wordsworth all day'. One has got to steer a middle path
> between these two angles . . . children have got to be
> introduced to different registers of speech, both spoken and
> written. . . . (former head of English department, School D;
> now deputy head of another school).

> I love Mr Labov because he pointed out that his little Harlem
> kiddies were not thick, they could think in the abstract. They
> were bilingual. They were capable of very sophisticated ideas,
> of dealing with very sophisticated concepts. The fact that they
> didn't 'speak proper' didn't mean to say that they could not
> deal with it. . . . There was this notion that became very
> dominant in the 60s: if you couldn't say it, you couldn't think
> it (very crudely). The working-class child hasn't got the
> language, therefore he can't do it, therefore you must teach
> him things he can do. What you're really doing, then, is
> pulling cast-iron shutters down on the *tremendous* capabilities
> of a lot of those kids. But nevertheless, I teach in the real
> world and my kids live in the real world and they have to go
> out and work in that world. So, whilst respecting the
> language (the specific vocabulary they have which is useful) I
> thought it was a consistent responsibility to stretch that
> vocabulary, to make them sensitive to words. . . . If they
> could describe that which they wanted to say in a sufficiently

succinct manner by themselves, who's complaining? The fact is that when they came to deal with other kinds of language and to communicate with different areas of society, they needed to extend their vocabulary (former head of English department, School I).

Those teachers of English who exhibited 'radical doubt' about the curriculum tended to express it in these terms. They rejected conservative accounts of their activities as caricatures and argued that concern for the basics of spelling and punctuation was the responsibility of *all* teachers, a responsibility which all teachers were slow to accept: 'I don't encourage them to be creative at the expense of these basics, I and other English teachers try to instruct them in the basics, but on our own we're not going to achieve much. It has to be part of a co-ordinated policy across the school.' (Head of English department, School E.)

School E, in keeping with its more militant image, provided one of the very few examples where curriculum objectives in English were explicitly related to political concerns by a young Marxist teacher:

> *Critical literacy* describes the things we are trying to do in this department. I see it mainly in terms of building up the kid's self-confidence through his ability to express himself. In those terms, formal grammar or the exact way in which the work is written or spoken is not relevant. What is most relevant is that he communicates effectively. If bad spelling is a barrier to communication then, of course, you correct it (and I regularly have spelling tests). If bad handwriting is a barrier to communication then you have to work at it to get the kids to write properly. But the criteria all the time is whether they, themselves, are expressing themselves properly and by 'properly' I mean doing justice to what they want to say.
>
> You've also got to try to get it across to the kids that *spoken* language is important. . . . If kids can't express themselves when they leave school, they're going to be sat on, right, left and centre. If they can express themselves, it increases their self-confidence and their ability to stand up for themselves, to fight and organize.

Whilst this account represented very well the position adopted by the few active socialist teachers involved in this research, it in no sense typified the ideology of English departments as such. Where their concerns extended beyond liberalism, they did so in a language which celebrated cultural variety and pupil self-confidence, without explicit political commitments. 'Radical doubt' English teachers were both aware of and sympathetic towards arguments concerning the dangers of cultural imposition in inner-city schools. At the same time they were aware of the constraints of the 'real world', in terms of external expectations for the attributes and competences of their pupils. Caught in this dilemma, they sought for some resolution of it in a principle of cultural comprehensiveness and for ways in which this principle might be legitimated. Such attempts at resolution and legitimation brought into sharp focus for these teachers, as for others in a similar situation, issues of evaluation, autonomy and constraint.

Evaluation, autonomy and constraint

The modern principle of teacher autonomy (understood to be the relatively unimpeded right of the teacher to select pedagogic subject material and to decide upon the mode of its transmission) has its origins in the socio-political crises of 1926 (see chapter 5). Its contemporary nature and its possible future are central issues of current educational and socio-political debate, sharpened in urban contexts by the recent 'crisis' of the William Tyndale School in Islington (Auld, 1976). As already noted in earlier chapters, that the teachers of the urban working class *once the most closely controlled sector* of the occupational group, should appear in contemporary schools to enjoy an extensive autonomy, constitutes a major paradox. *In fact, the notion of teacher autonomy is implicated in a series of paradoxes.*

The first and most obvious concerns the conservative reaction to it. Emerging historically to an important extent out of conservative fears of 'Bolshevik' central direction of curricula, teacher autonomy is now constituted as an important element in Black Paper critiques of urban schools. Autonomy is now seen to be an ill-advised and undemocratic freedom for 'political teachers' (i.e. socialist teachers) to subvert inner-city schools and their pupils. Calls for 'accountability', 'core curriculum' and 'greater parental choice' mark some of the policy implications of this position. Thus, from a conservative stance the autonomy of inner-city teachers is a real and dangerous feature of contemporary urban education in Britain, and measures must be taken to curtail it.

Within various liberal ideologies of education, the autonomy of such teachers is celebrated as a real and necessary feature of urban education and is one of the distinctive achievements of the British educational system. Teacher autonomy is seen to permit that wide range of curricula and pedagogic innovation, experimentation and flexibility which inner-city conditions require. The paradox for liberalism is that with such autonomy and with such potential for change, many of the pupils in urban schools remain bored and alienated. *If teacher autonomy implies the power to change the educational experiences of pupils and of their responses to the school, then the failure of this to be realized to any large extent remains to be explained.*

Radical critiques have an answer to this paradox, but are still enmeshed in their own. For radical critics of urban schools, teacher autonomy is *not* a real feature of urban education and it does not imply the power to change significantly the educational experiences of pupils. Essentially, from this view, it involves nothing more than a liberal rhetoric which breaks down and is exposed as a sham when any serious changes are attempted, especially when these have to do with changed evaluations of knowledge, of competences and of social relations. Thus *autonomy is a pervasive state of false consciousness among teachers, rather than any accurate description of their working situation.*

While this position, at the level of ideology critique, is clear enough, there are paradoxes to be faced at the level of practice. If autonomy is not real why should conservative attacks upon it be 'resisted'? If it is to become real, what would be the nature of the relationship between the autonomy of radical teachers and the expectations of conservative parents and pupils? It can be noted, for instance, that radical teachers at William Tyndale School utilized arguments concerning teacher autonomy and teacher professionalism to legitimate innovations in the face of conservative parental opposition (Auld, 1976; Ellis *et al.* 1976). These considerations raise the general question of what would be the status of teacher autonomy in a *radically* changed educational system?

The teachers in this study generally celebrated a sense of autonomy in their work situations: a sense that selection of appropriate subject material and appropriate modes of pedagogy were relatively unimpeded by external interference. This was understood to be, in most schools, an expression of the liberal norm of British schools.

At School E it was variously suggested that autonomy had been won by a militant teacher stance, or that its existence indicated general indifference to what went on in such schools:

> Subjectively, I feel no constraints whatsoever. . . . I'm not interfered with at all by anybody in the school. If anyone did interfere with me they'd get pretty short shrift. Nobody has ever told me off in the school, nobody has ever interfered with my lessons. Because I keep my kids relatively quiet, they think I'm doing a good job. . . . I could be giving them lessons on how to make petrol bombs for all they knew (English teacher, School E).

> Autonomy in many cases is just a posh word for saying, 'Do what you like' and as long as you don't assault the kids or hit them too hard, no one will care what you're doing . . . (head of English, School E).

Some teachers suggested that the autonomy they had enjoyed was particularly related to the high crisis period of inner-city schools in the early 1970s. The appointment of new headteachers and the introduction of new co-ordinated policies was now making itself felt:

> In this school I have always been able to do what I've wanted to do. Funnily enough, that was against the chaotic background when people always did their own thing. Under the new régime it seems possible that I shall be less able to do what I want to do because now we are thinking in terms of whole school policies, and the contributions each area is making to the whole and where it's going. So, although we're having discussions and deciding what contributions we will make, and how they'll fit together, it is very likely that in a year or so I'll have less freedom to do what I want to do. I'll have to put it before committees and discuss it . . . (head of social education, School F).

Thus, in some schools the teachers' sense of autonomy could be explained in terms of particular institutional conditions which were now in the process of change.

The central meaning of autonomy for most of the teachers was a sense of freedom from interference (for whatever reason) *within* their immediate work situation: the classroom. The enjoyment of such freedom engendered the *experience* of autonomy. Young (1971, p. 22) has, however, suggested that such experience constitutes only one dimension of autonomy and that 'this autonomy is in practice extremely limited by the control of sixth form (and, therefore, lower form) curricula by the universities, both through their entrance requirements and their domination of all but one of the school examination boards. . . .'

To what extent had the teachers experienced the external examining system as a real constraint upon their activities? Some experienced no sense of constraint because they regarded the systems of evaluation embodied in external examinations as part of the taken-for-granted order of the educational world. Far from being constraints, such systems of evaluation were seen to be necessary and essential to provide 'motivation' and 'purpose' for both pupils and teachers. External examinations contributed towards a sense of structure which such teachers valued and thought particularly useful for inner-city schools. Others were convinced that contemporary systems of evaluation involving a variety of examining boards and modes of school-based assessment provided liberal possibilities for 'playing the system' or 'beating the system'. This view was epitomized by a head of year at School B:

> It seems to me that it is up to each school to try to change and mould its curriculum to suit its own intake, particularly with the Mode 3 CSEs. The variety of courses that schools can have and the linking with FE colleges of one sort of another is considerable. It is very possible for schools to work out their own individual curriculum. Curriculum seems to me to be something that is continually coming under scrutiny and continually changing from year to year to meet the needs of particular groups of kids. . . .

Despite this strong 'liberal faith'[10] in the reality of autonomy and flexibility in curricula and evaluation procedures, some of the teachers involved in innovation were more sceptical. From this perspective, introducing Mode 3 assessments meant, in practice, putting in 'a helluva lot of work'; incurring extra departmental costs: 'We've got to come to terms with putting aside £80–£100 a year for it, instead of buying a set of books' (School H); having considerable persistence: 'we still have to go to the MREB juggernaut and it's all a very slow business and they make it very inhuman' (School E); and in some schools being exposed to critical comment from colleagues:

> We provoked so much (almost personal) hostility to what we were doing. We had instituted Mode 3 exams in 'O' level and CSE and that was unfavourably viewed. We had implications that we only did it so that we could fix the marks to get better results than anybody else (former head of English, School D).

For a minority of teachers, therefore, who felt that they were *challenging* fundamental categories and assumptions of the evaluation process, of 'what counts as knowledge', the experience of constraint was real. It was not that radical change was impossible, but that it required 'hero-innovators' to accomplish.

Inner-city schools and the 'crisis' of curriculum

This chapter has attempted to make explicit the ways in which the contemporary crisis of the curriculum is constituted and experienced by teachers in ten working-class inner-city schools in London. It has sought also to go beyond description and to extract the fundamental principles which provide the rationale for various conflicting curriculum structures and modes of pedagogy.

The Victorian definers of schooling for the urban masses, while divided on strategies and priorities, were essentially united on the fundamental principles of order, civilization and functional competence, which would form and mould the curriculum and pedagogy of urban schools. Contemporary urban schools, however, are arenas for the making visible of conflict of fundamental principles and of a 'crisis of validity' in curriculum and pedagogy. Within such schools groups of teachers advance different constructs as to what constitutes an appropriate educational experience for the pupils. For some, the imperatives are traditional disciplines, excellencies and competence; for some, relevance, interest and community relatedness; for some principles of modernization and efficiency; for some, the need for cultural comprehensiveness; for some, the development of a critical consciousness and an active, self-confident intelligence; for some, a sense of integration and meaning and for some, a sense of working-class solidarity and socio-historical location.

Different principles, however, are related to differential amounts

212

of power and sources of institutional and other support and the question of which sets of principles dominate within any one school becomes an important subject for empirical inquiry.[11] Crucial, also, is the question of departmental and individual autonomy. This study would suggest that the autonomy enjoyed by inner-city teachers in relation to curriculum content, pedagogy and (to some degree) evaluation, is a *real and considerable freedom of their work situation.*[12] Such freedom may be an unintended consequence of recent crisis conditions in inner-city schools or of a variety of other factors, but its presence permits the *co-existence within some schools of a remarkably wide range of curricula and pedagogic principles.* Whether such a measure of autonomy will survive policies in inner-city schools related to accountability, greater involvement of parents and employers, curriculum co-ordination and moves to integrated studies, is obviously a matter of urgent contemporary concern. At present, however, the structure of the curriculum – particularly the existence of relatively autonomous subject departments, creates a context in which innovations in curriculum, pedagogy, pupil grouping and evaluation procedures *are a possibility.* Such innovations can be introduced even against wider institutional disapproval (as at School D). The realization of these possibilities, however, has to take place within a framework of constraints, the most important of which are the requirements of examination boards; the availability of resources (including, crucially, space) and also crucially, the ability of inner-city teachers, hard-pressed by other preoccupation, to find the time and the energy to become innovators rather than merely survivors.

It is clear that if these constraints were significantly modified, a much fuller realization of the possibilities of curricula and pedagogic innovation would take place in urban schools. Teacher autonomy, would then come to have that reality which a present 'liberal faith' now attributes to it. In such an event (and perhaps the William Tyndale School provides an example), very complex questions are raised concerning the nature of teacher autonomy, the 'rights' of pupils, parents and of the community and the nature of the proper location of curriculum control, in a society which claims to be pluralist and democratic.

The ultimate question to be faced is, to what extent will any social formation permit a variety of principles to be realized within its formal educational process, particularly those which raise radical questions concerning its own legitimacy?

213

Chapter 11

Conclusions

There appears to be general agreement among sociologists working in education, albeit from different theoretical and political positions, of the necessity of attempting some form of structural location of teachers in any given social formation. Bernstein (1977, p. 192), in examining the relationships which exist between education and production, with particular reference to 'that fraction of the middle-class who function as agents of cultural reproduction', points to the ambiguous position within a class structure of 'the agents of symbolic control'. From a different perspective, Sharp and Green (1975, p. 227) argue that 'unless and until educators are able to comprehend their own structural location . . . they will continue to be unwilling victims of a structure that undermines the moral concerns they profess. . . .' Young and Whitty (1977, p. 230) conclude in *Society, State and Schooling: readings on the possibilities for radical education* with the observation that 'we therefore face a considerable theoretical and political task in developing a concrete understanding of the class position of teachers'.

This study has provided some empirical grounds for a consideration of such issues, with especial reference to a particularly strategic group of educators: the teachers of the urban working class. It has attempted to do this by utilizing various approaches to the problem of location, those which entail an 'objective' account (i.e. in this case, the historical origins of the occupational group and its historical and contemporary relation to a particular form of ideological struggle) and those which entail a 'subjective' account (i.e. the constitution of teachers' consciousness in relation to their work situations and their pupils). It seems probable that unless these approaches are integrated in questions of occupational location, the result will be either *a disembodied structuralism or an unrelated world of consciousness.*

Substantively this study has shown that the origins of the occupational group under examination can be explicitly located in Victorian middle-class preoccupation with an urban problem, as constituted by the threat of 'anarchy' incipient in an urban working class. Thus the teachers of the urban working class were quite clearly a crucial sector of 'the agents of symbolic control' within nineteenth-century capitalist society. As such, their selection involved careful screening; their occupational socialization was bland and apolitical and their day-to-day activities were closely monitored. The ideology of professionalism and respectability and the process of 'being cultured' served to distance the teachers from their own socio-cultural origins and from any dangerous associations with the organized working class.

However, while they were undoubtedly caught up in a massive apparatus of control, urban teachers were never entirely determined by, or rendered the social puppets of this apparatus. Ideological conflict within the middle class over the form of education appropriate to an urban working class provided some space for manoeuvre and some possibility for alternative pedagogies. Teacher organizations and unions were able to utilize for their own ends the ideology of professionalism in the long historical struggle to attain a greater measure of autonomy. It remains the case, however, that well into this century features of control and constraint were dominant over features of autonomy for the teachers of the urban working class.

The structural location of contemporary urban teachers is a more complex issue. As this study has shown, the occupational group is now more *differentiated* in terms of the social and cultural origins of its members; the contexts and contents of their socialization and the principles which they are attempting to realize in their teaching activity. In particular, the entry in significant numbers of young graduate teachers (with short periods of professional preparation) into the schools of the urban working class marks an important change in both the composition and the orientation of the contemporary 'agents of symbolic control'.

Conclusions

The contemporary ideological struggle in which urban teachers are located is itself more differentiated and more profound. In place of a conflict of prescriptions for schooling, all designed to produce some notion of order within given social forms, the conflict is now one involving radically different models of man and radically different models of society. Whereas the ideological struggles of Victorian popular urban education were essentially fought out *around* the schools, the contemporary struggle has become mediated by different groups of teachers working *within* the schools, especially in inner-city localities. That such a situation could have arisen necessarily suggests *some alteration in the structural location of urban teachers, some alteration in the apparatus or modality of control and some alteration in the autonomy of urban schools.* It seems likely that such alterations have been in the main the *unintended consequences* of other forms of institutional, social and political action. The introduction of the comprehensive school (albeit in nominal form) has resulted in a greater social, cultural and ideological differentiation among the teachers of the urban working class than was ever the case previously and, as Holly (1977) has pointed out, this has had important implications for the social relations of education.[1]

This study has shown that the teaching group within inner-city schools now contains articulate members who consciously resist, in various ways, what they take to be the undesirable features of state education. It has shown that a fraction of this group resists its own socio-historical location as agents of symbolic control within society as constituted and seeks variously to become agents of radical change, either in terms of a liberated personal consciousness or in terms of a radically transformed social and political structure. To signal that intention, such teachers adopt a stance of fraternity in relation to the pupils and their parents and reject the ideology of professionalism with its implied social distance from manual workers. They assert explicitly that the time has come for teachers to recognize that they are *workers* and that their interests and those of their pupils will only be realized in association with other workers.[2]

This fraction, however, is by no means typical of the occupational group as a whole. Within inner-city schools there are influential and powerful conservative groups of teachers and frequently dominant groups of liberal teachers, who hold to an ethic of professionalism as appropriate to the educator's status and as

216

symbolizing his necessarily impartial and non-political stance.[3] Both groups locate the educational enterprise and themselves as teachers as being essentially *outside* of social and political structures and relatively autonomous in relation to them. The majority of the teachers who co-operated in this study appeared to locate themselves in an autonomous space within the social structure, a space which permitted them to realize those principles which they believed to be crucial for the education of inner-city children. These principles might be those of 'excellencies transcending class'; principles of relevance and interest; of integration and wholeness, or of cultural comprehensiveness. Such teachers believed that in realizing their particular principles they were acting in the best interests of urban working-class pupils and in an 'appropriate' and 'professional' way. Characteristically they did not and would not locate themselves as being fraternally united with working-class pupils and parents in any notion of a wider struggle to change society, since this was overtly political and regarded as inappropriate to their autonomous and impartial position as educators. They were able to maintain this position with conviction because they had experienced in their work situations *very little overt control* of their activities and, consequently, *notions of a 'dominant order' or of a 'controlling apparatus' and of the necessity for struggle against it were insubstantial in their consciousness, whereas notions of autonomy were real and actual.*[4] This was the crucial issue which effectively divided the liberal majority of contemporary inner-city teachers in this study from their radical and Marxist colleagues and this division makes substantive some central questions. Is the liberal majority to be dismissed as the victims of a false consciousness when 'in fact' they are as controlled in all the essentials as were their nineteenth-century predecessors? On the other hand, is the radical and Marxist view on the reality of control to be dismissed as ideological since, 'in fact', it is apparent that urban working-class schools and their teachers currently have (for all sorts of reasons) a large amount of autonomy within the existing social structure?

This study gives no support to either a naïve educational liberalism on the one hand, or to a determinist schooling thesis on the other. Empirically, it suggests that what can be observed from a socio-historical examination of urban schools and their teachers is a *significant change in the modality of control in urban education.* This change, partly the result of conscious political action, partly the consequence of the action of organized teachers and partly the consequence of crisis conditions in inner-city schools has had two important outcomes. It has involved the achievement of a real, although limited, measure of autonomy for urban teachers; an autonomy currently under critical scrutiny and some would say, attack. At the same time, it has involved *a movement from essentially visible and centralized control to essentially invisible and diffused control.*

The contemporary teacher of the urban working class is not, like his nineteenth-century predecessor, the object of an explicit and visible apparatus of control but of a more subtle and diffuse network of controls and constraints. This invisible control is constituted among other things, by the activities of examination boards and of their definitions of valid knowledge; by the constraints of the work situation and, crucially, by what 'being a good teacher' and 'being professional' are taken to imply. These controls are invisible to the majority of teachers in so far as they form a part of the taken-for-granted and unchallenged social world within which they operate. Within this study only those teachers who had challenged one or more of these features had a sense of the reality of control. This study has shown that despite the existence of a relative autonomy for teachers in urban schools, the constraints of the work situation and the contemporary implications of 'being a good teacher' had effectively precluded the majority of teachers from the possibility of challenge or even the possibility of much critical reflection about their own activities. Thus, this strategic section of the 'agents of symbolic control' are themselves still controlled. Controlled in the sense that their actual opportunities to question the conventional wisdom or dominant ideas within the system in which they operate, are very limited. Controlled in the sense that their ability to formulate radical alternatives is very circumscribed and controlled in the sense that 'being professional' inhibits the considerations of the relations between education and the socio-political structure. Such controls may have currently no very clear, conscious or unitary origin, but their existence serves a conservative function. The particular irony of the situation is that members of an occupational group who are, by their own rhetoric, engaged in explaining the world, *critically and in a relational sense*, are to an important extent precluded from doing this in relation to their own situation. At the same time, contemporary and influential developments in in-service higher education for teachers make available for

218

some modes of analysis and modes of thinking which encourage such a critical stance.[5]

What appears to be crucial at the present time is whether a significant number of urban teachers will *challenge* various features of what we have called the network of invisible control or whether they will continue to operate quiescently within it. Will such teachers challenge the definitions of knowledge and competence which are legitimized by examination boards? Will they challenge the constraints of their work situation and the institutional arrangements of the school? Will they challenge dominant constructs of the 'good teacher' and will they challenge the implications of professionalism? The combined effects of 'encounters with critical literature' and of significant changes in the work situation of urban schools (involving potential redundancy and greater 'accountability') may provide the conditions for a widespread radicalizing of inner-city teachers. If such radicalization occurs, this may be the beginning, in one arena, of a process of 'the making visible of fundamental social contradictions' and through this process, of generating wider social and political transformation. It may, on the other hand, provoke a firm reassertion of the founding purposes of working-class schools in urban areas. Those who wish to facilitate the first of these possibilities and to resist the latter, may find that while analysing the world is no substitute for changing the world, it can contribute towards that end.

Appendices

Table 1. The Schools

School	Size	Type	% Pupil poverty[1]	% 'immigrant' pupils[2]	Social Priority Status
School A	1,150	Boys	20	15	No
School B	1,250	Boys/Girls	25	22	Yes
School C	1,250	Boys/Girls	43	29	Yes
School D	1,300	Girls	15	11	No
School E	1,200	Boys	33	20	Yes
School F	900	Boys/Girls	56	16	Yes
School G	870	Boys/Girls	33	56	Yes
School H	1,260	Girls	25	18	No
School I	500	Boys	50	13	Yes
School J	800	Girls	Not available	49	Yes

[1] Defined by entitlement to free school meals.
[2] DES definition: LEA figures for 1973.

223

Table 2. The Teachers

Total interview sample was 80 (designated and non-designated)

School	No.	Age 20–29	30–39	40–49	50–59*	Teaching experience (years) 0–5	6–10	11–15	16–20	20+*	Preparing instit.¹ Univ.	College	English	Science	History²	Mathematics	P.E.	Art	Geography	Mod. langs.	Tech. studies	Home econ.	Remedial	Music	Sociology	Gen. subjects	Position Head of Year	Head of Dept.	Other
A	17³	6	8	2	1	8	4	4	–	1	9	8	5	2	3	1	–	–	–	–	1	–	2	1	–	1	4	7	6
B	7	2	2	3	–	1	3	2	–	1	2	5	1	–	1	1	1	1	–	–	–	1	–	–	–	–	3	1	3
C	7	2	3	2	–	2	2	1	2	–	–	7	1	–	1	1	–	1	–	–	–	–	–	1	–	–	–	6	1
D	8	1	1	5	1	2	2	2	2	1	5	3	–	3	1	–	1	–	1	–	–	–	1	–	–	–	1	4	3
E	7	1	4	2	–	1	2	4	–	–	3	4	2	–	1	–	–	–	1	–	1	–	1	–	–	–	2	4	1
F	7	–	3	1	3	–	1	2	1	3	1	6	3	1	–	–	–	1	–	–	–	–	–	–	–	1	1	5	1
G	8	3	3	1	1	2	3	1	1	2	1	7	2	2	1	–	–	1	1	–	1	–	–	–	–	–	5	2	1
H	8	4	2	1	1	4	3	–	–	1	4	4	1	1	1	1	1	–	–	2	–	–	–	–	2	–	1	6	1
I	5	2	2	1	–	–	4	–	–	1	–	5	1	–	–	1	–	–	–	–	1	–	–	–	–	2	3	2	1
J	6	1	3	2	–	2	4	–	–	–	3	3	1	–	–	1	–	–	1	–	–	2	1	–	–	–	–	5	1
10	80	22	31	20	7	22	27	16	5	10	28	52	17	10	8	6	4	4	4	2	4	3	5	2	2	4	20	42	18

* Head of integrated studies (School A)
Head of community service (School B)
Head of community education (sociology) (School E)
Head of social projects (School F)
Head of careers and social education (School D)

¹ Where the first qualification for teaching was obtained.

² Two teachers held the combined positions of head of history/head of humanities.

³ The numbers at School A are partly the result of a higher than average level of designation of 'outstanding' teachers by the headteachers and the deputy (ii) and partly by greater opportunities for the researcher to interview other teachers (6).

Table 3. Formal Interview Sample: 70 designated 'outstanding' teachers

School	No. designated	Age 20–29	Age 30–39	Age 40–49	Age 50+	Exp 0–5	Exp 6–10	Exp 11–15	Exp 16–20	Exp 21+	Prep. Univ.	Prep. College	English	Science	Hist.[2]	Mathematics	P.E.	Art	Geog.	Mod. Lang.	Tech. Studies	Home Econ.	Remedial	Music	Sociology	Gen. Subjects	Head of Year	Head of Dept.	Other	No. of full-time staff
A	11	3	7	1	—	5	2	4	—	—	5	6	3	—	2	1	—	—	—	—	1	—	1	1	—	1	3	5	3	70
B	7	2	2	3	—	1	3	2	—	1	2	5	1	1	1	1	1	1	—	—	—	1	—	—	—	—	3	1	3	84
C	7	2	3	2	—	2	2	1	2	—	—	7	1	1	1	1	1	1	—	—	—	—	1	—	—	—	—	6	1	73
D	8	1	1	5	1	2	1	2	2	1	5	3	—	3	1	—	1	—	—	—	—	—	1	—	—	—	1	4	3	75
E	6	1	4	1	—	1	1	3	1	—	3	3	2	—	1	—	—	—	1	—	—	—	1	—	—	1	2	3	1	65
F	6	—	3	1	2	—	2	2	—	2	1	5	2	1	—	—	—	1	1	—	1	—	—	—	—	—	—	5	1	58
G	8	3	3	1	1	2	3	1	—	2	1	7	2	1	1	—	—	1	1	—	1	—	—	—	1	—	5	2	1	50
H	6	2	2	1	1	2	3	—	—	1	3	3	1	1	—	1	—	—	—	2	—	—	—	—	—	2	1	5	—	70
I	5	2	2	1	—	—	4	—	—	1	—	5	1	—	—	1	—	—	—	—	1	2	—	—	—	—	3	2	—	29
J	6	1	3	2	—	2	4	—	—	—	3	3	1	—	—	1	—	—	1	—	—	—	1	—	—	—	—	5	1	48
10	70	17	30	18	5	17	25	15	5	8	23	47	14	8	7	6	3	4	4	2	4	3	4	2	1	4	18	38	14	622

* Head of integrated studies (School A)
Head of community service (School B)
Head of careers and social education (School D)
Head of social projects (School F)

[1] Where the first qualification for teaching was obtained.

[2] Two teachers held the combined positions of head of history/head of humanities.

[3] Refers to the teacher's original field of qualification. It does not necessarily imply that teachers were chosen for the excellence of their teaching in this subject field. See chapters 7 and 8.

[4] Also includes deputies.

Table 4. Informal Interview Sample: 10 non-designated teachers

No.	Age	Teaching experience	Preparing instit.	Subject area	Position	Selection principle[1]
1	28	4	U	Remedial	Assistant	Random
2	58	28	C	English	Head of Year	'Experience'
3	31	10	U	Science	Head of Dept.	Random
4	42	12	U	Science	Head of Dept.	'Radicalism'
5	32	5	U	English	Youth Tutor	'Radicalism'
6	26	1	C	History	Assistant	Random
7	41	11	C	Community Edu./ Sociology	Head of Dept.	'Radicalism'
8	57	28	C	English	Head of Year	'Experience'
9	29	5	U	Sociology	Assistant	'Radicalism'
10	30	7	C	P.E.	Head of Dept.	'Radicalism'

[1] There was a bias, in forming this small sub-sample, towards those non-designated teachers who were *strongly critical* of various aspects of the constitution of schools ('radicalism'). This decision was made after it became clear that few of such teachers were being formally designated by the headteachers.

Table 5. Formal Interview Sample: 10 headteachers' vocabulary of designation for 'outstanding' teachers

School	Age	Teaching experience	Experience[1] present sch.	Preparing institution	Main criteria used re 'outstanding' teachers (vocabulary of designation)[2]
A	38	12	2	U	Energetic and enthusiastic; secure identity; balanced
B	65	37	6	U	Good relationships; dedication and commitment; initiative and drive
C	59	28	2	U	High expectations; making demands; being involved
D	52	28	14	U	Good organization; energy; being leaders
E	38	15	2	U	Positive personality; professionalism; consistency
F	35	13	2	U	Clarity; imagination; outcomes
G	52	30	11	C	Sympathy and understanding; professionalism
H	37	15	2	C	High expectations; enthusiasm; stable personality
I	62	28	10	U	Management; discipline; strong personality
J	50	25	9	U	Empathy; rapport; purposeful; good management

[1] Experience as headteacher.
[2] Recurrent markers in the discourse of headteachers when typifying *generally* the correlates of 'outstanding' teachers in inner-city schools. See detailed individual accounts chapters 7 and 8.

Table 6. Formal Interview Sample: 15 deputy headteachers' vocabulary of designation for 'outstanding' teachers

School	Age	Teaching experience	Experience present sch.	Preparing institution	Main criteria re 'outstanding' teachers (vocabulary of designation)
A	59	25	25	C	Not given
B*	35	14	5	C	Relationships; commitment; resilience; organized (well-structured)
B*	35	12	1	U	Not given
C*	54	34	2	C	Commitment
C*	39	13	2	U	Not given
D	53	33	33	U	Not given
E*	62	28	28	U	Not given
E*	37	15	7	C	Extrovert; quite tough; committed to interest of the kids
F*	50	28	4	C	Persons who care; involved
F*	54	28	4	C	Personal relationships
G*	47	11	3	U	Likeable personality; relationships; totally dedicated
G*	33	12	3	C	Out-going personality; common sense/down-to-earth attitude
H	45	20	11	U	High expectations; tough-mindedness
I	46	24	2	C	Stable personality; professionalism; discipline
J	39	18	3	C	Hard-working; conscientious; results

* Schools in which first and second deputy headteachers were interviewed.

Table 7. Formal Interview Sample: 10 headteachers' vocabulary of designation for 'poor' teachers

School	Age	Teaching experience	Experience present sch.	Preparing institution	Main criteria used *re* 'poor' teachers (vocabulary of designation)
A	38	16	2	U	No spark; teachers who don't understand what the commitments need to be
B*	65	37	6	U	Failure to relate to the children; don't keep abreast of social and educational change
C*	59	28	2	U	Not given
D	52	28	14	U	Inability to think ahead (lacks organization); a political slant
E	38	15	2	U	Bad classroom manager; inconsistency; no personality
F*	35	13	2	U	Laziness; not liking children; internal insecurity
G	52	30	11	C	Superficial culture; lacks professionalism; lazy and ineffective
H	37	15	2	C	Inability to communicate to the kids; negative personality, colourless
I	62	28	10	U	Lazy; cannot keep order; dissident
J	50	25	9	U	Absence of self-criticism; fear of accountability; forming of way out and rather militant groups

* At these schools it was suggested that some teachers who might have been 'good' in a previous school context (i.e. secondary modern) might in a sense now be regarded as 'poor' teachers in so far as they had been unable to respond to changed conditions. Such teachers might actually hold senior positions within the schools.

Interview Procedures

Teachers

The interviews were semi-structured, in that certain standard items for discussion were introduced by the researcher but, at the same time, an attempt was made to respond to what the teachers indicated (either explicitly or by their emphasis) to be important concerns of their working world. Standard items introduced by the researcher were:

1 *Biographical and professional background of the teacher* including professional preparation; own social origin and educational experience; pattern of teaching experience; political and union affiliations.

2 *Experience of teaching* including typifications of pupils; teacher-pupil relations; satisfactions and frustrations; qualities needed in the teacher; views on professional preparation.

3 *Features of school* including attitude to comprehensive principle; influence of size and teacher turnover; staff relations; staff-hierarchy relations (role of head); school-community relations; pastoral care systems; internal government of schools.

4 *Curriculum and pedagogy* including attitudes to curriculum change; questions of 'cultural imposition'; questions of 'relevance'; integrated studies; boundary and structure; 'best' mode of pedagogy; mode of grouping pupils; evaluation; experience of autonomy or constraint.

The teachers were asked to co-operate in the 'making explicit' of various aspects of the world of inner-city schools. They were *not* aware that they had been designated as 'outstanding' teachers.

Headteachers and Deputy Headteachers

Interviews followed the same general format with the addition of questions concerning the qualities of 'outstanding' teachers (and, in some cases, of 'poor' teachers) and the ways in which these evaluations were arrived at.

Notes

Introduction

1. As exemplified, for instance, in Young and Whitty (1977).
2. Agents of symbolic control are understood to be that fraction of the middle class whose function it is in the field of cultural reproduction to legitimate and render 'normal' a given social order. For a discussion of the agents of symbolic control see Bernstein (1977) 'Symbolic control and the identification of the new middle-class', pp. 127–30.
3. Harold Silver (1977, pp. 57–68) has recently demonstrated how many crucial aspects of the study of popular education have been neglected in socio-historical research and has called for a radical reorientation of research effort. A valuable 'answer' to that call has been provided in McCann (1977). It can, however, be noted that even here the 'teachers of the people' are essentially ignored.
4. While Marxist writers such as Castells (1969) suggest that 'urban sociology is an ideology' (1976, p. 60), which mystifies and obscures the social contradictions of capitalism, such a view is resisted. As Pahl (1975, p. 237) observes, urban sociology and urban studies have considerable potential to 'illuminate the workings of capitalism as a system'. For an example of this, see Harvey (1973). It is clear that this debate within urban sociology has considerable relevance for any discussion concerned with the status of urban education as a field of study.
5. The most recent and visible example of such confrontation and struggle have been the events concerning the William Tyndale Junior School in Islington. See Auld (1976). See also Ellis *et al.* (1976).
6. There is already a useful literature of 'critical' historical studies especially from American sources. See for instance: Katz (1968); Lazerson (1971); Kaestle (1973); Ravitch (1974). For Britain see Reeder (1977).
7. For a critical examination of the theory of ideology, mainly within the Marxist tradition, see *Working Papers in Cultural Studies 10; On Ideology*, Centre for Contemporary Cultural Studies, University of Birmingham, 1977.
8. See, for instance, the arguments of Frith and Corrigan (1977 pp. 253–68).

231

9. The writer acknowledges the fruitful influence here of Stuart Hall (1974).
10. Material for this section is derived from an SSRC research project 'Teaching in the Inner-City Comprehensive School' which was undertaken between 1975–77.

Chapter 1 Teachers of the Urban Working Class: socio-historical location

1. For discussions of the heterogeneous nature of the 'middle classes' and of the 'working classes' in nineteenth-century Britain, see Neale (1972) and Stedman-Jones (1971).
2. Harold Silver (1977, p. 62) warns us against the danger of confusing statements of *intent* with statements concerned with *practice* and is critical of Johnson for not going beyond 'a starting point for an analysis of real situations. . . .'
3. There is no suggestion here of a conscious intention, but an examination of the forms of 'social science' later admitted to the curriculum of teachers' colleges strongly suggests that they provided a 'scientific' as opposed to a moralistic vocabulary for describing various deficiencies of working-class life and child socialization.
4. See Squibb (1973). See also Taylor (1969, p. 12); 'the dominant value orientation of teacher education during the past six decades of the present century have been those of social and literary romanticism.'
5. Asher Tropp's (1957) study remains the most valuable single collection of socio-historical material concerned with elementary school teachers. Its influence upon this chapter and upon chapter 2 will be obvious.
6. The strongly 'vocational' aspects of professionalism are still represented by the Professional Association of Teachers which is pledged to the notion that strike action *can never be admissible* for teachers.
7. For an examination of these conflicting interests, see Tropp (1957), chapters 2 to 7).
8. For a discussion of the nature of the sociology of education at this time, see M. F. D. Young, 'An Approach to the Study of Curricula as Socially Organized Knowledge' in Young (1971, pp. 24–6). For an alternative account see Bernstein, 'The sociology of education: a brief account' in Bernstein (1977, pp. 146–62).
9. Its treatment here is brief because a considerable literature already exists concerned with the relationships between religious interests and education provision.
10. For a study which makes explicit the social control preoccupations of some religious interests in popular education in urban areas, see P. McCann, 'Popular education, socialization and social control: Spitalfields 1812–1824' in McCann (1977, pp. 1–40).
11. For two recent historical studies concerned with making the working classes 'rational' see Goldstrom (1977) and Jones (1977).
12. Quoted in Harrison (1961, pp. 79–82) as part of a discussion of political economy in working-class education.
13. This is, it must be admitted, a frankly speculative interpretation.
14. W. E. Forster, quoted in West (1975, p. 231).
15. For a discussion of 'the special mission of the English teacher' see Mathieson (1975, pp. 37–55).
16. Committee of Council on Education 1866 (Report of Rev. Mitchell), p. 125.
17. Committee of Council on Education 1867–68 (Report of Rev. Mitchell), p. 129.

18. Committee of Council on Education 1875 (Report of HMI Alderson), p. 31.
19. Committee of Council on Education 1881 (Report of HMI Stokes), pp. 445–7.
20. Committee of Council on Education 1873 (Report of HMI Alderson), pp. 28–9.
21. HMI Stewart noted on truancy rates that (Committee of Council on Education 1877, p. 548):

> Children are, after all, good judges of the value of the schools they attend; they know very well when lessons are interesting and what teachers look after them as they ought to do; they are quite capable of feeling an affectionate respect for those who do their duty and the attendance at a school is often a very fair test of its character. In well-managed schools I have never heard much said about bad attendance and where the loudest complaints have been laid against children, I have been inclined to take part with them.

22. HMI Alderson, for instance, argued against the power of 'subjects' (Committee of Council on Education 1881, p. 177):

> Subjects are not the object of education. Subjects are means not ends; pursued as ends they germinate feebly and lose their reproductive power . . . subjects which remain to the learner always subjects instead of passing by the process of assimilation into his system and forming a common fund of useful and durable knowledge have no educational value. The result of teaching 'subjects' too exclusively is that the scholar carries his knowledge so to say in compartments . . . [there is a] . . . need of a greater interpenetration of subjects.

Chapter 2 The Working World of the 'Teachers of the People'

1. For comparative purposes it can be pointed out that the accounts derived later from contemporary urban teachers (see chapters 7 to 10) are from a sample taken to be representative of 'successful' teachers.
2. Committee of Council on Education 1882 (Report of HMI Fitch), p. 313.
3. The notion of 'paramount reality' is taken from the work of Schutz and Luckmann (1974).
4. Committee of Council on Education 1883 (Report of HMI Stokes), p. 404.
5. Teachers' insecurity concerning the imputed limitations of *their own* social and cultural background may be related (along with the expectations of visiting inspectors) to a strong preoccupation with 'correctness', especially in spoken and written English. Certainly, elementary school teachers were frequently exposed to derogatory comments concerning their 'lack of culture'.
6. *English Journal of Education*, vol. IV, 1850, p. 5.
7. Ibid., p. 6.
8. Ibid., p. 7.
9. Ibid., p. 13.
10. Ibid., p. 231.
11. Ibid., p. 14.
12. Ibid., p. 78.
13. For a contemporary comparison, see the sense of revulsion expressed by some inner-city teachers in Howard Becker's (1952) study of Chicago slum schools reprinted in Cosin *et al.* (1971).

14. *English Journal of Education*, vol. IV, 1850, p. 230.
15. Then as now 'the pupil as conservative' was a problem to those teachers attempting innovation in curriculum, pedagogy or the social relations of schooling. For a contemporary discussion of 'the pupil as conservative' see John Spradbury's essay 'Conservative pupils? Pupil resistance to a curriculum innovation in mathematics' (Whitty and Young, 1977).
16. Corporal punishment was an issue which often estranged teachers from the radical sections of the working class. Most teachers took the view that in the conditions in which they had to work, corporal punishment was a necessity and great bitterness was expressed against 'theorists' who thought it could be otherwise. James Runciman (1887, p. 249) expressed the teachers' case with vigour:

> I saw a boy promptly draw a nine-inch knife and dash it into the back of another. The blade ran along a rib, slipped in and barely missed the base of the lung. What does the sentimentalist say to a youth of that kind?
>
> Again there are boys and girls who have a perfect mania for scribbling the most horrible indecencies, and blasphemies on walls. They must be watched like felons or the mania overpowers them. Then there are boys and girls with a taste for unspeakable vices; others who are cruel to a degree which an Apache Indian could not excel; others who are brutally insolent, rankly foul-mouthed, murderously revengeful and callous; others who are cowardly young fiends, who lay themselves out hour by hour to torture a struggling assistant and who twit him with hints of the police court if he dares to utter a stern word.
>
> The London Board take for granted that there are no wicked children; the gushers talk of moral persuasion; but practical men know that you cannot try moral persuasion on a young wretch who has not even an elementary conception of morality and whose mind cannot assimilate the faintest idea of goodness. You must use the one argument that he understands; you MUST employ the short, sharp discipline of pain.

17. While the account is fictional, it seems reasonable to interpret it as having been firmly grounded in D. H. Lawrence's own experiences of elementary school classrooms. See *The Rainbow*, Penguin, Harmondsworth, 1975, p. 395.
18. For another examination of the influence of the rural and small-town origins of social analysts, see C. Wright Mills (1967).
19. The 'wit' of urban working-class children was frequently acknowledged and seen to be an unsocialized intelligence which resisted the powers of schooling.
20. This volatility was commented upon frequently by writers of the time who attributed these characteristics *to the effects of urban living*. HMI Alderson wrote to the Committee of Council on Education in 1873:

> the surroundings of the London child, the whirl and distraction incident to life in a great city are unfavourable to subjects of study requiring patient drudgery, fixed attention, concentration and thought. They are favourable to subjects into the learning of which imagination and mental vivacity largely enter.

An early work in the sociology of the urban environment gave systematic attention to these issues. For the town child it was suggested (Bray, 1907, pp. 17–18):

> the stream of thought, in place of being formed of a few clear-cut impressions, is a confused torrent of chaotic perspectives. There is no definite centre around which these thousand sights revolve, nothing to hold them together, give them unity, nothing to produce the consciousness of cause and effect.

The writer observed that the city environment did produce 'a phenomenal sharpness and readiness of resources' and 'acute perception of all that happens in the neighbourhood'. Volatility was similarly explained (Bray, 1907, p. 47): 'children who have acquired the habit of sharing the life of a crowd find the routine existence of the individual insipid and distasteful; they become more noisy and uncontrolled in their ways, less tolerant of any restraint'. *Anarchy was an ever present threat* (Bray, 1907, pp. 145–7): 'the crowd of a town in a moment thrashes into a delirious mob and swept away on a torrent of excitement and reckless of appearance, plunges into acts of unmitigated folly'.

The writer proposed that schools in such a context should instil habits (Bray, 1907, p. 205):

> we want habits, because habits alone render tolerable the drudgery and the routine of life and secure stability of character. Looking at the life of the town child . . . we need chiefly habits of regularity, habits of accuracy, habits of obedience, habits of attention, habits of order, habits of self-control, habits of cleanliness using the last term in its widest significance.

It is only fair to report that in other parts of the work, the author argues the need for 'habits of resistance and habits of dissatisfaction'.

21 The term 'hero-innovator' is taken from the work of N. J. Georgiades (1975). While charismatic and heroic qualities might have been needed to initiate change in such conditions, these same qualities tended to emphasize the individualistic and isolated nature of such change. Edward O'Neill for instance appeared to regard most other teachers as 'idiots' and consistently refused to join the NUT.

22. There is evidence, however, that he had read and been influenced by Edward Holmes's book *What Is And What Might Be* (1911). See G. Holmes (1952, p. 35).

23. Ballard, (1937, pp. 72–5) reports a typical case of such commitment.

24. The unattractive environments of inner-urban schools and their many 'problems' made it difficult to ensure that 'the right sort' of teachers were appointed.

Chapter 3 Change and Continuity in Urban Education

1. For different interpretations of the meanings of 'apathy', see Yeo (1974, pp. 279–311).

2. For a discussion of this, see Easthope (1975).

3. This formulation is used to suggest that ideological conflict within education cannot be interpreted *solely* in class or political terms (as it is in vulgar forms of Marxist analysis) or *solely* in terms of conflicting 'educational theories' (as it is in forms of naïve liberalism). The term matrix is used to convey the sense of complex interrelation of class, educational and political issues which impinge upon schooling. That class relations 'determine in the last instance' is not disputed.

4. The term 'curriculum as practice' is taken from Young (1975).

5. 'Conscientization' – understood to mean 'the process in which men, not as recipients, but as knowing subjects, achieve a deepening awareness, both of the socio-cultural reality which shapes their lives and of their capacity to transform that reality' – is taken from the work of Paulo Freire. See Freire (1972, p. 51).

6. This is not to suggest that organized groups within the working class do not concern themselves with educational issues, but that as an active arena for conflict, education

is more of a middle-class preoccupation.

7. What is referred to here as 'liberal romanticism' is given a more conservative character by Sharp and Green (1975, p. 227):

> We are suggesting that modern child-centred education is an aspect of romantic radical conservatism which involves an emotional turning away from society and an attempt within the confines of education to bring about that transformation of individual consciousness which is seen to be the key to social regeneration.

8. For a critical discussion of social democratic ideology in education, see Finn, Grant and Johnson (1977).

9. 'Radicalism' refers to a very heterogeneous collection of critiques and prescriptions. While these writings have diverse theoretical locations, an ideological unity is seen to inhere in common commitments to notions of human liberation and of the need to activate a critical consciousness among 'the people'. At the same time, these formulations *do not contain an explicit political framework or set of prescriptions*. Forms of such radicalism in education may be derived from the work of Illich (1973) and of other de-schoolers; from the writings of Freire (1972a, b, 1974) or from forms of critical sociology or philosophy.

10. 'Interests' as used here is taken to refer to *situations advantageous to a particular social group*. Interests may be conceived of as class interests and while this is one of the most powerful uses of the term, it is not the only one. Within classes, there are interest groups which have an 'investment' in particular states of affairs, modes of organization and recognition of particular forms of expertise. At the same time there are groups which have an 'investment' in overthrowing or changing these conditions.

It is not suggested that such groups act *solely* in relation to 'situations advantageous to them' but that such considerations are implicated in ideological positions which they may hold. See the discussion of 'Social groups: interests and ideologies' in Plamenatz (1970, pp. 93–122).

11. Bourdieu (1974, p. 38) remarks: 'Teachers are the products of a system whose aim is to transmit an aristocratic culture and are likely to adopt its values with greater ardour in proportion to the degree to which they owe it their own academic and social success.'

12. This stance of 'radical doubt' and of non-attachment often brings down upon radicals the fury of the organized political Left, who see such manifestations as evidence of romantic bourgeois individualism. See, for instance, the criticism by Gintis (1972, p. 95) that Illich 'rejects politics in favour of individual liberation'.

13. These divisions within the Left have been commented upon in various articles in the journal *Radical Education*. This journal is concerned with attempts to promote greater unity among radical and socialist teachers. The formation of the Socialist Teachers' Alliance is seen to be 'the belated recognition by the left of the need for an organisation which . . . recognises the importance of dealing with the educational crisis as a whole' (*Radical Education*, no. 9, Summer 1977, pp. 5–6).

14. An important distinction must be made here between what *appears* to be the fundamental problem to those in the situation – in this case, teachers trying to find a definition of the situation which 'works' in the classroom – and what may be objectively the fundamental problem, i.e. the ways in which school arrangements are constituted and their relationship to wider aspects of the social framework.

15. Marxist writers, such as Frith and Corrigan (1977), argue that the potential of classroom struggle for the development of a radical political consciousness has not been fully recognized by the Left.

Chapter 4　The 'Problem' of the Urban School: conservative and liberal formulations

1. It is important to note that notions of progressive education are utilized in different ideological positions, with different sets of meanings. The conservative critique associated progressive education with lack of control and rigour in schooling and with subversive egalitarian potential in its weakening of the strength of boundaries and of visible hierarchies in the schooling process.

　On the other hand, some Left critiques, associate progressive education with bourgeois romantic individualism and attack it as inappropriate to working-class traditions, situations and 'needs'.

2. See Boyson's (1974) account of his success: 'I always watch what is going on in the school with an eye to a press release' (p. 116).

3. Within the conservative critique of urban schools, it is apparent that calls for greater 'accountability' are associated with an analysis of the *politicizing* of schools, especially inner-city schools i.e. that the number of radical and socialist teachers in such schools is increasing. See Butt (1975).

4. See, for instance, the critical examination of pastoral care in *Teachers' Action*, no. 3, and in *Teachers' Action*, no. 5.

5. For two recent examinations of this conflict see Hill (1976) and Leavold (1977). The latter represents one of the few empirical studies available of 'sanctuary' units now being established in urban schools.

6. See Holly (1977) for a distinction between liberal romantic progressivism in education and socialist progressivism.

7. While acknowledging the potential of progressive pedagogy and integrated curricula to realize new forms of social solidarity; to change the principles of social control and in important ways to contribute towards the liberation of the person, there is apparent in Bernstein's writings a deep scepticism about the whole enterprise. This is revealed in references to 'the strategies of spurious casualness' and in Bernstein's (1977, pp. 13, 21) persistent exploration 'of implicit forms of control which I believed were at the bottom of so-called spontaneous behaviour'.

8. This argument against a 'special areas approach' is essentially similar to that of Castells (1976) in his critique of urban sociology. Both argue the diversionary effect of such policies and such study. However, what is overlooked is the possibility that a 'special areas approach' may provide a concrete and vivid means for the *realization* of wider structural inequalities and contradictions.

9. While insisting on the claim that the E P A is a viable administrative unit for positive discrimination, we would not wish to deny that in the end the appropriate unit is the individual and his family. In other words the use of the district as a means of identifying problems and allocating resources is held by us to be no more than a convenient framework within which closer and more detailed work has to be done with schools, school classes, individuals and families. . . .

For a criticism of area policies, see Townsend (1976).

10. See the review of 'Poverty and American Contemporary Education', in Halsey (1972, pp. 13–30).

Chapter 5   The 'Problem' of the Urban School: radical and Marxist formulations

1. Freire's notion of critical literacy is, perhaps, best expressed in the following (1974, p. 81):

> Literacy makes sense only in these terms, as the consequence of men's beginning to reflect about their own capacity for reflection, about the world, about their work, about their power to transform the world. . . . I can see validity only in a literacy programme in which men understand words in their true significance: as a force to transform the world.

2. Thus Paton (1973, p. 49) argues:

> in one sense of the word 'politics' is a bottomless well of self sacrifice by militants; an alienated realm of human relationships where the ultimate question is who has more POWER. I am not interested in this sort of politics . . . I am interested in the new politics, the politics of liberation understood as both social and personal liberation. . . . The politics of liberation is a politics of the experiential, a politics of the quality of relationships and of everyday life.

3. Where urban schools are 'in crisis' – particularly in inner-city areas, the potential impact of libertarian ideology is enhanced in terms of its claim to provide a realistic alternative when conventional systems have failed. These possibilities might occur in inner London, New York City or other metropolitan centres.

   For a libertarian teacher's account of such a crisis in New York City see Rebecca Staton's article in *Liberation* (1976). She argues that 'the only hope for urban education at this point is complete decentralization'. (I am grateful to Michael F. D. Young for bringing this article to my attention.)

4. Such a description of the 'new' sociology of education is not taken to imply that it has the monopoly of 'being critical', but that the practice of criticism is central to its activity and that it explicitly recognizes the need for praxis.

5. The existence of the journal *Teaching London Kids*, which originated from conferences organized by the London Association for the Teaching of English in 1972, is seen to provide evidence of organized radical intentions. The journal, which is produced by a group of London classroom teachers, tries 'to relate socialist theory to the daily practice of teachers in school and out' and is 'above all concerned with presenting radical strategies for action'. See *Radical Education*, no. 1, 1974, p. 13.

6. Critical sociology of education has itself been criticised from a wide range of perspectives. For different accounts see: Pring (1972); Simon (1974); Shipman (1973); Bernbaum (1977).

7. Mode 3 examination makes it possible for teachers to devise their own syllabus, set examination papers or forms of assessment based upon this and undertake primary marking. It is widely interpreted as showing concrete evidence of teacher autonomy. Young (1971, pp. 7–8) argues that in practice this is a myth: 'the most striking feature of Mode 3 syllabuses is their similarity to each other and to the Mode 1 syllabuses they were designed to replace. This seems to indicate that the boards while seeming to welcome innovations, use existing Mode 1 syllabuses as their standard for judging the acceptability of alternatives'.

8. The 'overwhelmingly conservative' nature of the majority of teachers is frequently commented upon in radical and Marxist analyses of education. Thus the writer of the editorial in *Radical Education*, no. 2, concerned with questions of racialism in schools, remarks:

238

let us not kid ourselves that teachers are an enlightened bunch who would go to the stake rather than implement reactionary, repressive and indeed cruel policies in school. The survey published by the *Times Education Supplement* (4 October 1974) indicated that only 30 per cent of the teachers would vote Labour . . . put more significantly, this means that 70 per cent of teachers found Harold Wilson and Roy Jenkins too left wing.

The survey referred to – *Teachers in the British General Election of October 1974*, Times Publishing, London, 1974 – did, in fact, conclude (p. 33):

We are dealing with a profoundly Conservative profession. It is also a conservative one. Not only does it have a tendency to vote Conservative in preference to any other party, but it also strongly resists change.

9. However, such works have become more widely available to teachers following Open University courses.

10. See publications of Teachers' Action Collective (2 Turquand St, London S E 17).

11. Radical Education, founded in Autumn, 1974 exists to 'put education-as-radical back on the agenda of the working-class movement' and to serve 'in countering a certain fragmentation which characterizes the radical movement in education' (see *Radical Education*, no. 1).

Chapter 6 Situating the Inquiry

1. 'Teacher consciousness', as used throughout this study, is taken to refer to the particular way in which the social world of the school is constituted in the mind of the teacher. Some part of this constitution is made explicit and manifest in discourse, particularly in the typifications which are employed to 'make sense' of that world.

2. Most of the available material is American in origin and relates to the particular characteristics of inner-city schools in metropolitan cities. The studies tend not to have a formal theoretical framework, but of a generally descriptive and 'case study' orientation. See, for instance:
Moore (1967); Fuchs (1968); Kohl (1971).

3. Sharp and Green (1975, pp. 68–70) make a useful distinction between *teacher ideology* and *teacher perspectives*. *Teacher ideology* is defined as 'a connected set of systematically related beliefs and ideas about what are felt to be the essential features of teaching . . . a broad definition of the task and a set of prescriptions for performing it, all held at a relatively high level of abstraction' and *teacher perspectives* as '. . . a lower order of beliefs . . . rather similar to what Strauss (1964) conceptualises as an "operational philosophy". . . . We will define it as "a co-ordinated set of ideas, beliefs and actions a person uses in coping with a problematic situation".'

4. The co-operating group ('sample') consisted in total of eighty teachers: fifteen deputy headteachers and ten headteachers. For further details, see Appendices, Tables 1 and 6.

5. Although certain empirical material was obtained concerning the constructs of a 'good' teacher and a 'good' school held by pupils and parents in the area under investigation, it was not possible to utilize this in the present study. The essential focus here, therefore, is upon the constructs held by headteachers and deputy headteachers.

6. The preliminary interviews with the headteachers were undertaken with the purposes of enlisting their co-operation in the project and explaining in particular its

focus upon 'what it is to be' an 'outstanding' teacher in an inner-city school (the project had already been formally approved by headteacher and teacher consultative committees within ILEA).

The headteachers in general felt that the concerns of the project were important subjects for research and all but one of those approached agreed to co-operate.

The procedure of gaining access to the teachers revealed in itself an interesting difference among the schools. Whereas, for most of the schools, once the head-teacher's general support had been obtained, meetings were held with the designated teachers to canvas their individual co-operation, *at School E the research request had to be submitted in writing to the Staff Council whose approval was necessary before any research could proceed at the school.* This was an early indication that the teachers at School E had established a relatively greater influence over school decisions than was the case generally.

7. For some approaches to constructs of the 'good teacher' see:
Biddle and Elena (1964); Taylor (1962); Musgrove and Taylor(1969); Musgrove (1971); McNeill and Popham (1973).

8. For full details, see chapters 7 and 8 and Appendices, Tables 3 and 4.

9. The 'informal' sample consisted of ten teachers. See Appendices, Table 4. For details of interviews see Appendices, Interview Procedures.

10. See, for instance:
Scott and Lyman (1968); Harre and Secord (1972); Elliott and Adelman (1975).
Harre and Secord (1972, p. 7) write:

> The things that people say about themselves and other people should be taken seriously as reports of data relevant to phenomena that really exist and which are relevant to the explanation of behaviour. It is through reports of feelings, plans, intentions, beliefs, reasons and so on that the meanings of social behaviour and the rules under-lying social acts can be discovered.

11. These strategies have been variously suggested as ways to achieve greater 'authenticity' in the collection of qualitative data. The possibility of joint accounts is discussed by Bartholomew (1974), triangulation by Denzin (1970), and returning accounts by Dale (1973).

12. The term is derived from Glaser and Strauss (1967, p. 61) who use it to refer to situations of joint collection and analysis of data where 'saturation' 'means that no additional data are being found whereby the sociologist can develop properties of the category'. The term is used here in a different sense to refer to the reseacher's attempt to 'take on' the theory and the world view of another through very detailed knowledge of their discourse.

13. Where this happened some judgment of dominant emphasis had to be made.

14. This crude quantification suggested that of the seventy teachers designated by their headteachers as 'outstanding' within an inner-city school: approximately thirty could be identified with a conservative stance in education; approximately thirty-five adopted liberal/reformist positions of various kinds; only five or six teachers were associated with radical or explicitly Marxist positions.

15. For further details of the schools, see Appendices, Table 1.

16. The 'new middle-class' are 'those who are the new agents of symbolic control' e.g. those who are filling the ever-expanding major and minor professional class concerned with the servicing of persons' (Bernstein, 1977, p. 136). The implication is that this social group is broadly favourable to the spread of a 'progressive' pedagogy and forms of comprehensive organization within the state system of education and, indeed, that

they are active in the diffusion of both.

There was evidence in this inquiry that such a group did play a crucial role in affecting the destinies of some inner-city schools.

17. For the five other schools in this division, the average was 27 per cent of pupils from skilled manual working-class backgrounds.

Chapter 7 The Social Construction of the 'Good' Teacher: a study in one school

1. These levels might be compared with Keddie's (1971) 'Educationist' and 'Teacher' contexts.
2. It is interesting that during the preliminary stages of the research the (early) retiring head of one of the schools did, in fact, suggest that there were *no* outstandingly good teachers in the school, which was described with unusual candour as 'an under-subscribed, unpopular school'. Subsequently a new headteacher, in consultation with the two deputies was to designate six teachers as outstandingly good.
3. The notion of 'busyness' is taken from Sharp and Green (1975) but applied here to the activity of the teacher rather than the pupil.
4. Mr C.'s response to the critique of pastoral care by the Teachers' Action Collective revealed the difficulties and uncertainties but also the basic rationale of liberal pastoral care teachers in urban schools:

> I see their point of view – I disagree with it. It's basically the same argument at
> a political level as wanting a violent revolution – any piecemeal improvement is
> harmful because it's hiding the injustices and preventing the day when we can
> have the revolution. I don't support that. There are times when I feel perhaps
> that it is the best way, but basically I don't support it. I suppose it is regarded as
> helping these kids in the short term but in the long term it's not helping a future
> generation of kids. All right, I'm a short-term operator in that case. I feel we've
> got to do everything we can to help these kids individually. I know obviously
> there are vast social implications in it and I don't know what the answer is.

5. There was evidence that pressure of school work made it difficult for teachers to sustain further courses of part-time study. Two of the teachers had enrolled for MA courses but subsequently abandoned them for this reason.
6. This was true not only for Mrs R. but also for Mr W., Mrs I., Miss Y. and the first deputy of the school, Mr N.
7. It would be wrong to suggest that Mrs R. took an entirely passive role in relation to the CSE Examination Board. She recognized that Biology had a difficult technical language and was critical of examination emphasis upon this:

> I write to the CSE Board each year that there is too much emphasis upon words.
> I don't think it matters that a child knows the tube from the mouth to his ear is
> called the eustachian tube. That the child knows the tube is there and the
> purpose of that tube – that, to me, is important and not the name of it.

8. While Mr H. had liberal/radical ideas about the curriculum, *these did not extend to working relationships with his staff*. Mr H. admitted to implementing change within his department in an autocratic manner and he exhibited a low tolerance of alternative positions:

241

Most of the problems which I face here are those which come directly from relationships with staff, rather than children. The children are the easy part of the job, it's getting conflicting personalities to work together in unity. . . . There are certain people who will never resolve themselves to the situation . . . then their only recourse is to look for another job. I'm not prepared to have the progress of this faculty held back because of one or two people who don't want to do it. . . . I have one or two people on the staff who believe that everything should be democratically arrived at. There must be a unanimous decision on everything. I don't work that way and I'm not prepared to do so . . . I'm not prepared to take time for the lengthy process of total democracy. In any case, I suspect that the motives, at times, for this kind of democratic action aren't necessarily the same as my motives. They are not necessarily to build up the faculty. It is often a political awareness in the place.

9. Miss L. observed:

Recently TV people came to make a film and used some of our kids. The children didn't understand what the people were talking about—they couldn't articulate their views about this area, what they thought about the houses coming down. They couldn't find the words. In that situation, with somebody with a *very* middle-class way of speaking, they were nervous. The group of children had very little to say: 'What's he talking about?' In a very much more informal situation, with somebody talking to them in the way they speak, they would probably have more to say about it.

10. It should be noted here that formal reports and references concerning the professional ability of teachers within the ILEA are 'open' documents, available to the teachers and subject to a right of appeal.

11. Mr N., a graduate, was a late entrant to teaching, having previous clerical experience. He had taught in two other London comprehensive schools (total of six years) and had been first deputy at School G for three years. He was thought of as a promising candidate for a headship.

12. Miss E. during this time had obtained, by part-time study, a degree from London University.

13. It was possible to establish this, during the course of discussions with the designated teachers and with others who had knowledge of the school.

Chapter 8 Defining 'Good' Teachers in Ten Schools

1. The notion of 'professional knowledge' used here is taken to imply what Alfred Schutz has described as 'recipe knowledge'. For a discussion of this, in relation to teachers, see *The Social Organization of Teaching and Learning*, Units 5–8, Open University Press, Milton Keynes, 1972, pp. 30–3.

2. Throughout the inquiry a salient notion associated with the typification of 'good' teachers was 'getting on with the job'. This priority of 'busyness' can be seen to be structurally generated by the exigencies of the teachers' work situation (size of classes; variety of classes; mixed ability teaching; time pressures; administrative responsibility; etc.). The demands of 'busyness' preclude much opportunity in the work situation to reflect upon, theorize about, or be critical of the ends to which the activity is directed. It is conceivable that 'getting on with the job' as a teacher characteristic is valued by

some headteachers, not only because of the imperatives of the situation, but because it implies lack of criticism (actively expressed) of existing arrangements.

3. The average length of teaching appointment in School D for these teachers was eleven years and the range was from six to twenty years.

4. This remark had a particular irony in that the school was located in an area in which *absence of privilege and presence of deprivation was most obvious.*

5. The headmaster of School I was clearly sceptical about what could be achieved intellectually with inner-city children:

> The old argument that so many children in poor areas were losing their chance because they weren't given opportunities to do this and that, doesn't cut any ice. The odd one will lift himself up, but the large majority won't. . . . But educational achievements are of secondary importance to their having a basic moral and ethical code of behaviour (by my inclinations, based on Christianity). . . . Whenever I speak in assembly . . . the words 'social' and 'society' and the boys' place in it is my main text . . . that is the main aim — I expect the place to be socially civilized.

6. The teacher in question had a very confident manner and positive style and 'no discipline problems'. For these qualities she was esteemed by the headteacher. It seems likely that the headteacher was unacquainted with her comparatively radical educational and political views.

7. The radicalizing effect of working in an inner-city school was described by this particular teacher in these terms:

> School I impinged itself on me. . . . I had certain notions of equality and justice, but going to work in a school like I, where you actually live with the people from day to day, confirmed certain things, revealed a whole load of new things, and my political consciousness came very much out of working with the parents and the kids and seeing the things that weren't done and seeing values that weren't recognized and wanting to do something about it. . . . I became very, very aware of the inequalities of the education system, and of course I became politically angry and I could see things in the structure of our society which were wrong. . . .

8. Being 'over-subscribed' was widely taken to be the indicator of a school's success and, significantly, the term is used in this sense in Rhodes Boyson's account of his inner-city school, *Oversubscribed: The Story of Highbury Grove*. In a competitive market situation for pupil intake and with parental choice and a declining school population to be considered, a school which is under-subscribed runs the risk of acquiring a 'sink school' reputation and the possibility of ultimate closure. The headteachers were, thus, understandably preoccupied with questions of school image.

9. A constant theme throughout the inquiry was that smaller schools would facilitate better control. While these remarks were usually made in relation to the pupils, it is clear that there are also control implications in relation to teachers.

10. In this sense some use was made of a methodology of triangulation. See Denzin (1970).

11. There were accounts from other sources which rendered problematic the headteacher's claim to be a facilitator of ideas within the school. These accounts suggested on the contrary: that he was an impediment to them.

12. In an early research discussion, this teacher had been designated by the previous headmaster and this designation was 'accepted' by the current headmaster. At the time of the main research activity this teacher was not employed at the school.

13. This teacher had also left the school because she felt that the new headmaster was unsympathetic to the development of integrated studies.

14. Among some sections of the staff at School A there was a strong feeling that the school's hierarchy (the head, two deputies and a senior master) were only minimally involved in actual classroom teaching, and this led them to believe that bureaucratic functions counted for more than pedagogic functions.

15. It was suggested by other teachers in the locality that a 'local middle-class Mafia' had exercised a significant influence on the school's destinies.

16. Despite her acceptance of examination results as an imperative of the situation, the headteacher registered her criticism of the situation in which she found herself:

> While I deplore the emphasis that is given to academic qualifications at all levels, and am very cynical about what exam results really tell you about a person, nonetheless, I recognize that in this particular society, increasingly, academic qualifications equal life-chances in the form of job opportunity. . . .

17. Overall, there was no evidence in this inquiry to support a simple connection between a teacher's social origin and the holding of any particular educational ideologies or sets of expectations.

18. These distinctions which focus upon the curriculum and 'purpose' of urban working-class schools and which contrast an imperative for the liberation of the few through scholarship success with an imperative for the 'conscientization' of the many through critical study or forms of community education, present a serious dilemma to some inner-city teachers who are critical of a conventional wisdom.

19. These were added by the headteacher and the deputy at a later date, 'after further reflection'.

20. It seems likely that this comprehensive representation of ideological positions was partly a consequence of School E's wide ideological spectrum and partly a consequence of the internal politics of the school, i.e. the staff council had given approval for the research to proceed and might raise further questions about which teachers had been interviewed. The headteacher used the principle of 'consistency' as a basic criterion — 'it may not be my sort of consistency, but it is theirs'.

21. Except in the case of the headmaster of School C.

22. In general, the headteachers saw the work of their schools to be under attack by misrepresentations from the 'Right' and the 'Left'. They saw Black Paper attacks as distorted sensationalism which failed to take into account the problems of the socio-economic context in which they worked and the many organizational and pedagogic problems which they had faced during a period of teacher shortage and high teacher mobility in inner-city areas.

On the other hand, they rejected as caricatures those typifications of their schools from a radical or Marxist stance which suggested that these were primarily concerned with socialization for conformity to the given cultural, political and economic order.

23. See previous note.

Chapter 9 Pupils, Localities and the Experience of Teaching

1. For a discussion of Victorian theories of urban corruption and urban degeneration see Stedman-Jones (1971).

2. Bray's (1907, p. 145) of the incipient anarchy of city life echoes the early accounts of Kay-Shuttleworth:

There remains to be considered another habit . . . though required every moment of the day it finds its most bitter foe in the environment of a town; it is the habit of self-control . . . perhaps the most remarkable effect of an urban environment is to be sought in the disappearance of the habit of self-control . . . the crowd of a town in a moment thrashes into a delirious mob and swept away on a torrent of excitement and reckless of appearance, plunges into acts of unmitigated folly. . . . To bring back, in some measure, the traditional self-control of the race must be regarded as not the least important of the many tasks we lay upon the modern schoolmaster. . . .

The whole book constitutes a fascinating and neglected early study in 'urban education'. On a similar theme of the absence of 'steadiness' and 'application' in the London labour force compared with provincial workers, see Stedman-Jones (1971).
3. The distinction between 'social type' and 'person' is central to Bernstein's (1977) examination of differing modes of socialization and of pedagogy in 'Class and Pedagogies: visible and invisible'.
4. This was characteristically expressed in the form, 'if we *must* talk about social class, then. . . .' The general impression created was that the teacher was prepared to utilize the term 'social class' under protest and only because it appeared to signify something real in the social world of the researcher.
5. The deputy headmaster at school C, who had a wide range of teaching experience, was concerned that teachers who had taught only in London inner-city comprehensives might come to 'normalize' low standards:

Many inexperienced teachers just do not know how to pitch the lesson. . . . I don't think, in the main, they have had sufficient training in making demands upon children. . . . This is why I would like to see people from all backgrounds coming in to London schools. There are many comprehensive schools outside London which are very, very effective indeed.

6. While the sincerity of the teachers is not in question, it seems reasonable to ask:
(a) If the conditions of their work situation permitted them *in practice* to treat every pupil as an individual?
(b) Whether their preoccupation with individualism did not give them a partial and limited view of their *social situation*?
7. In this and subsequent chapters material is utilized from the accounts of both designated 'outstanding' teachers and the small informal sample of those not so designated. Where the material quoted is taken from the account of a non-designated teacher, this will be indicated in the notes. In this case, the teacher is non-designated.
8. There was a strong belief among some teachers that problems of under-achievement and restlessness in secondary schools were to an important extent 'produced' by deficient junior school experience. This was commented upon strongly by experienced teachers in two of the more 'conservative' schools (Schools D and I):

I find it appalling that in next year's first year (I've got the profiles on them now) we've still got something like 30 per cent of these children with reading ages of seven. . . . A lot of it is due to the new progressive education, I believe that because I've got some first year boys who have never actually been made to sit down for half an hour. Now, if you don't sit down for half an hour in any one day, you can't concentrate on anything. They have butterfly minds. . . . I have a group of kids who think that everything is running around and playing games, etc. To counter that you have to impose an iron discipline. . . . The

secondary schools haven't failed – we get them like that in the beginning.
(School I)

9. This teacher was *not*, however, designated as 'outstanding' by the headteacher of School A.
10. These attitudes and conflicts are examined later in this chapter as 'resisting immersion'.
11. One young male teacher explained his use of physical sanction, 'a clip round the ear', in these terms:

> It is all very well saying we must get this group to see us as friends and helpers and confidantes, rather than as strict disciplinarian people 'out there'. When I left college, at the end of the sociology course, these were very much my views. It was great – until I found I couldn't even get quiet in a classroom until something physical was done, because it's no good talking about establishing relationships with children who will not listen to you. Until you can get absolute quiet or until you can establish a degree of quietness so you can talk either to individuals without being drowned out, or to the group as a whole, then the radical philosophy is totally redundant.

He also made explicit his experience of 'sense of insult' in his first year at School A:

> I laboured under the misapprehension that the children would behave to me in a certain way because I was a teacher. When they didn't it made me angry, insecure and very depressed. I had a naïveté (which must be true of most people) that having worked for a few years (i.e. before teaching), having worked hard at college and come out with an honours degree and a distinction in teaching practice, that now I had earned my mark in the teaching profession and I could hold my head up. I felt an injustice in the situation, that it was very unfair of the children: 'how dare they not recognize my status'.

12. The sheer exhaustion of teaching in inner-city schools, especially in the period of teacher shortage and high rates of teacher mobility, was stressed in many accounts.
13. Another teacher (School I) characterized immersion as 'the sheer on-going flow of work during the school term which militates against thinking, feeling, responding and questioning – and in the end you give up'.
14. This sense of individual salvation was modified in those schools where subject departments were cohesive and supportive and exceptionally in one school (School B), where a group-dynamics approach to teacher morale was taken seriously.
15. Three features of 'the school' had salient associations with a sense of obstruction among those attempting radical innovation. These were:
1 *Administration* – a sense that senior staff were preoccupied with questions of system maintenance and bureaucratic tidiness to the detriment of facilitating pedagogic change.
2 *Time* – a sense that time allocation was essentially premised upon a traditional collection code curriculum which was inappropriate for the context and inimical to the social relations of pedagogy and to the development of real engagement with a subject.
3 *'Old guard' conservatism* – this applied to relatively few schools since no definable 'old guard' existed in most of them, but it was claimed to be a real factor particularly at School D.
16. This possibility requires empirical investigation, since radical critics of urban

schools claim that serious innovation in curriculum, pedagogy or evaluation is stifled, while 'official' sources as represented by headteachers and, in this case, ILEA spokesmen, claim that innovation is encouraged and is a real and visible feature of many inner-city schools. Clearly, disagreement as to what constitutes *radical innovation* is central to the existence of these conflicting accounts.

17. Teachers whose commitment to school work was de-limited by political or by domestic commitments were generally seen not to fulfil the requirements of the ideal teacher role.

18. Pupils were frequently typified as 'honest' in human relations terms, though not necessarily in other terms!

19. Some teachers argued that inner-city children had been *over-exposed to change* in many aspects of their social environment and that, as a consequence, stability and continuity, rather than change, were desirable features of their schools.

In this way the existence of change and uncertainty as a prevalent feature of inner-city localities and of the lives of the pupils, was used as a *rationale* for a countervailing school experience which provided a sense of 'structure' and certainty. This point is developed more fully in the following chapter.

Chapter 10 Curriculum and Pedagogy

1. Many teachers claimed to be either irritated or confused by curriculum discussions which involved unexplicated notions of 'middle-class culture/values' or 'working-class culture/values'. These were seen to be slogans rather than analytically useful concepts.

2. Teachers were ambivalent in relation to the notion of 'interest'. In some cases there were frank admissions, such as 'this school bores them [the pupils] to death'. At the same time, a growing tendency in the pupils 'to want to be entertained' was morally censured.

3. Social education could become the context within which the liberal teacher encountered working-class conservatism or prejudice. The teacher in charge of social education at School F observed:

> Social education is getting kids to talk in groups about various things. In a lot of this, I'm deeply depressed by the result. We discuss community relations, poverty, etc. It often uncovers things which I find very disturbing. It reveals attitudes that are then very difficult to discuss. They're quite prepared to put forward their attitudes. Then, when you attempt to say, 'Let's look at these attitudes and how they're formed', you find they are very rigidly engrained in them and their parents.

4. While such action might be labelled as 'indoctrination' by conservative defenders of the traditional curriculum, this interpretation was rejected by one young teacher who claimed (a) that 'History and other subjects have been so biased that I don't see any harm in setting the balance right' and (b) that inner-city pupils were resistant to *any* notion of indoctrination: 'I don't believe you can indoctrinate kids; that goes back again to a deficit view of kids. They've got their own ideas about things.'

5. Thus a senior teacher of mathematics at School H argued, 'we have lost our way; there is a need to return to teaching traditional subjects in a traditional way, to some sort of order. Children need a clear filing system (a feature of the old body of knowledge we had previously). There is a need to return to a structured position'.

247

6. The resources provided by the ILEA in every school were seen to be generous. Major obstacles to integration were problems of physical and temporal space and of departmental or individual non-cooperation.

7. Suggestions that forms of integrated curricula or of 'progressive' pedagogy might be problematic in inner-city schools were rejected by such innovators:

> Bearing in mind that the working-class child in this school tends to be noisy, generally exciteable, *not* the type of child who wants to sit down for very long . . . once you have this more moveable type of teaching, with inquiry going on and people moving about, it leads to a great deal of chaos, it can do. You have to ride through that, it's a matter of them learning the system. Initially it looks and sounds gruesome, there's no doubt about that. But in the long term it will have very positive results, I think.
>
> The one thing is that the other system, which has certainly been applied in this school (the very rigid, traditional, grammar school type of structure) has been *a complete failure*, in the sense that very few children here have succeeded in external exams. Large numbers of children have left here without even the basic skills in the past. It's an awful thing to say, but it's true. The traditional form has not succeeded (School F).

8. More 'troublesome' first year intakes of pupils were seen to be partly a result of progressive pedagogy in the junior schools and partly a result of increased 'stress' in inner-city areas generally. Secondary school 're-socialization' appeared to take two forms in response to this. The more conservative and traditional schools (e.g. Schools D and I) engaged in direct confrontation with this 'problem', with policies of clear definition of a new situation. In other schools (e.g. Schools A and E) integrated studies appeared to provide a 'space' for re-socialization.

9. The theme of institutional or bureaucratic 'corruption' is strong in radical literature concerned with schools. At the same time, there is a recognition that state schools are 'where the action is' and where radicals ought to be.

10. The term 'liberal faith' is used here because many teachers appeared to be prepared to argue this position without direct personal experience of introducing innovations.

11. Empirical or socio-historical studies of cultural transmission within urban working-class schools are still very few and a considerable research endeavour is required in this area.

12. The autonomy of contemporary urban teachers in Britain is a real and considerable freedom of their work situation when compared with:
(1) the conditions of their predecessors (2) the conditions of teachers in many other societies (3) the conditions of most other workers.

Chapter 11 Conclusions

1. Holly (1977, p. 186) points to 'the new situation of the urban comprehensive with a growing complement of graduate teachers. . . .' and suggests that the new "comprehensive" teachers are apt to question the routine skill-training view of education for working-class students'.

2. This position is also argued by Whitty and Young (1977, p. 5):

As long as radical teachers remain isolated within their schools and fail to develop links of solidarity with other teachers or work out ways of concretely identifying themselves with the broader working-class movement for the transformation of society, they will lack both the support and understanding of those groups upon whose power their capacity to resist the establishment will ultimately depend.

3. It is clear that among a whole complex of meanings assigned to the term 'professionalism', one has to do with the attempt by liberal educators to attain to some state of objectivity and possible impartiality in their teaching. Many teachers believe that they are attempting to realize this sense of professionalism in their work. In many cases, however, as this study has shown, what passes for professionalism is an avoidance of the controversial and a naïve belief that 'being political' is 'being socialist'. Thus, it is comparatively easy for radical critics of the schools to suggest that the 'professionalism' of the educator is a conservative or, at least, neutralizing device.

4. It can be observed that a great deal of the energies of organized teachers has been absorbed in the struggle for better salaries.

5. It is significant in this connection that certain courses of the Open University have been accused of 'Marxist bias'.

Bibliography

Althusser, L. (1971), 'Ideology and ideological state apparatuses', reprinted in B. R. Cosin (ed.), *Education: Structure and Society*, Penguin, Harmondsworth, 1972.

Arnold, M. (1935), *Culture and Anarchy*, J. Dover Wilson (ed.), Cambridge University Press.

Auld, R. (1976), *William Tyndale School Public Inquiry* (Auld Report), ILEA.

Ballard, P. B. (1937), *Things I Cannot Forget*, University of London Press.

Bantock, G. H. (1975), 'Progressivism and the content of education' in C. B. Cox and R. Boyson (eds), *Black Paper, 1975*, Dent, London.

Barker, R. (1972), *Education and Politics 1900–1951: A Study of the Labour Party*, Oxford University Press, London.

Bartholomew, J. (1974), 'Sustaining hierarchy through teaching and research' in M. Flude and J. Ahier (eds), *Educability, Schools and Ideology*, Croom Helm, London.

Becker, H. (1952), 'Social class variations in the teacher-pupil relationships' reprinted in B. R. Cosin *et al.* (eds), *School and Society: A Sociological Reader*, Routledge & Kegan Paul, London/Open University Press, Milton Keynes, 1971.

Bernbaum, G. (1977), *Knowledge and Ideology in the Sociology of Education*, Macmillan, London.

Bernstein, B. (1973), 'Education cannot compensate for society' in J. Raynor and J. Harden (eds), *Equality and City Schools: Readings in Urban Education*, vol. 2, Routledge & Kegan Paul, London.

Bernstein, B. (1975, 1977), *Class, Codes and Control*, vol. 3, Routledge & Kegan Paul, London.

Biddle, B. J. and Elena, W. (1964), *Contemporary Research on Teacher Effectiveness*, Holt, Rinehart & Winston, London.

250

Bourdieu, P. (1976), 'The school as a conservative force: scholastic and cultural inequalities' in R. Dale, G. Esland and M. MacDonald (eds), *Schooling and Capitalism: A Sociological Reader*, Routledge & Kegan Paul, London/Open University Press, Milton Keynes.

Bowles, S. and Gintis, H. (1977), *Schooling in Capitalist America: Educational Reform and the Contradictions of Economic Life*, Routledge & Kegan Paul, London.

Boyson, R. (1974), *Oversubscribed: The Story of Highbury Grove*, Ward Lock, London.

Boyson, R. (1975), *The Crisis in Education*, Woburn Press, London.

Bray, R. A. (1907), *The Town Child*, Fisher-Unwin, London.

Butt, R. (1975), 'Politics and education' in C. B. Cox and R. Boyson (eds), *Black Paper, 1975*, Dent, London.

Castells, M. (1969), 'Is there an urban sociology?' and 'Theory and Ideology in urban sociology' reprinted in C. Pickvance (ed.), *Urban Sociology: Critical Essays*, Tavistock, London, 1976.

Central Advisory Council For Education (1967), *Children and their Primary Schools* (Plowden Report), vol. 1, HMSO.

Centre For Contemporary Cultural Studies (1977), *Working Papers in Cultural Studies 10: On Ideology*, University of Birmingham.

Christian, G. A. (1922), *English Education from Within*, Gandy.

Coleridge, D. (1862), *The Teachers of the People*, Rivingtons, London.

Connell, W. F. (1950), *The Educational Thought of Matthew Arnold*, Routledge & Kegan Paul, London.

Cosin, B. R., Dale, I. R., Esland, G. M. and Swift, D. F. (eds) (1971), *School and Society: A Sociological Reader*, Routledge & Kegan Paul, London/Open University Press, Milton Keynes.

Cox, C. B. and Boyson, R. (eds), *Black Paper, 1975*, Dent, London.

Dale, R. (1973), 'Phenomenological perspectives and the sociology of the school', *Educational Review*, vol. 25, no. 3.

Denzin, N. K. (1970), *Sociological Methods: A Sourcebook*, Butterworth, London

Easthope, G. (1975), *Community, Hierarchy and Open Education*, Routledge & Kegan Paul, London.

Elliott, J. and Adelman, C. (1975), 'Teacher's accounts and the objectivity of classroom research', *London Educational Review*, vol. 4, nos 2/3.

Ellis, T., McWhirter, J., McGregan, D. and Haddow, B. (1976), *William Tyndale: The Teachers' Story*, Writers' and Readers' Publishing Cooperative, London.

Esland, G. (1972), *The Social Organisation of Teaching and Learning*, units 5–8, Open University Press, Milton Keynes.

Fay, B. (1975), *Social Theory and Political Practice*, Allen & Unwin, London.

Field, F. (ed.) (1977), *Education and the Urban Crisis*, Routledge & Kegan Paul, London.

Bibliography

Finn, D., Grant, N. and Johnson, R. (1977), 'Social democracy, education and the crisis' in *Working Papers in Cultural Studies 10: On Ideology*, Centre for Contemporary Studies, University of Birmingham.

Flude, M. and Ahier, J. (1974), *Educability, Schools and Ideology*, Croom Helm, London.

Freire, P. (1972), *Cultural Action For Freedom*, Penguin, Harmondsworth.

Freire, P. (1972), *Pedagogy of the Oppressed*, Penguin, Harmondsworth.

Freire, P. (1974), *Education For Critical Consciousness*, Sheed & Ward, London.

Frith, S. and Corrigan, P. (1977), 'The politics of education' in M. F. D. Young and G. Whitty (eds), *Society, State and Schooling: Readings on the Possibilities for Radical Education*, Falmer Press, London.

Fuchs, E. (1968), *Teacher Talk: A View from within the Inner-city Schools*, Doubleday, London.

Gautrey, T. (1937), *Lux Mihi Laus: School Board Memories*, Link House, London.

Georgiades, N. J. (1975), 'What's wrong with our schools?', *New Behaviour*, 2 October.

Gintis, H. (1972), 'Towards a political economy of education', *Harvard Educational Review*, vol. 42, no. 1.

Glaser, B. G. and Strauss, A. L. (1967), *The Discovery of Grounded Theory*, Aldine, Chicago.

Glatter, R. (1972), *Management Development for the Education Profession*, Harrap, London.

Goffman, E. (1970), 'On the characteristics of total institutions' in E. Goffman, *Asylums*, Penguin, Harmondsworth.

Goldstrom, J. M. (1977), 'The content of education and the socialization of the working-class child 1830–1860' in P. McCann (ed.), *Popular Education and Socialization in the Nineteenth Century*, Methuen, London.

Goodman, P. (1966), *Compulsory Mis-Education and the Community of Scholars*, Vintage Books, New York.

Gouldner, A. W. (1976), *The Dialectic of Ideology and Technology: The Origins, Grammar and Future of Ideology*, Macmillan, London.

Hall, S. (1974), 'Education and the crisis of the urban school' in J. Raynor (ed.), *Issues in Urban Education*, Open University Press, Milton Keynes.

Halsey, A. H. (1972), *Educational Priority: EPA Problems and Policies*, vol. 1, HMSO.

Halsey, A. H. (1975), 'Sociology and the equality debate', *Oxford Review of Education*, vol. 1, no. 1.

Hargreaves, D. H., Hester, S. and Mellor, F. (1975), *Deviance in Classrooms*, Routledge & Kegan Paul, London.

Harre, R. and Secord, P. F. (1972), *The Explanation of Social Behaviour*, Blackwell, Oxford.

Harrison, J. F. C. (1961), *Learning and Living 1790–1960*, Routledge & Kegan Paul, London.

Harvey, D. (1973), *Social Justice and the City*, Arnold, London.

Higdon, T. (1924), *The Burston Rebellion*, National Labour Press, London.

Hill, T. (1976), 'Perspectives on the class base of resistance to schooling and the reaction it provokes'. Unpublished MA thesis, University of London.

Hoare, Q. (1967), 'Education: programme and men', *New Left Review*, vol. 32.

Holly, D. (1977), 'Education and the social relations of a capitalist society' in M. F. D. Young and G. Whitty (eds), *Society, State and Schooling: Readings on the Possibilities for Radical Education*, Falmer Press, London.

Holly, D. (1977), 'Politics of learning', *Radical Education*, no. 6.

Holmes, E. (1911), *What Is and What Might Be*, Constable, London.

Holmes, G. (1952), *The Idiot Teacher*, Faber, London.

Hughes, G. W. (1936), 'The social and economic status of the elementary school teacher 1833–1870'. Unpublished MEd thesis, Manchester University.

Illich, I. (1973), *Deschooling Society*, Penguin, Harmondsworth.

Jackson, P. W. (1968), *Life in Classroom*, Holt, Rinehart & Winston, London.

Johnson, R. (1970), 'Educational policy and social control in early Victorian England', *Past and Present*, vol. 49.

Johnson, R. (1976), 'Really useful knowledge', *Radical Education*, nos 7 and 8.

Johnson, T. (1972), *Professions and Power*, Macmillan, London.

Jones, D. K. (1977), 'Socialization and social science: Manchester model secular school 1854–61' in P. McCann (ed.), *Popular Education and Socialization in the Nineteenth Century*, Methuen, London.

Kaestle, C. F. (1973), *The Evolution of an Urban School System*, Harvard University Press.

Karabel, J. and Halsey, A. H. (eds) (1977), *Power and Ideology in Education*, Oxford University Press, London

Katz, M. (1968), *The Irony of Early School Reform*, Harvard University Press.

Kay-Shuttleworth, J. (1862), *Four Periods of Public Education*, Lowland Green.

Keddie, N. (1971), 'Classroom knowledge' in M. F. D. Young (ed.), *Knowledge and Control*, Collier Macmillan, London.

Keddie, N. (ed.) (1973), *Tinker, Tailor: The Myth of Cultural Deprivation*, Penguin, Harmondsworth.

Labov, W. (1973), 'The logic of non-standard English' in N. Keddie (ed.), *Tinker, Tailor: The Myth of Cultural Deprivation*, Penguin, Harmondsworth.

Lawrence, D. H. (1975), *The Rainbow*, Penguin, Harmondsworth.

Lawson, W. R. (1908), *John Bull and his Schools*.

Bibliography

Lazerson, M. (1971), *Origins of the Urban School*, Harvard University Press.

Leavold, J. M. (1977), 'Care, control and the urban school: a study of downtown sanctuary'. Unpublished MA thesis, University of London.

McCann, P. (ed.) (1977), *Popular Education and Socialization in the Nineteenth Century*, Methuen, London.

McLennan, G. (ed.) (1977), *Working Papers in Cultural Studies 10: On Ideology*, Centre for Contemporary Cultural Studies, University of Birmingham.

Macnamara, T. J. (1896), *Schoolmaster Sketches*. Cassell, London.

McNeill, J. and Popham, W. (1973), 'The assessment of teacher competence' in R. Travers (ed.), *Second Handbook of Research on Teaching*, Rand McNally, Chicago.

Marland, M. (1974), *Pastoral Care: Organising the Care and Guidance of the Individual Pupil in a Comprehensive School*, Heinemann, London.

Marland, M. (1975), *The Craft of the Classroom: A Survival Guide to Classroom Management*, Heinemann, London.

Martin, B. (1971), 'Progressive education versus the working class', *Critical Quarterly*, Winter.

Martin, B. (1975), 'The mining of the ivory tower' in C. B. Cox and R. Boyson (eds), *Black Paper, 1975*, Dent, London.

Marx, K. and Engels, F. (1965), *The German Ideology*, Lawrence & Wishart, London.

Mathieson, M. (1975), *The Preachers of Culture: A Study of English and its Teachers*, Allen & Unwin, London.

Merson, M. and Campbell, R. (1974), 'Community Education: instruction for inequality', *Education for Teaching*, no. 93, Spring.

Midwinter, E. (1973), *Patterns of Community Education*, Ward Lock, London.

Midwinter, E. (1975), *Education and Community*, Allen & Unwin, London.

Moore, G. A. (1967), *Realities of the Urban Classroom*, Doubleday, London.

Morton, D. C. and Watson, D. R. (1973), 'Contemporary education and contemporary liberalism in the United States: a sociological view' in J. Raynor and J. Harden (eds), *Equality and City Schools: Readings in Urban Education*, vol. 2, Routledge & Kegan Paul, London/Open University Press, Milton Keynes.

Musgrove, F. (1971), *Patterns of Power and Authority in English Education*, Methuen, London.

Musgrove, F. and Taylor, P. H. (1969), *Society and the Teacher's Role*, Routledge & Kegan Paul, London.

Neale, R. S. (1972), *Class and Ideology in the Nineteenth Century*, Routledge & Kegan Paul, London.

Newcastle Commission, Report to the Popular Education Commission, 1861, vols. 2 and 4, HMSO.

254

O'Neill, E. (1918), 'Developments in self-activity in an elementary school', *Conference on New Ideals in Education*, Oxford.

Pahl, R. E. (1975), *Whose City: and Further Essays on Urban Society*, Penguin, Harmondsworth.

Paton, K. (1973), *The Great Brain Robbery*, Moss Side Press, London.

Pickvance, C. (ed.) (1976), *Urban Sociology: Critical Essays*, Tavistock, London.

Plamenatz, J. (1970), *Ideology*, Macmillan, London.

Plant, R. (1974), *Community and Ideology*, Routledge & Kegan Paul, London.

Platt, A. (1969), *The Child Savers*, University of Chicago Press.

Pring, R. (1972), 'Knowledge out of control', *Education for Teaching*, no. 89, Autumn.

Rainwater, L. (1967), 'The revolt of the dirty workers', *Trans-Action*, November.

Ravitch, D. (1974), *The Great School Wars: New York City 1805-1973—A History of the Public Schools as Battlefield of Social Change*, Basic Books, New York.

Raynor, J. (ed.) (1974), *Issues in Urban Education*, Open University Press, Milton Keynes.

Reeder, D. (ed.) (1977), *Urban Education in the Nineteenth Century*, Taylor & Francis, London.

Right To Learn (1973), 'A contribution to the Green Paper Discussion by practising teachers in the ILEA',

Right To Learn (1974), 'School does matter: organisation for achievement in the inner-city'.

Rosenberg, C., *Education and Society*, Rank and File Teachers.

Runciman, K. (1887), *Schools and Scholars*, Chatto & Windus, London.

Schutz, A. and Luckmann, T. (1974), *The Structures of Life World*, Heinemann, London.

Scott, M. B. and Lyman, S. (1968), 'Accounts', *American Sociology Review*, vol. 33.

Searle, C. (1975a), 'All in the same class', *The Times Educational Supplement*, 10 October.

Searle, C. (1975b), *Classrooms of Resistance*, Writers' and Readers' Publishing Cooperative, London.

Selleck, R. (1972), *English Primary Education and the Progressives 1914-1939*, Routledge & Kegan Paul, London.

Sharp, R. and Green, A. (1975), *Education and Social Control. A Study of Progressive Primary Education*, Routledge & Kegan Paul, London.

Shipman, M. (1973), 'Bias in the sociology of education', *Educational Review*, vol. 25, no. 3, January.

Silver, H. (1977), 'Aspects of neglect: the strange cast of Victorian popular education', *Oxford Review of Education*, vol. 3, no. 1.

Bibliography

Simon, B. (1965), *Education and the Labour Movement 1870–1920*, Lawrence & Wishart, London.

Simon, B. (1972), *The Radical Tradition in Education in Britain*, Lawrence & Wishart, London.

Simon, J. (1974), 'New direction sociology and comprehensive schooling', *Forum*, vol. 17, no. 1, Autumn.

Smith, L. and Geoffrey, W. (1968), *The Complexities of the Urban Classroom*, Holt, Rinehart & Winston, London.

Spencer, F. H. (1938), *An Inspector's Statement*, English Universities Press, London.

Spradbury, J. (1977), 'Conservative pupils? Pupil resistance to a curriculum innovation in mathematics' in G. Whitty and M. F. D. Young (eds), *Explorations in the Politics of School Knowledge*, Nafferton Books, London.

Spring, J., 'Anarchism and education', *Libertarian Teacher*, no. 9.

Staton, R. (1976), 'Yo, Teach!', *Liberation*, Spring, pp. 79–83.

Stebbins, R. A. (1975), *Teachers and Meaning: Definitions of Classroom Situations*, Brill, London.

Stedman-Jones, G. (1971), *Outcast London: A Study in the Relationship between Classes in Victorian Society*, Oxford University Press, London.

Squibb, P. (1973), 'The college of education: a sociological view', *Occasional Papers in Sociology of Education*, ATCDE.

Taylor, P. H. (1962), 'Children's evaluations of the characteristics of a good teacher', *British Journal of Educational Psychology*, vol. 32.

Taylor, W. (1969), *Society and the Education of Teachers*, Faber, London.

Teachers' Action Collective, 'Teachers are workers', *Teachers' Action*, vol. 1.

Teachers' Action Collective, 'Pastoral care: concern or control?', *Teachers' Action*, vol. 3.

Teachers' Action Collective, 'Pastoral care: the system of control', *Teachers' Action*, vol. 5.

Townsend, P. (1976), 'Area Deprivation Politics', *New Statesman*, 6 Aug.

Tropp, A. (1957), *The School Teachers: the Growth of the Teaching Profession in England and Wales from 1800 to the Present Day*, Heinemann, London.

Turner, R. H. (1962), 'Role taking: process versus conformity' in A. Rose (ed.), *Human Behaviour and Social Processes*, Routledge & Kegan Paul, London.

Van Der Eyken, W. and Turner, B. (1969), *Adventures in Education*, Allen Lane, London.

Waller, W. (1965), *The Sociology of Teaching*, Wiley, Chichester.

Watson, D. (1973), 'Urban education and cultural competence: competing theoretical models in social science', *Urban Education*, vol. 8, no. 1.

West, E. G. (1975), *Education and the Industrial Revolution*, Batsford, London.

White, J. (1975), 'The end of the compulsory curriculum' in *The Curriculum: The Doris Lee Lectures 1975*, University of London.

Whitty, G. (1977), 'Sociology and the problem of radical educational change' in M. F. D. Young and G. Whitty (eds), *Society, State and Schooling: Readings on the Possibilities for Radical Education*, Falmer Press, London.

Whitty, G. and Young, M. F. D. (eds) (1976), *Explorations in the Politics of School Knowledge*, Nafferton Books, London.

Williams, R. (1971), *The Long Revolution*, Penguin, Harmondsworth.

Worsley, P. (1975), 'The reification of Marxism: rejoinder to Lazar', *Sociology*, vol. 9, no. 3.

Wright Mills, C. (1967), 'The professional ideology of social pathologists' in I. Horowitz (ed.), *Power, Politics and People*, Oxford University Press, London.

Wright Mills, C. (1970), *The Sociological Imagination*, Penguin, Harmondsworth.

Yeo, S. (1974), 'On the uses of apathy', *European Journal of Sociology*, vol. XV, no. 2.

Young, M. F. D. (ed.) (1971), *Knowledge and Control: New Directions for the Sociology of Education*, Collier Macmillan, London.

Young, M. F. D. (1974), 'Sociology and the politics of school knowledge'. Unpublished paper, University of London.

Young, M. F. D. (1975), 'Curriculum change: limits and possibilities', *Educational Studies*, vol. 1, no. 2, January. Reprinted in M. F. D. Young and G. Whitty (eds), *Society, State and Schooling: Readings on the Possibilities for Radical Education*, Falmer Press, 1977.

Young, M. F. D. (1976), 'Some thoughts on collaborative research with teachers'. Unpublished paper, University of London.

Young, M. F. D. and Whitty, G. (eds) (1977), *Society, State and Schooling: Readings on the Possibilities for Radical Education*, Falmer Press, London.

Index